Pickle the Spy

Andrew Lang

Pickle the Spy

Table of Contents

Pickle the Spy

Andrew Lang

PICKLE THE SPY or The Incognito of Prince Charles

Pickle the Spy

PICKLE THE SPY
or The Incognito of Prince Charles

'I knew the Master: on many secret steps of his career
I have an authentic memoir in my hand.'
THE MASTER OF BALLANTRAE

PREFACE

This woful History began in my study of the Pelham Papers in the Additional Manuscripts of the British Museum. These include the letters of Pickle the Spy and of JAMES MOHR MACGREGOR. Transcripts of them were sent by me to Mr. ROBERT LOUIS STEVENSON, for use in a novel, which he did not live to finish. The character of Pickle, indeed, like that of the Master of Ballantrae, is alluring to writers of historical romance. Resisting the temptation to use Pickle as the villain of fiction, I have tried to tell his story with fidelity. The secret, so long kept, of Prince Charles's incognito, is divulged no less by his own correspondence in the Stuart MSS. than by the letters of Pickle.

For Her Majesty's gracious permission to read the Stuart Papers in the library of Windsor Castle, and to engrave a miniature of Prince Charles in the Royal collection, I have respectfully to express my sincerest gratitude.

To Mr. HOLMES, Her Majesty's librarian, I owe much kind and valuable aid.

The Pickle Papers, and many despatches in the State Papers, were examined and copied for me by Miss E. A. IBBS.

In studying the Stuart Papers, I owe much to the aid of Miss VIOLET SIMPSON, who has also assisted me by verifying references from many sources.

It would not be easy to mention the numerous correspondents who have helped me, but it were ungrateful to omit acknowledgment of the kindness of Mr. HORATIO F. BROWN and of Mr. GEORGE T. OMOND.

I have to thank Mr. ALEXANDER PELHAM TROTTER for permission to cite the MS. Letter Book of the exiled Chevalier's secretary, ANDREW LUMISDEN, in Mr. TROTTER'S possession.

Miss MACPHERSON of Cluny kindly gave me a copy of a privately printed Memorial of her celebrated ancestor, and, by CLUNY'S kind permission, I have been allowed to see some letters from his charter chest. Apparently, the more important secret papers have perished in the years of turmoil and exile.

This opportunity may be taken for disclaiming any belief in the imputations against CLUNY conjecturally hazarded by 'NEWTON,' or KENNEDY, in the following pages. The Chief's destitution in France, after a long period of suffering in Scotland, refutes these suspicions, bred in an atmosphere of jealousy and distrust. Among the relics of the family are none of the objects which CHARLES, in 1766–1767, found it difficult to obtain from CLUNY'S representatives for lack of a proper messenger.

To Sir ARTHUR HALKETT, Bart., of Pitfirrane, I am obliged for a view of BALHALDIE'S correspondence with his agent in Scotland.

The Directors of the French Foreign Office Archives courteously permitted Monsieur LÉON PAJOT to examine, and copy for me, some of the documents in their charge. These, it will be seen, add but little to our information during the years 1749–1766.

I have remarked, in the proper place, that Mr. MURRAY ROSE has already printed some of Pickle's letters in a newspaper. As Mr. MURRAY ROSE assigned them to JAMES MOHR MACGREGOR, I await with interest his arguments in favour of this opinion in his promised volume of Essays.

The ornament on the cover of this work is a copy of that with which the volumes of Prince CHARLES'S own library were impressed. I owe the stamp to the kindness of Miss WARRENDER of Bruntsfield.

Among printed books, the most serviceable have been Mr. EWALD'S work on Prince Charles, Lord STANHOPE'S History, and Dr. BROWNE'S 'History of the Highlands and Clans.' Had Mr. EWALD explored the Stuart Papers and the Memoirs of d'Argenson, Grimm, de Luynes, Barbier, and the Letters of Madame du Deffand (edited by M. DE LESCURE), with the 'Political Correspondence of Frederick the Great,' little would have been left for gleaners in his track.

I must not forget to thank Mr. and Mrs. BARTELS for researches in old magazines and journals. Mr. BARTELS also examined for me the printed correspondence of Frederick the Great. To the kindness of J. A. ERSKINE CUNNINGHAM, Esq., of Balgownie I owe permission to photograph the portrait of Young Glengarry in his possession.

If I might make a suggestion to historical students of leisure, it is this. The Life of the Old Chevalier (James III.) has never been written, and is well worth writing. My own studies, alas! prove that Prince Charles's character was incapable of enduring misfortune. His father, less brilliant and less popular, was a very different man, and, I think, has everything to gain from an unprejudiced examination of his career. He has certainly nothing to lose.

Since this work was in type the whole of Bishop Forbes's MS., *The Lyon in Mourning*, has been printed for an Historical Society in Scotland. I was unable to consult the MS. for this book, but it contains, I now find, no addition to the facts here set forth.

November 5, 1896.

CHAPTER I—INTRODUCTORY TO PICKLE

Subject of this book—The last rally of Jacobitism hitherto obscure —Nature of the new materials—Information from spies, unpublished Stuart Papers, &c.—The chief spy—Probably known to Sir Walter Scott —'Redgauntlet' cited—'Pickle the Spy'—His position and services— The hidden gold of Loch Arkaig—Consequent treacheries—Character of Pickle—Pickle's nephew—Pickle's portrait—Pickle detected and denounced—To no purpose—Historical summary—Incognito of Prince Charles—Plan of this work.

The latest rally of Jacobitism, with its last romance, so faded and so tarnished, has hitherto remained obscure. The facts on which 'Waverley' is based are familiar to all the world: those on which 'Redgauntlet' rests were but imperfectly known even to Sir Walter Scott. The story of the Forty–five is the tale of Highland loyalty: the story of 1750–1763 is the record of Highland treachery, or rather of the treachery of some Highlanders. That story, now for the first time to be told, is founded on documents never hither to published, or never previously pieced together. The Additional Manuscripts of the British Museum, with relics of the government of Henry Pelham and his brother, the Duke of Newcastle, have yielded their secrets, and given the information of the spies. The Stuart Papers at Windsor (partly published in Browne's 'History of the Highland Clans' and by Lord Stanhope, but mainly virginal of type) fill up the interstices in the Pelham Papers like pieces in a mosaic, and reveal the general design. The letters of British ambassadors at Paris, Dresden, Berlin, Hanover, Leipzig, Florence, St. Petersburg, lend colour and coherence. The political correspondence of Frederick the Great contributes to the effect. A trifle of information comes from the French Foreign Office Archives; French printed 'Mémoires' and letters, neglected by previous English writers on the subject, offer some valuable, indeed essential, hints, and illustrate Charles's relations with the wits and beauties of the reign of Louis XV. By combining information from these and other sources in print, manuscript, and tradition, we reach various results. We can now follow and understand the changes in the singular and wretched development of the character of Prince Charles Edward Stuart. We get a curious view of the manners, and a lurid light on the diplomacy of the middle of the eighteenth century. We go behind the scenes of many conspiracies. Above all, we encounter an extraordinary personage, the great, highborn Highland chief who sold himself as a spy to the English Government.

His existence was suspected by Scott, if not clearly known and understood.

In his introduction to 'Redgauntlet,' {3} Sir Walter Scott says that the ministers of George III. 'thought it proper to leave Dr. Cameron's new schemes in concealment (1753), lest by divulging them they had indicated the channel of communication which, it is now well known, they possessed to all the plots of Charles Edward.' To 'indicate' that secret 'channel of communication' between the Government of the Pelhams and the Jacobite conspirators of 1749–1760 is one purpose of this book. Tradition has vaguely bequeathed to us the name of 'Pickle the Spy,' the foremost of many traitors. Who Pickle was, and what he did, a whole romance of prosperous treachery, is now to be revealed and illustrated from various sources. Pickle was not only able to keep the Duke of Newcastle and George II. well informed as to the inmost plots, if not the most hidden movements of Prince Charles, but he could either paralyse a serious, or promote a premature, rising in the Highlands, as seemed best to his English employers. We shall find Pickle, in company with that devoted Jacobite, Lochgarry, travelling through the Highlands, exciting hopes, consulting the chiefs, unburying a hidden treasure, and encouraging the clans to rush once more on English bayonets.

Romance, in a way, is stereotyped, and it is characteristic that the last romance of the Stuarts should be interwoven with a secret treasure. This mass of French gold, buried after Culloden at Loch Arkaig, in one of the most remote recesses of the Highlands, was, to the Jacobites, what the dwarf Andvari's hoard was to the Niflungs, a curse and a cause of discord. We shall see that rivalry for its possession produced contending charges of disloyalty, forgery, and theft among certain of the Highland chiefs, and these may have helped to promote the spirit of treachery in Pickle the Spy. It is probable, though not certain, that he had acted as the agent of Cumberland before he was sold to Henry Pelham, and he was certainly communicating the results of his inquiries in one sense to George II., and, in another sense, to the exiled James III. in Rome. He was betraying his own cousins, and traducing his friends. Pickle is plainly no common spy or 'paltry vidette,' as he words it. Possibly Sir Walter Scott knew who Pickle was: in him Scott, if he had chosen, would have found a character very like Barry Lyndon (but worse), very unlike any personage in the Waverley Novels, and somewhat akin to the Master of Ballantrae. The cool, good–humoured, smiling, unscrupulous villain of high rank and noble lineage; the scoundrel happily unconscious of his own unspeakable infamy, proud and sensitive upon the point of honour; the picturesque hypocrite in religion, is a being whom we do not meet in Sir Walter's romances. In Pickle he had such a character ready made to his hand, but, in the time of Scott, it would have been dangerous, as it is still disagreeable, to unveil this old mystery of iniquity. A friend of Sir Walter's, a man very ready with the pistol, the last, as was commonly said, of the Highland chiefs, was of the name and blood of Pickle, and would have taken up Pickle's feud. Sir Walter was not to be moved by pistols, but not even for the sake of a good story would he hurt the sensibilities of a friend, or tarnish the justly celebrated loyalty of the Highlands.

Now the friend of Scott, the representative of Pickle in Scott's generation, was a Highlander, and Pickle was not only a traitor, a profligate, an oppressor of his tenantry, and a liar, but (according to Jacobite gossip which reached 'King James') a forger of the King's name! Moreover he was, in all probability, one fountain of that reproach, true or false, which still clings to the name of the brave and gentle Archibald Cameron, the brother of Lochiel, whom Pickle brought to the gallows. If we add that, when last we hear of Pickle, he is probably engaged in a double treason, and certainly meditates selling a regiment of his clan, like Hessians, to the Hanoverian Government, it will be plain that his was no story for Scott to tell.

Pickle had, at least, the attraction of being eminently handsome. No statelier gentleman than Pickle, as his faded portrait shows him in full Highland costume, ever trod a measure at Holyrood. Tall, athletic, with a frank and pleasing face, Pickle could never be taken for a traitor and a spy. He seemed the fitting lord of that castellated palace of his race, which, beautiful and majestic in decay, mirrors itself in Loch Oich. Again, the man was brave; for he moved freely in France, England, and Scotland, well knowing that the *skian* was sharpened for his throat if he were detected. And the most extraordinary fact in an extraordinary story is that Pickle *was* detected, and denounced to the King over the water by Mrs. Archibald Cameron, the widow of his victim. Yet the breach between James and his little Court, on one side, and Prince Charles on the other, was then so absolute that the Prince was dining with the spy, chatting with him at the opera–ball, and presenting him with a gold snuff–box, at about the very time when Pickle's treachery was known in Rome. Afterwards, the knowledge of his infamy came too late, if it came at all. The great scheme had failed; Cameron had fallen, and Frederick of Prussia, ceasing to encourage Jacobitism, had become the ally of England.

These things sound like the inventions of the romancer, but they rest on unimpeachable evidence, printed and manuscript, and chiefly on Pickle's own letters to his King, to his Prince, and to his English employers—we cannot say 'pay–masters,' for *Pickle was never paid*! He obtained, indeed, singular advantages, but he seldom or never could wring ready money from the Duke of Newcastle.

To understand Pickle's career, the reluctant reader must endure a certain amount of actual history in minute details of date and place. Every one is acquainted with the brilliant hour of Prince Charles: his landing in Moidart accompanied by only seven men, his march on Edinburgh, his success at Prestonpans, the race to Derby, the retreat to Scotland, the gleam of victory at Falkirk, the ruin of Culloden, the long months of wanderings and distress, the return to France in 1746. Then came two years of baffled intrigues; next, the Treaty of Aix–la–Chapelle insisted on the Prince's expulsion from France; last, he declined to withdraw. On December 10, 1748, he was arrested at the opera, was lodged in the prison of Vincennes, was released, and made his way to the Pope's city of Avignon, arriving there in the last days of December 1748. On February 28, 1749, he rode out of Avignon, and disappeared for many months from the ken of history. For nearly eighteen years he preserved his incognito, vaguely heard of here and there in England, France, Germany, Flanders, but always involved in mystery. On that mystery, impenetrable to his father, Pickle threw light enough for the purposes of the English Government, but not during the darkest hours of Charles's incognito.

'Le Prince Edouard,' says Barbier in his journal for February 1750, 'fait l'admiration et la curiosité de l'Europe.' This work, alas! is not likely to add to the admiration entertained for the unfortunate adventurer, but any surviving curiosity as to the Prince's secret may be assuaged. In the days of 1749–1750, before Pickle's revelations begin, the drafts of the Prince's memoranda, notes, and angry love–letters, preserved in Her Majesty's Library, enable us to follow his movements. On much that is obscurely indicated in scarcely decipherable scrawls, light is thrown by the French memoirs of that age. The names of Madame de Talmond, Madame d'Aiguillon, and the celebrated Montesquieu, are beacons in the general twilight. The memoirs also explain, what was previously inexplicable, the motives of Charles in choosing a life 'in a hole of a rock,' as he said after the Peace of Aix–la–Chapelle (1748). It is necessary, however, to study the internal feuds of the Jacobites at this period, and these are illuminated by the Stuart Papers, the letters of James and his ministers.

The plan of our narrative, therefore, will be arranged in the following manner. First, we sketch the character of Prince Charles in boyhood, during his Scottish expedition, and as it developed in cruelly thwarting circumstances between 1746 and 1749. In illustrating his character the hostile parties within the Jacobite camp must be described and defined. From February 1749 to September 1750 (when he visited London), we must try to pierce the darkness that has been more than Egyptian. We can, at least, display the total ignorance of Courts and diplomatists as to Charles's movements before Pickle came to their assistance, and we discover a secret which they ought to have known.

After the date 1752 we give, as far as possible, the personal history of Pickle before he sold himself, and we unveil his motives for his villany. Then we display Pickle in action, we select from his letters, we show him deep in the Scottish, English, and continental intrigues. He spoils the Elibank Plot, he reveals the hostile policy of Frederick the Great, he leads on to the arrest of Archibald Cameron, he sows disunion, he traduces and betrays. He finally recovers his lands, robs his tenants, dabbles (probably) in the French scheme of invasion (1759), offers further information, tries to sell a regiment of his clan, and dies unexposed in 1761.

Minor spies are tracked here and there, as Rob Roy's son, James Mohr Macgregor, Samuel Cameron, and Oliver Macallester. English machinations against the Prince's life and liberty are unveiled. His utter decadence is illustrated, and we leave him weary, dishonoured, and abandoned.

'A sair, sair altered man
Prince Charlie cam' hame'

to Rome; and the refusal there of even a titular kingship.

The whole book aims chiefly at satisfying the passion of curiosity. However unimportant a secret may be, it is pleasant to know what all Europe was once vainly anxious to discover. In the revelation of manners, too, and in tracing the relations of famous wits and beauties with a person then so celebrated as Prince Charles, there is a certain amount of entertainment which may excuse some labour of research. Our history is of next to no political value, but it revives as in a magic mirror somewhat dim, certain scenes of actual human life. Now and again the mist breaks, and real passionate faces, gestures of living men and women, are beheld in the clear–obscure. We see Lochgarry throw his dirk after his son, and pronounce his curse. We mark Pickle furtively scribbling after midnight in French inns. We note Charles hiding in the alcove of a lady's chamber in a convent. We admire the 'rich anger' of his Polish mistress, and the sullen rage of Lord Hyndford, baffled by 'the perfidious Court' of Frederick the Great. The old histories emerge into light, like the writing in sympathetic ink on the secret despatches of King James.

CHAPTER II—CHARLES EDWARD STUART

Prince Charles—Contradictions in his character—Extremes of bad and good—Evolution of character—The Prince's personal advantages— Common mistake as to the colour of his eyes—His portraits from youth to age—Descriptions of Charles by the Duc de Liria; the President de Brosses; Gray; Charles's courage—The siege of Gaeta—Story of Lord Elcho—The real facts—The Prince's horse shot at Culloden—Foolish fables of David Hume confuted—Charles's literary tastes—His clemency—His honourable conduct—Contrast with Cumberland—His graciousness—His faults—Charge of avarice—Love of wine— Religious levity—James on Charles's faults—An unpleasant discovery —Influence of Murray of Broughton—Rapid decline of character after 1746—Temper, wine, and women—Deep distrust of James's Court— Rupture with James—Divisions among Jacobites—King's men and Prince's men—Marischal, Kelly, Lismore, Clancarty—Anecdote of Clancarty and Braddock—Clancarty and d'Argenson—Balhaldie—Lally Tollendal—The Duke of York—His secret flight from Paris—'Insigne Fourberie'—Anxiety of Charles—The fatal cardinal's hat—Madame de Pompadour—Charles rejects her advances—His love affairs—Madame de Talmond—Voltaire's verses on her—Her scepticism in religion—Her husband—Correspondence with Montesquieu—The Duchesse d'Aiguillon— Peace of

Aix–la–Chapelle—Charles refuses to retire to Fribourg—The gold plate—Scenes with Madame de Talmond—Bulkeley's interference— Arrest of Charles—The compasses—Charles goes to Avignon—His desperate condition—His policy—Based on a scheme of d'Argenson—He leaves Avignon—He is lost to sight and hearing.

'Charles Edward Stuart,' says Lord Stanhope, 'is one of those characters that cannot be portrayed at a single sketch, but have so greatly altered as to require a new delineation at different periods.' {12a} Now he 'glitters all over like the star which they tell you appeared at his nativity,' and which still shines beside him, *Micat inter omnes*, on a medal struck in his boyhood. {12b} Anon he is sunk in besotted vice, a cruel lover, a solitary tippler, a broken man. We study the period of transition.

Descriptions of his character vary between the noble encomium written in prison by Archibald Cameron, the last man who died for the Stuarts, and the virulent censures of Lord Elcho and Dr. King. Veterans known to Sir Walter Scott wept at the mention of the Prince's name; yet, as early as the tenth year after Prestonpans, his most devoted adherent, Henry Goring, left him in an angry despair. Nevertheless, the character so variously estimated, so tenderly loved, so loathed, so despised, was one character; modified, swiftly or slowly, as its natural elements developed or decayed under the various influences of struggle, of success, of long endurance, of hope deferred, and of bitter disappointment. The gay, kind, brave, loyal, and clement Prince Charlie became the fierce, shabby, battered exile, homeless, and all but friendless. The change, of course, was not instantaneous, but gradual; it was not the result of one, but of many causes. Even out of his final degradation, Charles occasionally speaks with his real voice: his inborn goodness of heart, remarked before his earliest adventures, utters its protest against the self he has become; just as, on the other hand, long ere he set his foot on Scottish soil, his father had noted his fatal inclination to wine and revel.

The processes in this change of character, the events, the temptations, the trials under which Charles became an altered man, have been very slightly studied, and, indeed, have been very obscurely known. Even Mr. Ewald, the author of the most elaborate biography of the Prince, {13} neglected some important French printed sources, while manuscript documents, here for the first time published, were not at his command. The present essay is itself unavoidably incomplete, for of family papers bearing on the subject many have perished under the teeth of time, and in one case, of rats, while others are not accessible to the writer. Nevertheless, it is hoped that this work elucidates much which has long been veiled in the motives, conduct, and secret movements of Charles during the years between 1749 and the death, in 1766, of his father, the Old Chevalier. Charles then emerged from a retirement of seventeen years; the European game of Hide and Seek was over, and it is not proposed to study the Prince in the days of his manifest decline, and among the disgraces of his miserable marriage. His 'incognito' is our topic; the period of 'deep and isolated enterprise' which puzzled every Foreign Office in Europe, and practically only ended, as far as hope was concerned, with the break–up of the Jacobite party in 1754–1756, or rather with Hawke's defeat of Conflans in 1759.

Ours is a strange and melancholy tale of desperate loyalties, and of a treason almost unparalleled for secrecy and persistence. We have to do with the back–stairs of diplomacy, with spies and traitors, with cloak and sword, with blabbing servants, and inquisitive ambassadors, with disguise and discovery, with friends more staunch than steel, or weaker than water, with petty jealousies, with the relentless persecution of a brave man, and with the consequent ruin of a gallant life.

To understand the psychological problem, the degradation of a promising personality, it is necessary to glance rapidly at what we know of Charles before his Scottish expedition.

To begin at the beginning, in physical qualities the Prince was dowered by a kind fairy. He was firmly though slimly built, of the best stature for strength and health. 'He had a body made for war,' writes Lord Elcho, who hated him. The gift of beauty (in his case peculiarly fatal, as will be seen) had not been denied to him. His brow was high and broad, his nose shapely, his eyes of a rich dark brown, his hair of a chestnut hue, golden at the tips. Though his eyes are described as blue, both in 1744 by Sir Horace Mann, and in later life (1770) by an English lady in Rome, though Lord Stanhope and Mr. Stevenson agree in this error, brown was really their colour. {15a} Charles inherited the dark eyes of his father, 'the Black Bird,' and of Mary Stuart. This is manifest from all the original portraits and miniatures, including that given by the Prince to his secretary, Murray of Broughton, now in my collection. In boyhood Charles's face had a merry, mutinous, rather reckless expression, as portraits prove. Hundreds of faces like his may be seen at the public schools; indeed, Charles had many 'doubles,' who sometimes traded on the resemblance, sometimes, wittingly or unwittingly, misled the spies that constantly pursued him. {15b} His adherents fondly declared that his natural air of distinction, his princely bearing, were too marked to be concealed in any travesty. Yet no man has, in disguises of his person, been more successful. We may grant 'the grand air' to Charles, but we must admit that he could successfully dissemble it.

About 1743, when a number of miniatures of the Prince were done in Italy for presentation to adherents, Charles's boyish mirth, as seen in these works of art, has become somewhat petulant, if not arrogant, but he is still 'a lad with the bloom of a lass.' A shade of aspiring melancholy marks a portrait done in France, just before the expedition to Scotland. Le Toque's fine portrait of the Prince in armour (1748) shows a manly and martial but rather sinister countenance. A plaster bust, done from a life mask, if not from Le Moine's bust in marble (1750), was thought the best likeness by Dr. King. This bust was openly sold in Red Lion Square, and, when Charles visited Dr. King in September 1750, the Doctor's servant observed the resemblance. I have never seen a copy of this bust, and the medal struck in 1750, an intaglio of the same date, and a very rare profile in the collection of the Duke of Atholl, give a similar idea of the Prince as he was at thirty. A distinguished artist, who outlined Charles's profile and applied it to another of Her present Majesty in youth, tells me that they are almost exact counterparts.

Next we come to the angry eyes and swollen features of Ozias Humphreys's miniature, in the Duke of Atholl's collection, and in his sketch published in the 'Lockhart Papers' (1776), and, finally, to the fallen weary old face designed by Gavin Hamilton. Charles's younger brother, Henry, Duke of York, was a prettier boy, but it is curious to mark the prematurely priestly and 'Italianate' expression of the Duke in youth, while Charles still seems a merry lad. Of Charles in boyhood many anecdotes are told. At the age of two or three he is said to have been taken to see the Pope in his garden, and to have refused the usual marks of reverence. Walton, the English agent in Florence, reports an outbreak of ferocious temper in 1733. {17a} Though based on gossip, the story seems to forebode the later excesses of anger. Earlier, in 1727, the Duc de Liria, a son of Marshal Berwick, draws a pretty picture of the child when about seven years old:–

'The King of England did not wish me to leave before May 4, and I was only too happy to remain at his feet, not merely on account of the love and respect I have borne him all my life, but also because I was never weary of watching the Princes, his sons. The Prince of Wales was now six and a half, and, besides his great beauty, was remarkable for dexterity, grace, and almost supernatural cleverness. Not only could he read fluently, but he knew the doctrines of the Christian faith as well as the master who had taught him. He could ride; could fire a gun; and, more surprising still, I have seen him take a crossbow and kill birds on the roof, and split a rolling ball with a shaft, ten times in succession. He speaks English, French, and Italian perfectly, and altogether he is the most ideal Prince I have ever met in the course of my life.

'The Duke of York, His Majesty's second son, is two years old, and a prodigy of beauty and strength.' {17b}

Gray, certainly no Jacobite, when at Rome with Horace Walpole speaks very kindly of the two gay young Princes. He sneers at their melancholy father, of whom Montesquieu writes, '*ce Prince a une bonne physiononie et noble. Il paroit triste, pieux.*' {18a} Young Charles was neither pious nor melancholy.

Of Charles at the age of twenty, the President de Brosses (the author of 'Les Dieux Fétiches') speaks as an unconcerned observer. 'I hear from those who know them both thoroughly that the eldest has far higher worth, and is much more beloved by his friends; that he has a kind heart and a high courage; that he feels warmly for his family's misfortunes, and that if some day he does not retrieve them, it will not be for want of intrepidity.' {18b}

Charles's gallantry when under fire as a mere boy, at the siege of Gaeta (1734), was, indeed, greatly admired and generally extolled. {18c} His courage has been much more foolishly denied by his enemies than too eagerly applauded by friends who had seen him tried by every species of danger.

Aspersions have been thrown on Charles's personal bravery; it may be worth while to comment on them. The story of Lord Elcho's reproaching the Prince for not heading a charge of the second line at Culloden, has unluckily been circulated by Sir Walter Scott. On February 9, 1826, Scott met Sir James Stuart Denham, whose father was out in the Forty–five, and whose uncle was the Lord Elcho of that date. Lord Elcho wrote memoirs, still unpublished, but used by Mr. Ewald in his 'Life of the Prince.' Elcho is a hostile witness: for twenty years he vainly dunned Charles for a debt of 1,500*l*. According to Sir James Stuart Denham, Elcho asked Charles to lead a final charge at Culloden, retrieve the battle, or die sword in hand. The Prince rode off the field, Elcho calling him 'a damned, cowardly Italian—.'

No such passage occurs in Elcho's diary. He says that, after the flight, he found Charles, in the belief that he had been betrayed, anxious only for his Irish officers, and determined to go to France, not to join the clans at Ruthven. Elcho most justly censured and resolved 'never to have anything more to do with him,' a broken vow! {19a} As a matter of fact, Sir Robert Strange saw Charles vainly trying to rally the Highlanders, and Sir Stuart Thriepland of Fingask gives the same evidence. {19b}

In his seclusion during 1750, Charles wrote a little memoir, still unpublished, about his Highland wanderings. In this he says that he was 'led off the field by those about him,' when the clans broke at Culloden. 'The Prince then changed his horse, his own having been wounded by a musket–ball in the shoulder.' {20a}

The second–hand chatter of Hume, in his letter to Sir John Pringle (February 13, 1773), is unworthy of serious attention.

Helvetius told Hume that his house at Paris had sheltered the Prince in the years following his expulsion from France, in 1748. He called Charles 'the most unworthy of mortals, insomuch that I have been assured, when he went down to Nantz to embark on his expedition to Scotland, he took fright and refused to go on board; and his attendants, thinking the matter gone too far, and that they would be affronted for his cowardice, carried him in the night time into the ship, *pieds et mains liés*.'

The sceptical Hume accepts this absurd statement without even asking, or at least without giving, the name of Helvetius's informant. The adventurer who insisted on going forward when, at his first landing in Scotland, even Sir Thomas Sheridan, with all the chiefs present, advised retreat, cannot conceivably have been the poltroon of Hume's myth. Even Hume's correspondent, Sir John Pringle, was manifestly staggered by the anecdote, and tells Hume that another of his fables is denied by the very witness to whom Hume appealed. {20b} Hume had cited Lord Holdernesse for the story that Charles's presence in London in 1753 (1750 seems to be meant) was known at the time to George II. Lord Holdernesse declared that there was nothing in the tale given by Hume on his authority! That Charles did not join the rallied clans at Ruthven after Culloden was the result of various misleading circumstances, not of cowardice. Even after 1746 he constantly carried his life in his hand, not only in expeditions to England (and probably to Scotland and Ireland), but in peril from the daggers of assassins, as will later be shown.

High–spirited and daring, Charles was also hardy. In Italy he practised walking without stockings, to inure his feet to long marches: he was devoted to boar–hunting, shooting, and golf. {21a} He had no touch of Italian effeminacy, otherwise he could never have survived his Highland distresses. In travelling he was swift, and incapable of fatigue. 'He has,' said early observer, '*the habit of keeping a secret*.' Many secrets, indeed, he kept so well that history is still baffled by them, as diplomatists were perplexed between 1749 and 1766. {21b}

We may discount Murray of Broughton's eulogies Charles's Greek, Latin, and Hebrew, and his knowledge of history and philosophy, though backed by the Jesuit Cordara. {21c} Charles's education had been interrupted by quarrels between his parents about Catholic or Protestant tutors. His cousin and governor, Sir Thomas Sheridan (a descendant of James II.), certainly did not teach him to spell; his style in French and English is often obscure, and, when it is clear, we know not whether he was not inspired by some more literary adviser. In matters of taste he was fond of music and archæology, and greatly addicted to books. De Brosses, however, considered him 'less cultivated than Princes should be at his age,' and d'Argenson says that his knowledge was scanty and that he had little conversation. A few of his books, the morocco tooled with the Prince of Wales's feathers, remain, but not enough to tell us much about his literary tastes. On these, however, we shall give ample information. In Paris, after Culloden, he bought Macchiavelli's works, probably in search of practical hints on state–craft. In spite of a proclamation by Charles, which Montesquieu applauded, he certainly had no claim to a seat in the French Academy, which Montesquieu playfully offered to secure for him.

In brief, Charles was a spirited, eager boy, very capable of patience, intensely secretive, and, as he showed in 1745–1746, endowed with a really extraordinary clemency, and in one regard, where his enemies were concerned, with a sense of honour most unusual in his generation. His care for the wounded, after Prestonpans, is acknowledged by the timid and Whiggish Home, in his 'History of the Rebellion,' and is very warmly and gracefully expressed in a letter to his father, written at Holyrood.' {23a} He could not be induced to punish miscreants who attempted his life and snapped pistols in his face. He could hardly be compelled to retort to the English offer of 30,000*l*. for his head by issuing a similar proclamation about 'the Elector.' 'I smiled and created it' (the proclamation of a reward of 30,000*l*. for his head) 'with the disdain it deserved, upon which they' (the Highlanders) 'flew into a violent rage, and insisted upon my doing the same by him.' This occurs in a letter from Charles to James, September 10, 1745, dated from Perth. A copy is found among Bishop Forbes's papers. Here Charles deplores the cruelties practised under Charles II. and James II., and the consequent estrangement of the Duke of Argyll. {23b}

In brief, the contest between Charles and Cumberland was that of a civilised and chivalrous commander against a foe as treacherous and cruel as a Huron or an Iroquois. On this point there is no possibility of doubt. The English Government offered a vast reward for Charles, dead or alive. The soldiers were told significantly, by Cumberland, that he did not want prisoners. On the continent assassins lurked for the Prince, and ambassadors urged the use of personal violence. Meanwhile the Prince absolutely forbade even a legitimate armed attack directed mainly against his enemy, then red–handed from the murder of the wounded.

With this loyalty to his foes, with this clemency to enemies in his power, Charles certainly combined a royal grace, and could do handsome things handsomely. Thus, in 1745, some of the tenants of Oliphant of Gask would not don the white cockade at his command. He therefore 'laid an arrest or inhibition on their corn–fields.' Charles, finding the grain hanging dead–ripe, as he marched through Perthshire, inquired the cause, and when he had learned it, broke the 'taboo' by cutting some ears with his sword, or by gathering them and giving them to his horse, saying that the farmers might now, by his authority, follow his example and break the inhibition. {24a}

Making every allowance for an enthusiasm of loyalty on the part of the narrators in Bishop Forbes's MS. 'Lyon in Mourning' (partly published by Robert Chambers in 'Jacobite Memoirs' {24b}), it is certain that the courage, endurance, and gay content of the Prince in his Highland wanderings deserve the high praise given by Smollett. Thus, in many ways we see the elements of a distinguished and attractive character in Charles. His enemies, like the renegade Dr. King, of St. Mary's Hall (ob. 1763), in his posthumous 'Anecdotes,' accused the Prince of avarice. He would borrow money from a lady, says King, while he had plenty of his own; he neglected those who had ruined themselves for his sake. Henry Goring accused the Prince of shabbiness to his face, but assuredly he who insisted on laying down money on the rocks of a deserted fishers' islet to pay for some dry fish eaten there by himself and his companions—he who gave liberally to gentle and simple out of the treasure buried near Loch Arkaig, who refused a French pension for himself, and asked favours only for his friends—afforded singular proofs of Dr. King's charge of selfish greed. The fault grew on him later. After breaking with the French Court in 1748, Charles had little or nothing of his own to give away. His Sobieski jewels he had pawned for the expenses of the war, having no heart to wear them, he said, 'on this side of the water.' He was often in actual need, though we may not accept d'Argenson's story of how he was once seen selling his pistols to a gun–maker. {25a} If ever he was a miser, that vice fixed itself upon him in his utter moral ruin.

Were there, then, no signs in his early life of the faults which grew so rapidly when hope was lost? There were such signs. As early as 1742, James had observed in Charles a slight inclination to wine and gaiety, and believed that his companions, especially Francis Strickland, {25b} were setting him against his younger brother, the Duke of York, who had neither the health nor the disposition to be a roysterer. {26a}

Again, on February 3, 1747, James recurs, in a long letter, to what passed in 1742, 'because that is the foundation, and I may say the key, of all that has followed.' Now in 1742 Murray of Broughton paid his first visit to Rome, and was fascinated by Charles. This unhappy man, afterwards the Judas of the cause, was unscrupulous in private life in matters of which it is needless to speak more fully. He was, or gave himself the air of being, a very stout Protestant. James employed him, but probably liked him little. It is to be gathered, from James's letter of February 3, 1747, that he suspected Charles of listening to advice, probably from Murray, about his changing his religion. 'You cannot forget how you were prevailed upon to speak to your brother' (the devout Duke of York) 'on very nice and delicate subjects, and that without saying the least thing to me, though we lived in the same house . . . You were then much younger than you are now, and therefore could be more easily led by specious arguments and pretences. . . . It will, to be sure, have been represented to you that our religion is a great prejudice to our interest, but that it may in some measure be remedied by a certain free way of thinking and acting.' {26b}

In 1749 James made a disagreeable discovery, which he communicated to Lord Lismore. A *cassette*, or coffer, belonging to Charles, had, apparently, been left in Paris, and, after many adventures on the road, was brought to Rome by the French ambassador. James opened it, and found that it contained letters 'from myself and the Queen.' But it also offered proof that the Prince had carried on a secret correspondence with England, long before he left Rome in 1744. Probably his adherents wished James to resign in his favour. {27a}

As to religion, Dr. King admits that Charles was no bigot, and d'Argenson contrasted his disengaged way of treating theology with the exaggerated devoutness of the Duke of

York. Even during the march into England, Lord Elcho told an inquirer that the Prince's religion 'was still to seek.' Assuredly he would never make shipwreck on the Stuart fidelity to Catholicism. All this was deeply distressing to the pious James, and all this dated from 1742, that is, from the time of Murray of Broughton's visit to Rome. Indifference to religious strictness was, even then, accompanied by a love of wine, in some slight degree. Already, too, a little rift in the friendship of the princely brothers was apparent; there were secrets between them which Henry must have communicated to James.

As for the fatal vice of drink, it is hinted at on April 15, 1747, by an anonymous Paris correspondent of Lord Dunbar's. Charles had about him 'an Irish cordelier,' one Kelly, whom he employed as a secretary. Kelly is accused of talking contemptuously about James. 'It were to be wished that His Royal Highness would forbid that friar his apartment, because he passes for a notorious drunkard . . . and His Royal Highness's character, in point of sobriety, has been a little blemished on this friar's account.' {28a}

The cold, hunger, and fatigue of the Highland distresses had, no doubt, often prompted recourse to the national dram of whiskey, and Charles would put a bottle of brandy to his lips 'without ceremony,' says Bishop Forbes. The Prince on one occasion is said to have drunk the champion 'bowlsman' of the Islands under the table. {28b}

What had been a jovial feast became a custom, a consolation, and a curse, while there is reason, as has been seen, to suppose that Charles, quite early in life, showed promise of intemperance. In happier circumstances these early tastes might never have been developed into a positive disease. James himself, in youth, had not been a pattern of strict sobriety, but later middle age found him almost ascetic.

We have sketched a character endowed with many fine qualities, and capable of winning devoted affection. We now examine the rapid decline of a nature originally noble.

Returned from Scotland in 1746, Prince Charles brought with him a head full of indigested romance, a heart rich in chimerical expectations. He now prided himself on being a plain hardy mountaineer. He took a line of his own; he concealed his measures from the spy–ridden Court of his father in Rome; he quarrelled with his brother, the Duke of York, when the Duke accepted a cardinal's hat. He broke violently with the French king, who would not aid him. He sulked at Avignon. He sought Spanish help, which was refused. He again became the centre of fashion and of disaffection in Paris. Ladies travelled from England merely to see him in his box at the theatre. Princesses and duchesses 'pulled caps for him.' Naturally cold (as his enemies averred) where women were concerned, he was now beleaguered, besieged, taken by storm by the fair. He kept up the habit of drinking which had been noted in him even before his expedition to Scotland. He allowed his old boyish scepticism (caused by a mixed Protestant and Catholic education) to take the form of studied religious indifference. After defying and being expelled by Louis XV., he adopted (what has never, perhaps, been observed) the wild advice of d'Argenson ('La Bête,' and Louis's ex–minister of foreign affairs), he betook himself to a life of darkling adventures, to a hidden and homeless exile. In many of his journeys he found Pickle in his path, and Pickle finally made his labours vain. The real source of all this imbroglio, in addition to an exasperated daring and a strangely secretive temperament, was a deep, well–grounded mistrust of the people employed by his father, the old 'King over the water.' Whatever James knew was known in London by next mail. Charles was aware of this, and was not aware that his own actions were almost as successfully spied upon and reported. He therefore concealed his plans and movements from James, and even—till Pickle came on the scene—from Europe and from England. The result of his reticence was an irremediable rupture between 'the King and the Prince of Wales—over the water,' an incurable split in the Jacobite camp.

The general outline here sketched must now be filled up in detail. The *origo mali* was the divisions among the Jacobites. Ever since 1715 these had existed and multiplied. Mar was thought to be a traitor. Atterbury, in exile, suspected O'Brien (Lord Lismore). The Earl Marischal and Kelly {30a} were set against James's ministers, Lord Sempil, Lord Lismore, and Balhaldie, the exiled chief of the Macgregors. Lord Dunbar (Murray, brother of Lord Mansfield) was in James's disgrace at Avignon. Sempil, Balhaldie, Lismore were 'the King's party,' opposed to Marischal, Kelly, Sheridan, Lally Tollendal, 'the Prince's party.' Each sect inveighed against the other in unmeasured terms of reproach. This division widened when Charles was in France, just before the expedition to Scotland.

One of James's agents in Paris, Lord Sempil, writes to him on July 5, 1745, with warnings against the Prince's counsellors, especially Sir Thomas Sheridan (Charles's governor, and left–handed cousin) and Kelly. They, with Lally Tollendal and others, arranged the descent on Scotland without the knowledge of James or Sempil, whom Charles and his party bitterly distrusted, as they also distrusted Lord Lismore (O'Brien),

James's other agent. While the Prince was in Scotland (1745–1746), even before Prestonpans, the Jacobite affairs in France were perplexed by the action of Lismore, Sempil, and Balhaldie, acting for James, while the old Earl Marischal (who had been in the rising of 1715, and the Glenshiel affair of 1719) acted for the Prince. With the Earl Marischal was, for some time, Lord Clancarty, of whom Sempil speaks as 'a very brave and worthy man.' {31a} On the other hand, Oliver Macallester, the spy, describes Clancarty, with whom he lived, as a slovenly, drunken, blaspheming rogue, one of whose eyes General Braddock had knocked out with a bottle in a tavern brawl! Clancarty gave himself forth as a representative of the English Jacobites, but d'Argenson, in his 'Mémoires,' says he could produce no names of men of rank in the party except his own. D'Argenson was pestered by women, priests, and ragged Irish adventurers. In September 1745, the Earl Marischal and Clancarty visited d'Argenson, then foreign minister of Louis XV. in the King's camp in Flanders. They asked for aid, and the scene, as described by the spy Macallester, on Clancarty's information, was curious. D'Argenson taunted the Lord Marischal with not being at Charles's side in Scotland. To the slovenly Clancarty he said, 'Sir, your wig is ill–combed. Would you like to see my perruquier? He manages wigs very well.' Clancarty, who wore 'an ordinary black tie–wig,' jumped up, saying in English, 'Damn the fellow! He is making his diversion of us.' {32a} The Lord Marischal was already on bad personal terms with Charles. Clancarty was a ruffian, d'Argenson was the adviser who suggested Charles's hidden and fugitive life after 1748. The singular behaviour of the Earl Marischal in 1751–1754 will afterwards be illustrated by the letters of Pickle, who drew much of his information from the unsuspicious old ambassador of Frederick the Great to the Court of Versailles. It is plain that the Duke of Ormonde was right when he said that 'too many people are meddling in your Majesty's affairs with the French Court at this juncture' (November 15, 1745). The Duke of York, Charles's brother, was on the seaboard of France in autumn 1745. At Arras he met the gallant Chevalier Wogan, who had rescued his mother from prison at Innspruck. {32b} Clancarty, Lord Marischal, and Lally Tollendal were pressing for a French expedition to start in aid of Charles. Sempil, Balhaldie, Lismore, were intriguing and interfering. Voltaire wrote a proclamation for Charles to issue. An expedition was arranged, troops and ships were gathered at Boulogne. Swedes were to join from Gothenburg. On Christmas Eve, 1745, nothing was ready, and the secret leaked out. A million was sent to Scotland; the money arrived too late; we shall hear more of it. {33a} The Duke of York, though he fought well at Antwerp, was kneeling in every shrine, and was in church when the news of Culloden was brought to him. This information he gave, in the present century, to one of the Stair family. {33b} The rivalries and enmities went on increasing and multiplying into cross–divisions after Charles made his escape to France in August 1746. He was filled with distrust of his father's advisers; his own were disliked by James. The correspondence of Horace Mann, and of Walton, an English agent in Florence, shows that England received all intelligence sent to James from Paris, and knew all that passed in James's cabinet in Rome. {33c} The Abbé Grant was suspected of being the spy.

Among so many worse than doubtful friends, Charles, after 1746, took his own course; even his father knew little or nothing of his movements. Between his departure from Avignon (February 1749) and the accession of Pickle to the Hanoverian side (Autumn 1749 or 1750), Charles baffled every Foreign Office in Europe. Indeed, Pickle was of little service till 1751 or 1752. Curious light on Charles's character, and on the entangled quarrels of the Jacobites, is cast by d'Argenson's 'Mémoires.' In Spring, 1747, the Duke of York disappeared from Paris, almost as cleverly as Charles himself could have done. D'Argenson thus describes his manuvre. 'He fled from Paris with circumstances of distinguished treachery' (*insigne fourberie*) towards his brother, the Prince. He invited Charles to supper; his house was brilliantly lighted up; all his servants were in readiness; but *he* had made his escape by five o'clock in the afternoon, aided by Cardinal Tencin. His Governor, the Chevalier Graeme, was not in the secret. The Prince waited for him till midnight, and was in a mortal anxiety. He believed that the English attempts to kidnap or assassinate himself had been directed against his brother. At last, after three days, he received a letter from the Duke of York, 'explaining his fatal design' to accept a cardinal's hat. 'Prince Charles is determined never to return to Rome, *but rather to take refuge in some hole in a rock.*'

Charles, in fact, saw that, if he was to succeed in England, he could not have too little connection with Rome. D'Argenson describes his brother Henry as 'Italian, superstitious, a rogue, avaricious, fond of ease, and jealous of the Prince.' Cardinal Tencin, he says, and Lord and Lady Lismore, have been bribed by England to wheedle Henry into the cardinalate, 'which England desires more than anything in the world.' Charles expressed the same opinion in an epigram. Lady Lismore, for a short time believed to be the mistress of Louis XV., was deeply suspected. Whatever may be the truth of these charges, M. de Puysieux, an enemy of Charles, succeeded at the Foreign Office to d'Argenson, who had a queer sentimental liking for the Prince. Cardinal Tencin was insulted, and was hostile; the Lismores were absolutely estranged, if not treacherous; there was a quarrel between James and Henry in Rome, and Charles, in Paris. {35a}

Such was the state of affairs at the end of 1747, while Pickle was still a prisoner in the Tower of London, engaged, he tells us, in acts of charity towards his fellow–captives!

Meanwhile Charles's private conduct demands a moment's attention. Madame de Pompadour was all powerful at Court. {35b} This was, therefore, a favourable moment for Charles, in a chivalrous affection for the injured French Queen (his dead mother's kinswoman), to insult the reigning favourite. Madame de Pompadour sent him *billets* on that thick smooth vellum paper of hers, sealed with the arms of France. The Prince tossed them into the fire and made no answer; it is Pickle who gives us this information. Maria Theresa later stooped to call Madame de Pompadour her cousin. Charles was prouder or less politic; afterwards he stooped like Maria Theresa.

For his part, says d'Argenson, the Prince 'now amused himself with love affairs. Madame de Guémené almost ravished him by force; they have quarrelled, after a ridiculous scene; he is living now with the Princesse de Talmond. He is full of fury, and wishes in everything to imitate Charles XII. of Sweden and stand a siege in his house like Charles XII. at Bender.' This was in anticipation of arrest, after the Treaty of Aix–la–Chapelle, in which his expulsion from France was one of the conditions. This Princesse de Talmond, as we shall see, was the unworthy Flora Macdonald of Charles in his later wanderings, his protectress, and, unlike Flora, his mistress. She was not young; Madame d'Aiguillon calls her *vieille femme* in a curious play, 'La Prison du Prince Charles Edouard Stuart,' written by d'Argenson in imitation of Shakespeare. {36a} The Princesse, *née* Marie Jablonowski, a cousin of the Queen of France and of Charles, married Anne Charles Prince de Talmond, of the great house of La Trimouille, in 1730. She must have been nearly forty in 1749, and some ten years older than her lover.

We shall later, when Charles is concealed by the Princesse de Talmond, present the reader with her 'portrait' by the mordant pen of Madame du Deffand. Here Voltaire's rhymed portrait may be cited:

Les dieux, en la donnant naissance
Aux lieux par la Saxe envahis,
Lui donnèrent pour récompense
Le goût qu'on ne trouve qu'en France,

Et l'esprit de tous les pays.

The Princesse, who frequented the *Philosophes*, appears to have encouraged Charles in free thinking and ostentatious indifference in religion.

'He is a handsome Prince, and I should love him as much as my wife does,' says poor M. de Talmond, in d'Argenson's play, 'but why is he not saintly, and ruled by the Congrégation de Saint Ignace, like his father? It is Madame de Talmond who preaches to him independence and incredulity. She is bringing the curse of God upon me. How old will she be before the conversion for which I pray daily to Saint François Xavier?'

Such was Madame de Talmond, an old mistress of a young man, flighty, philosophical, and sharp of tongue.

On July 18, 1748, Charles communicated to Louis XV. his protest against the article of the Peace of Aix–la–Chapelle which drove him out of every secular state in Europe. Louis broke a solemn treaty by assenting to this article. Charles published his protest and sent it to Montesquieu. He complained that Montesquieu had not given him the new edition of his book on the Romans. 'La confiance devroit être mieux établi entre les auteurs: j'espère que ma façon de penser pour vous m'attirera la continuation de votre bonne volonté pour moi.' {37a} Montesquieu praised Charles's 'simplicity, nobility, and eloquence': 'comme vous le dites très bien, vous estes un auteur.' 'Were you not so great a Prince, the Duchesse de Guillon' (d'Aiguillon) 'and I would secure you a place in the Academy.'

The Duchesse d'Aiguillon, who later watched by Montesquieu's death–bed, was a friend of Charles. She and Madame de Talmond literally 'pull caps' for him in d'Argenson's play. But she was in favour of his going to Fribourg with a pension after the Peace: Madame de Talmond encouraged resistance. Louis's minister, M. de Cousteille, applied to Fribourg for an asylum for Charles on June 24, 1748. On September 8, Burnaby wrote, for England, a long remonstrance to the 'Laudable States of Fribourg,' calling Charles 'this young Italian!' The States, in five lines, rebuked Burnaby's impertinence, as 'unconfined in its expressions and so unsuitable to a Sovereign State that we did not judge it proper to answer it.' {38a}

To Fribourg Charles would not go. He braved the French Court in every way. He even insisted on a goldsmith's preferring his order for a great service of plate to the King's, and, having obtained the plate, he feasted the Princesse de Talmond, his friend and cousin, the Duc de Bouillon, and a crowd of other distinguished people. {38b} In his demeanour Charles resolutely affronted the French Ministers. There were terrible scenes with Madame de Talmond, especially when Charles was forbidden the house by her husband. Charles was led away from her closed door by Bulkeley, the brother–in–law of Marshal Berwick, and a friend of Montesquieu's. {39a} Thus the violence which afterwards interrupted and ended Charles's *liaison* with Madame de Talmond had already declared itself. One day, according to d'Argenson, the lady said, 'You want to give *me* the second volume in your romance of compromising Madame de Montbazon [his cousin] with your two pistol–shots.' No more is known of this adventure. But Charles was popular both in Court and town: his resistance to expulsion was applauded. De Gèvres was sent by the King to entreat Charles to leave France; 'he received de Gèvres gallantly, his hand on his sword–hilt.' D'Argenson saw him at the opera on December 3, 1748, 'fort gai et fort beau, admiré de tout le public.'

On December 10, 1748, Charles was arrested at the door of the opera house, bound hand and foot, searched, and dragged to Vincennes. The deplorable scene is too familiar for repetition. One point has escaped notice. Charles (according to d'Argenson) had told de Gèvres that he would die by his own hand, if arrested. Two pistols were found on him; he had always carried them since his Scottish expedition. But a *pair of compasses* was also found. Now it was with a pair of compasses that his friend, Lally Tollendal, long afterwards attempted to commit suicide in prison. The pistols were carried in fear of assassination, but what does a man want with a pair of compasses at the opera? {40a}

After some days of detention at Vincennes, Charles was released, was conducted out of French territory, and made his way to Avignon, where he resided during January and February 1749. He had gained the sympathy of the mob, both in Paris and in London. Some of the French Court, including the Dauphin, were eager in his cause. Songs and poems were written against Louis XV, D'Argenson, as we know, being out of office, composed a play on Charles's martyrdom. So much contempt for Louis was excited, that a nail was knocked into the coffin of French royalty. The King, at the dictation of England, had arrested, bound, imprisoned, and expelled his kinsman, his guest, and (by the Treaty of Fontainebleau) his ally.

Applause and pity from the fickle and forgetful the Prince had won, but his condition was now desperate. Refusing to accept a pension from France, he was poor; his jewels he had pawned for the Scottish expedition. He had disobeyed his father's commands and mortally offended Louis by refusing to leave France. His adherents in Paris (as their letters to Rome prove) were in despair. His party, as has been shown, was broken up into hostile camps. Lochiel was dead. Lord George Murray had been insulted and estranged. The Earl Marischal had declined Charles's invitation to manage his affairs (1747). Elcho was a persistent and infuriated dun. Clancarty was reviling Charles, James, Louis, England, and the world at large. Madame de Pompadour, Cardinal Tencin, and de Puysieux were all hostile. The English Jacobites, though loyal, were timid. Europe was hermetically sealed against the Prince. Refuge in Fribourg, where the English threatened the town, Charles had refused. Not a single shelter was open to him, for England's policy was to drive him into the dominions of the Pope, where he would be distant and despised. Of advisers he had only such attached friends as Henry Goring, Bulkeley, Harrington, or such distrusted boon companions as Kelly—against whom the English Jacobites set all wheels in motion. Charles's refuge at Avignon even was menaced by English threats directed at the Pope. The Prince tried to amuse himself; he went to dances, he introduced boxing matches, {41a} just as years before he had brought golf into Italy. But his position was untenable, and he disappeared.

From the gossip of d'Argenson we have learned that Charles was no longer the same man as the gallant leader of the race to Derby, or the gay and resourceful young Ascanius who won the hearts of the Highlanders by his cheerful courage and contented endurance. He was now embittered by defeat; by suspicions of treachery which the Irish about him kindled and fanned, by the broken promises of Louis XV., by the indifference of Spain. He had become 'a wild man,' as his father's secretary, Edgar, calls him—'Our dear wild man.' He spelled the name 'L'ome sauvage.' He was, in brief, a desperate, a soured, and a homeless outcast. His chief French friends were ladies—Madame de Vassé, Madame de Talmond, and others. Montesquieu, living in their society, and sending wine from his estate to the Jacobite Lord Elibank; rejoicing, too, in an Irish Jacobite housekeeper, 'Mlle. Betti,' was well disposed, like Voltaire, in an indifferent well-bred way. Most of these people were, later, protecting and patronising the Prince when concealed from the view of Europe, but theirs was a vague and futile alliance. Charles and his case were desperate.

In this mood, and in this situation at Avignon, he carried into practice the counsel which d'Argenson had elaborated in a written memoir. 'I gave them' (Charles and Henry) 'the best possible advice,' says La Bête. 'My "Mémoire" I entrusted to O'Brien at Antwerp. Therein I suggested that the two princes should never return to Italy, *but that for some years they should lead a hidden and wandering life between France and Spain*. Charles might be given a pension and the vicariat of Navarre. This should only be allowed to slip out by degrees, while England would grow accustomed to the notion that they were *not* in Rome, and would be reduced to mere doubts as to their place of residence. Now they would be in Spain, now in France, finally in some town of Navarre, where their authority would, by slow degrees, be admitted. Peace once firmly established, it would not be broken over this question. They would be in a Huguenot country, and able to pass suddenly into Great Britain.' {43}

This was d'Argenson's advice before Henry fled Rome to be made a cardinal, and before the treaty of Aix–la–Chapelle, closing Europe against Charles, was concluded. The object of d'Argenson is plain; he wished to keep Charles out of the Pope's domains, as England wanted to drive the Prince into the centre of 'Popery.' If he resided in Rome, Protestant England would always suspect Charles; moreover, he would be remote from the scene of action. To the Pope's domains, therefore, Charles would not go. But the scheme of skulking in France, Spain, and Navarre had ceased to be possible. He, therefore, adopted 'the fugitive and hidden life' recommended by d'Argenson; he secretly withdrew from Avignon, and for many months his places of residence were unknown.

'Charles,' says Voltaire, 'hid himself from the whole world.' We propose to reveal his hiding–places.

CHAPTER III—THE PRINCE IN FAIRYLAND—FEBRUARY 1749–SEPTEMBER 1750—I. WHAT THE WORLD SAID

Pickle the Spy

Europe after Peace of Aix-la-Chapelle—A vast gambling establishment —Charles excluded—Possible chance in Poland—Supposed to have gone thither—'Henry Goring's letter'—Romantic adventures attributed to Charles—Obvious blunders—Talk of a marriage—Count Brühl's opinion —Proposal to kidnap Charles—To rob a priest—The King of Poland's ideas—Lord Hyndford on Frederick the Great—Lord Hyndford's mare's nest—Charles at Berlin—'Send him to Siberia'—The theory contradicted—Mischievous glee of Frederick—Charles discountenances plots to kill Cumberland—Father Myles Macdonnell to James—London conspiracy—Reported from Rome—The Bloody Butcher Club—Guesses of Sir Horace Mann—Charles and a strike—Charles reported to be very ill—Really on the point of visiting England—September 1750.

Europe, after the Peace of Aix-la-Chapelle, was like a vast political gambling establishment. Nothing, or nothing but the expulsion of Prince Charles from every secular State, had been actually settled. Nobody was really satisfied with the Peace. The populace, in France as in England, was discontented. Princes were merely resting and looking round for new combinations of forces. The various Courts, from St. Petersburg to Dresden, from London to Vienna, were so many tables where the great game of national *faro* was being played, over the heads of the people, by kings, queens, abbés, soldiers, diplomatists, and pretty women. Projects of new alliances were shuffled and cut, like the actual cards which were seldom out of the hands of the players, when Casanova or Barry Lyndon held the bank, and challenged all comers. It was the age of adventurers, from the mendacious Casanova to the mysterious Saint-Germain, from the Chevalier d'Eon to Charles Edward Stuart. That royal player was warned off the turf, as it were, ruled out of the game. Where among all these attractive tables was one on which Prince Charles, in 1749, might put down his slender stake, his name, his sword, the lives of a few thousand Highlanders, the fortunes of some faithful gentlemen? Who would accept Charles's empty alliance, which promised little but a royal title and a desperate venture? The Prince had wildly offered his hand to the Czarina; he was to offer that hand, vainly stretched after a flying crown, to a Princess of Prussia, and probably to a lady of Poland.

At this moment the Polish crown was worn by Augustus of Saxony, who was reckoned 'a bad life.' The Polish throne, the Polish alliance, had been, after various unlucky

adventures since the days of Henri III. and the Duc d'Alençon, practically abandoned by France. But Louis XV. was beginning to contemplate that extraordinary intrigue in which Conti aimed at the crown of Poland, and the Comte de Broglie was employed (1752) to undermine and counteract the schemes of Louis's official representatives. {46a}
As a Sobieski by his mother's side, the son of the exiled James (who himself had years before been asked to stand as a candidate for the kingdom of Poland), Charles was expected by politicians to make for Warsaw when he fled from Avignon. It is said, on the authority of a Polish manuscript, 'communicated by Baron de Rondeau,' that there was a conspiracy in Poland to unseat Augustus III. and give the crown to Prince Charles. {46b} In 1719, Charles's maternal grandfather had declined a Russian proposal to make a dash for the crown, so the chivalrous Wogan narrates. In 1747 (June 6), Chambrier had reported to Frederick the Great that Cardinal Tencin was opposed to the ambition of the Saxon family, which desired to make the elective crown of Poland hereditary in its house. The Cardinal said that, in his opinion, there was a Prince who would figure well in Poland, *le jeune Edouard* (Prince Charles), who had just made himself known, and in whom there was the stuff of a man. {46c} But Frederick the Great declined to interfere in Polish matters, and Tencin was only trying to get rid of Charles without a rupture. In May 1748, Frederick refused to see Graeme, a Jacobite who was sent to demand a refuge for the Prince in Prussia. {46d} Without Frederick and without Sweden, Charles in 1749 could do nothing serious in Poland.

The distracted politics of Poland, however, naturally drew the attention of Europe to that country when Charles, on February *28*, vanished out of Avignon 'into fairyland,' like Frederick after Molwitz. Every Court in Europe was vainly searched for 'the boy that cannot be found.' The newsletters naturally sent him to Poland, so did Jacobite myth.

The purpose of this chapter is to record the guesses made by diplomatists at Charles's movements, and the expedients by which they vainly endeavoured to discover him. We shall next lift, as far as possible, the veil which has concealed for a century and a half adventures in themselves unimportant enough. In spite of disappointments and dark hours of desertion, Charles, who was much of a boy, probably enjoyed the mystery which he now successfully created. If he could not startle Europe by a brilliant appearance on any stage, he could keep it talking and guessing by a disappearance. He obviously relished secrecy, pass–words, disguises, the 'properties' of the conspirator, in the spirit of Tom Sawyer and Huckleberry Finn. He came of an evasive race. His grandfather, as Duke of York, had fled from England disguised as a girl. His father had worn many disguises in many adventures. *He* had been 'Betty Burke.'

Though it is certain that, in March 1749 (the only month when he almost evades us), Charles could not have visited Berlin, Livadia, Stockholm, the reader may care to be reminded of a contemporary Jacobite romance in which he is made to do all these things. A glance should be cast on the pamphlet called 'A Letter from H. G—-g, Esq.' (London, 1750). The editor announces that the letter has been left in his lodgings by a mistake; it has not been claimed, as the person for whom it was meant has gone abroad, and so the editor feels free to gratify 'the curiosity of the town.' The piece, in truth, is a Jacobite tract, meant to keep up the spirits of the faithful, and it is probable that the author really had some information, though he is often either mistaken, or fables by way of a 'blind.' About February 11, says the scribe (nominally Henry Goring, Charles's equerry, an ex–officer of the Queen of Hungary), a mysterious stranger, the 'Chevalier de la Luze,' came to Avignon, and was received by the Prince 'with extraordinary marks of distinction.' 'He understood not one word of English,' which destroys, if true, the theory that the Earl Marischal, or Marshal Keith, is intended. French and Italian he spoke well, but with a foreign accent. Kelly ventured to question the Prince about the stranger, but was rebuffed. One day, probably February 24, the stranger received despatches, and vanished as he had come. The Prince gave a supper (d'Argenson's 'ball'), and, when his guests had retired, summoned Goring into his study. He told Goring that 'there were spies about him' (the Earl Marischal, we know, distrusted Kelly); he rallied him on a love–affair, and said that Goring only should be his confidant. Next morning, very early, they two started for Lyons, disguised as French officers. As far as Lyons, indeed, the French police actually traced them. {49a} But, according to the pamphlet, they did not stop in Lyons; they rested at a small town two leagues further on, whence the Prince sent dispatches to Kelly at Avignon. Engaging a new valet, Charles pushed to Strasbourg, where he again met La Luze, now described as 'a person whose extraordinary talents had gained him the confidence one of the wisest Princes in Europe,' obviously pointing to Frederick of Prussia, the master of Marshal Keith, and the friend and host of his brother, the Earl Marischal. At Strasbourg, Charles rescued a pretty young lady from a fire; she lost her heart at once to the 'Comte d'Espoir' (his travelling title), but the Prince behaved like Scipio, not to mention a patriarch famous for his continence. 'I am no stoic,' said His Royal Highness to La Luze, 'but I have always been taught that pleasures, how pardonable soever in themselves, become highly criminal when indulged to the prejudice of another,' adding many other noble and unimpeachable sentiments.

After a romantic adventure with English or Scottish assassins, in which His Royal Highness shot a few of them, the travellers arrived at Leipzig. La Luze now assumed his real name, and carried Charles, by cross roads, to 'a certain Court,' where he spent ten days with much satisfaction. He stayed at the house of La Luze (Berlin and the Earl Marischal appear to be hinted at, but the Marischal told Pickle that he had never seen Charles at Berlin), secret business was done, and then, through territories friendly or hostile, 'a certain port' was reached. They sailed (from Dantzig?), were driven into a hostile port (Riga?), escaped and made another port (Stockholm?) where they met Lochgarry, 'whom the Prince thought had been one of those that fell at Culloden.'

This is nonsense. Lochgarry had been with Charles after Culloden, and had proposed to waylay Cumberland, which the Prince forbade. Murray of Broughton, in his examination, and Bishop Forbes agree on this point, and James, we know, sent, by Edgar, a message to Lochgarry on Christmas Eve, 1748. {50a} Charles, therefore, knew excellently well that Lochgarry did *not* die at Culloden. After royal, but very secret entertainment 'in this kingdom' (Sweden?), Charles went into Lithuania, where old friends of his maternal ancestors, the Sobieskis, welcomed him. He resumed a gaiety which he had lost ever since his arrest at the opera in Paris, and had 'an interview with a most illustrious and firm friend to his person and interest.' Though his marriage, says the pamphleteer, had been much talked of, 'he has always declined making any applications of that nature himself. It was his fixed determination to beget no royal beggars.' D'Argenson reports Charles's remark that he will never marry till the Restoration, and, no doubt, he was occasionally this mood, among others. {51a} The pamphleteer vows that the Prince 'loves and is loved,' but will not marry 'till his affairs take a more favourable turn.' The lady is 'of consummate beauty, yet is that beauty the least of her perfections.'

The pamphlet concludes with vague enigmatic hopes and promises, and certainly leaves its readers little wiser than they were before. In the opinion of the Messrs. 'Sobieski Stuart' (who called themselves his grandsons), Charles really did visit Sweden, and his jewel, as Grand Master of the Grand Masonic Lodge of Stockholm, is still preserved there. {51b} The castle where he resided in Lithuania, it is said, is that of Radzivil. {51c} The affectionate and beautiful lady is the Princess Radzivil, to whom the newspapers were busy marrying Charles at this time. The authors of 'Tales of the Century,' relying on some vague Polish traditions, think that a party was being made to raise the Prince to the Polish crown. In fact, there is not a word of truth in 'Henry Goring's letter.'

We now study the perplexities of Courts and diplomatists. Pickle was not yet at hand with accurate intelligence, and, even after he began to be employed, the English Government left their agents abroad to send in baffled surmises. From Paris, on March 8, Colonel Joseph Yorke (whom d'Argenson calls by many ill names) wrote, 'I am told for certain that he [the Prince] is now returned to Avignon.' {52a} Mann, in Florence, hears (March 7) that the Prince has sent a Mr. Lockhart to James to ask for money, but that was really done on December 31, 1748. {52b} On March 11, Yorke learned from Puysieux that the Prince had been recognised by postboys as he drove through Lyons towards Metz; probably, Puysieux thought, on 'an affair of gallantry.' Others, says Yorke, 'have sent him to Poland or Sweden,' which, even in 1746, had been getting ready troops to assist Charles in Scotland. {52c} On March 20, Yorke hints that Charles may be in or near Paris, as he probably was. Berlin was suggested as his destination by Horace Mann (April 4). Again, he has been seen in disguise, walking into a gate of Paris (April 11). {52d} On April 14, Walton, from Florence, writes that James has had news of his son, is much excited, and is sending Fitzmorris to join him. The Pope knows and is sure to blab. {52e} On May 3, Yorke mentions a rumour, often revived, that the Prince is dead. On May 9, the Jacobites in Paris show a letter from Oxford inviting Charles to the opening of the Radcliffe, 'where they assure him of better reception than the University has had at Court lately.' {53a} Mann (May 2) mentions the Radzivil marriage, arranged, in a self–denying way, by the Princesse de Talmond. On May 17, Yorke hears from Puysieux that the French ambassador in Saxony avers that Charles is in Poland, and that Sir Charles Williams has remonstrated with Count Brühl. On May 1, 1749, Sir Charles Hanbury Williams wrote from Leipzig to the Duke of Newcastle. He suspects that Charles is one of several persons who have just passed through Leipzig on the way to Poland; Count Brühl is 'almost certain' of it. {53b} On May 5 (when Charles was really in or near Venice), Hanbury Williams sends a copy of his remonstrance with Brühl.

'I asked Count Brühl whether, in the present divided and factious state of the nobility of Poland, His Polish Majesty would like to have a young adventurer (who can fish in no waters that are not troubled, and who, by his mother, is allied to a family that once sat upon the Polish throne) to go into that country where it would be natural for him to endeavour to encourage factions, nourish divisions, and foment confederations to the utmost of his power, and might not the evil–minded and indisposed Poles be glad to have such a tool in their hands, which at some time or other they might make use of to answer their own ends? To this Count Brühl answered in such terms as I could wish, and I must do him the justice to say that he showed the best disposition to serve His Majesty in the affair in question; but I am yet of opinion that, whatever is done effectually in this case, must be done by the Court of Petersburg, and I would humbly advise that, as soon as it is known for certain that the Pretender's son is in Poland, His Majesty should order his minister at the Court of Petersburg to take such steps as His Majesty's great wisdom shall judge most likely to make the Czarina act with a proper vigour upon this occasion.

'Your Grace knows that the republic of Poland is at present divided into two great factions, the one which is in the interest of Russia, to which the friends of the House of Austria attach themselves; the other is in the interest of France and Prussia. As I thought it most likely, if the Pretender's son went into Poland, he would seek protection from the French party, I have desired and requested the French ambassador that he would write to the French resident at Warsaw, and to others of his friends in Poland, that he might be informed of the truth of the Pretender's arrival, and the place that he was at in Poland, as soon as possible, and that when he was acquainted with it he would let me know what came to his knowledge, all which he has sincerely promised me to do, and I do not doubt but he will keep his word. . . . It is publicly said that the Pretender's son's journey to Poland is with a design to marry a princess of the House of Radzivil.

'As soon as I hear anything certain about the Pretender's son being in Poland, I will most humbly offer to your Grace the method that I think will be necessary for His Majesty to pursue with respect to the King and republic of Poland, in case His Majesty should think fit not to suffer the Pretender's son to remain in that country.

'C. HANBURY WILLIAMS.'

On May 12, Williams believes that Charles is *not* in Poland. On May 18, he guesses (wrongly) that the Prince is in Paris. On May 25, he fancies—'plainly perceives'—that the French ambassador at Dresden believes in the Polish theory. On June 9, Brühl tells Williams (correctly) that Charles is in Venice. On June 11, Hanbury Williams proposes to have a harmless priest seized and robbed, and to kidnap Prince Charles! I give this example of British diplomatic energy and chivalrous behaviour.

From Sir Charles Hanbury Williams.
'Dresden: June 11, N.S. 1749.

' . . . Count Brühl has communicated to me the letters which he received by the last post from the Saxon resident at Venice, who says that the Pretender's son had been at Venice for some days; that he has received two expresses from his father at Rome since his being there; but that nobody knew how long he intended to stay there. . . Mons. Brühl further informs me that he hears from Poland that the Prince of Radzivil, who is Great General of Lithuania, has a strong desire to marry his daughter to the Pretender's son. The young lady is between eleven and twelve years old, very plain, and can be no great fortune, for she has two brothers; but yet Mons. Brühl is of opinion that there is some negotiation on foot for this marriage, which is managed by an Italian priest who is a titular bishop, whose name is Lascarisk (*sic*), and who lives in and governs the Prince Radzivil's family. This priest is soon to set out for Italy, under pretence of going to Rome for the Jubilee year, but Mons. Brühl verily thinks that he is charged with a secret commission for negotiating the above–mentioned marriage. If His Majesty thinks it worth while to have this priest watched, I will answer for having early intelligence of the time he intends beginning his journey, and then it would be no difficult matter to have him stopped, and his papers taken from him, as he goes through the Austrian territories into Italy. The more I think of it the more I am persuaded that the Pretender's son will not go into Poland for many reasons, especially for one, which is that for a small sum of money I will undertake to find a Pole who will engage to seize upon his person in any part of Poland, and carry him to any port in the north that His Majesty shall appoint. I have had offers of this sort already made me, to which your Grace may be sure I gave no answer, except thanking the persons for the zeal they showed for the King, my master, but I am convinced that the thing is very practicable.

'I had this day the honour to dine with the King of Poland, and, as I sat next to him at table, he told me that he was very glad to hear that the Pretender's son was at length found to be at Venice, for that he would much rather have him there than in Poland; to which I answered that I was very glad, upon His Polish Majesty's account, that the Pretender's son had not thought fit to come into any of His Majesty's territories, since I believed the visit would be far from being agreeable. To which the King of Poland replied that *it would be a very disagreeable visit to him*, and after that expressed himself in the handsomest manner imaginable with respect to His Majesty, and the regard he had for his Sacred person and Royal House; and I am convinced if the Pretender's son had gone into Poland, His Polish Majesty and his minister would have done everything in their power to have drove him out of that kingdom as soon as possible.

'C. HANBURY WILLIAMS.

'P.S.—Since my writing this letter, Count Brühl tells me that the news of the Pretender's son's being at Venice is confirmed by letters from his best correspondent at Rome, but both accounts agree in the Pretender's son's being at Venice incognito, and that he appears in no public place, so that very few people know of his being there. . . . C. H. W.'

In 1751, Hanbury Williams renewed his proposal about waylaying Lascaris.

Charles, as we shall see, was for a short time at Venice in May 1749. Meanwhile the game of hide and seek through Europe went on as merrily as ever. Lord Hyndford, so well known to readers of Mr. Carlyle's 'Frederick,' now opens in full cry from Moscow, but really on a hopelessly wrong scent. As illustrating Hyndford's opinion of Frederick, who had invested him with the Order of the Thistle, we quote this worthy diplomatist:

Lord Hyndford to the Duke of Newcastle. {58a}
'Moscow: June 19, 1749.

' . . . I must acquaint your Grace of what I have learnt, through a private canal, from the last relation of Mr. Gross, the Russian minister at Berlin, although I dare say it is no news to your Grace. Mr. Gross writes that, some days before the date of his letter, the Pretender's eldest son arrived at Potsdam, and had been very well received by the King of Prussia, General Keith, and his brother, the late Earl Marshal; and all the other English, Scotch, and Irish Jacobites in the Prussian service were to wait upon him. This does not at all surprise me; but Mons. Valony, the French minister, went likewise to make his compliments at a country house, hired on purpose for this young vagabond. This is all that I know as yet of this affair in general, for the Chancellor has not thought proper as yet to inform me of the particulars. However, this public, incontestable proof of the little friendship and regard the King of Prussia has for His Majesty and His Royal Family, and for the whole British nation, will, I hope, open the eyes of the people who are blind to that Prince's monstrous faults, if any such are still left amongst us, and I doubt not but it will save His Majesty the trouble of sending Sir C. Hanbury Williams or any other minister to that perfidious Court.

'HYNDFORD.'

This was all a mare's nest; but Hyndford is for kidnapping the Prince. He writes:

'Moscow: June 26, 1749.

'My Lord,—Since the 19th inst., which was the date of my last letter to your Grace, I have been with the Chancellor, who made his excuses that he had not sooner communicated to me the intelligence which Mr. Gross, the Russian minister at Berlin, had sent him concerning the Pretender's eldest son. The Chancellor confirmed all that I wrote to your Grace on the 19th upon that subject, and he told me that he had received a second letter from Mr. Gross, wherein that minister says that the Young Pretender had left the country house where he was, in the neighbourhood of Berlin, and had entirely disappeared, without its being hitherto possible for him, Mr. Gross, or Count Choteck, the Austrian minister, to find out the route he has taken, although it is generally believed that he is gone into Poland; and that now the King of Prussia and his ministers deny that ever the Pretender's son was there, and take it mightily amiss of anybody that pretends to affirm it. I am sorry that the Russian troops are not now in Poland, for otherwise I believe it would have been an easy matter to prevail upon this Court to catch this young knight errant and to send him to Siberia, where he would not have been any more heard of; and if the Court of Dresden will enter heartily into such a scheme, it will not be impossible yet to apprehend him, and as it is very probable that the King of Prussia has sent him into Poland to make a party and breed confusion, it appears to be King Augustus's interest to secure him.

'HYNDFORD.'

Many months later, on Feb. 2, 1749–1750, Lord Hyndford, writing from Hanover, retracted. The rumour of Charles's presence at Berlin, he found, was started by Count de Choteck, the Austrian ambassador. In fact, Choteck used to meet a fair lady secretly in a garden near Berlin, and near the house of Field–Marshal Keith and his brother, Lord Marischal. Hard by was an inn, where a stranger lodged, a rich and handsome youth, whom Choteck, meeting, took for Prince Charles. He was really a young Polish gentleman, into whose reasons for retirement we need not examine.

Frederick, in his mischievous way, wrote about all this from Potsdam, on June 24, 1749:

'We have played a trick on Choteck; he spends much on spies, and, to prove that he is well served, he has taken it into his head that young Edouard, really at Venice, is at Berlin. He has been very busy over this, and no doubt has informed his Court.'

On July 7, 1749, Frederick, in a letter to his minister at Moscow, said that only dense ignorance could credit the Berlin legend. {61}

These documents certainly demonstrate that the Prince fluttered the Courts, and that the Jacobite belief in English schemes to kidnap or murder him was not a mere mythical delusion. Only an opportunity was wanted. He had spared the Duke of Cumberland's life, even after the horrors of Culloden. But Hanbury Williams knows a Pole who will waylay him; Hyndford wants to carry him off to Siberia. It was not once only, on the other hand, but twice at least, that Charles protected the Butcher, Cumberland. In 1746 he saved his enemy from Lochgarry's open attempt. In 1747 (May 4), a certain Father Myles Macdonnell wrote from St. Germain to James in Rome. He dwells on the jealousies among the Jacobites, and particularly denounces Kelly, then a trusted intimate of Charles. Kelly, he says, is a drunkard, and worse! It was probably he who raised 'a scruple' against a scheme relating to 'Cumberland's hateful person.' 'Honest warrantable people from London' came to Paris and offered 'without either fee or reward' to do the business. What was the 'business,' what measures were to be taken against 'Cumberland's hateful person'? Father Myles Macdonnell, writing to James, a Catholic priest to a Catholic King, does not speak of *assassination*. He talks of 'the scruple raised against securing Cumberland's person.' 'I suspect Parson Kelly of making a scruple of an action the most meritorious that could possibly be committed,' writes Father Myles. {62a} The talk of kidnapping, in such cases as those of Cumberland and Prince Charles—men of spirit and armed—is a mere blind. Murder is meant! Father Myles's letter proves that (unknown to James in Rome) there was a London conspiracy to kill the Butcher, but Prince Charles again rejected the proposal. He was less ungenerous than Hyndford and Hanbury Williams. The amusing thing is that the English Government knew, quite as well as Father Macdonnell or James, all about the conspiracy to slay the Duke of Cumberland. Here is the information, which reached Mann through Rome. {62b}

From Mr. Thomas Chamberlayne to Sir H. Mann.

'Capranica: November 18, 1747.

' . . . The family at Rome . . . was informed, by one who arrived there last October from London, that there are twelve persons, whose names I could not learn, but none of distinction, that are formed in a club or society, and meet at the Nag's Head in East Street, Holborn. They have bound themselves under most solemn oaths that this winter they will post themselves in different parts of the City of London mostly frequented by His Royal Highness, the Duke of Cumberland, in his night visits [to whom?], and are resolved to lay violent hands on his royal person. The parole among the different parties in their respective posts is *The Bloody Butcher*. They are all resolute fellows, who first declared at their entering in this conspiracy to despise death or torture. This motive is worthy of your care, so I am certain you'll make proper use of it . . .

'THOMAS CHAMBERLAYNE.'

If Charles afterwards attempted to repay in kind the attentions of his royal cousins, or of their ministers, this can hardly be reckoned inhuman. If he was fluttering the Courts, they—Prussia, Russia, France, Poland—were leading him the life of a tracked beast. They were determined to drive him into the Papal domains; even in Venice he was harried by spies. {63} On May 30, to retrace our steps, Mann, from Florence, reports that Charles has arrived at the Papal Nuncio's in Venice, attended by one servant in the livery of the Duke of Modena. Walton adds that he has not a penny (June 6). Walton (July 11) writes from Florence that the Prince is reported from Venice to have paid assiduous court to the second daughter of the Duke of Modena, a needy potentate, but that he suddenly disappeared.' {64} On Sept. 5, 1749, Walton says he is in France. On Sept. 26, Walton writes that he is offering his sword to the Czarina, who declines. He is at Lübeck, or (Oct. 3) at Avignon. On Oct. 20, Mann writes that, from Lübeck, Charles has asked the Imperial ambassador at Paris to implore the Kaiser to give him an asylum in his States. On Oct. 31, Mann only knows that the Pope and James 'reciprocally ask each other news about' the Prince. On Jan. 23, 1750, poor Mann is 'quite at a loss.' James receives letters from the Prince, but never with date of place, otherwise Mann would have been better informed. Walton hears that James believes Charles to be imprisoned in a French fortress. From Paris, Jan. 17, 1750, Albemarle wrote that he heard the Prince was in Berlin. The Prince later told Pickle that he had been in Berlin more than once, and, as we shall see, Frederick amused him with hopes of assistance. Kelly has left Charles's followers in distress at Avignon. Kelly, in fact, received his *congé*; he was distrusted by the Earl Marischal, and Carte, the historian. On Jan. 28, Albemarle hears that Charles has been in Paris 'under the habit of a Capuchine Fryar,' and this *was* a disguise of his, according to Pickle.

Meanwhile the French Government kept protesting their total ignorance. On April 3, 1750, Walton announces that James has had a long letter from Charles containing his plans and those of his adherents, for which he demands the Royal approval. James has sent a long letter to Charles by the courier of the Duc de Nivernais, the French ambassador in Rome. By the middle of June, James is reported by Walton to be full of hope, and to have heard excellent news. But these expectations were partly founded on a real scheme of Charles, partly on a strike of colliers at Newcastle. A mob orator there proclaimed the Prince, and the Jacobites in Rome thought that His Royal Highness was heading the strike! {65a} In July, the same illusions were entertained. On August 12, Albemarle, from Paris, reports the Prince to be dangerously ill, probably not far from the French capital. He was really preparing to embark for England. Albemarle, by way of trap, circulated in the English press a forged news–letter from Nancy in Lorraine, dated August 24, 1750. It announced Charles's death of pneumonia, in hopes of drawing forth a Jacobite denial. This stratagem failed. On August 4, James, though piqued by being kept in the dark, sent Charles a fresh commission of regency. {65b} Of the Prince's English expedition of September 1750, the Government of George II. knew nothing. Pickle was in Rome at the moment, not with Charles; what Pickle knew the English ministers knew, but there is a difficulty in dating his letters before 1752, and I am not aware that any despatches of his from Rome are extant.

We have now brought the history to a point (September 1750) where the Prince, for a moment, emerges from fairyland, and where we are not left to the perplexing conjectures of diplomatists in Paris, Dresden, Florence, Hanover, and St. Petersburg. In September 1750, Charles certainly visited London. There is a point of light. We now give an account of his actual movements in 1749–1750.

CHAPTER IV—THE PRINCE IN FAIRYLAND. II.—WHAT ACTUALLY OCCURRED

Charles mystifies Europe—Montesquieu knows his secret—Sources of information—The Stuart manuscripts—Charles's letters from Avignon— A proposal of marriage—Kennedy and the hidden treasure—Where to look for Charles— *Cherchez la femme*!—Hidden in Lorraine— Plans for entering Paris—Letter to Mrs. Drummond—To the Earl Marischal—Starts for Venice—At Strasbourg—Unhappy Harrington— Letter to James—Leaves Venice 'A bird without a nest'—Goes to Paris —The Prince's secret revealed—The convent of St. Joseph—Curious letter as Cartouche—Madame de Routh—Cartouche again—Goring sent to England—A cypher—Portrait of Madame de Talmond—Portrait of Madame d'Aiguillon—Intellectual society—Mademoiselle Luci—'Dener Bash'—The secret hoard—Results of Goring's English mission— Timidity of English Jacobites—Supply of money—Charles a *bibliophile*—'My big muff'—A patron of art—Quarrels with Madame de Talmond—Arms for a rising—Newton on Cluny—Kindness to Monsieur Le Coq—Madame de Talmond weary of Charles—Letters to her— Charles reads Fielding's novels—Determines to go to England—Large order of arms—Reproached by James—Intagli of James— *En route* for London—September 1750.

The reader has had an opportunity of observing the success of Charles in mystifying Europe. Diplomatists, ambassadors, and wits would have been surprised, indeed, had they known that one of the most famous men of the age possessed the secret for which they were seeking. The author of 'L'Esprit des Lois' could have enlightened them, for Charles's mystery was no mystery to Montesquieu, who was friendly with Scottish and English Jacobites. The French Ministers, truly or falsely, always professed entire ignorance. They promised to arrest the Prince wherever he might be found on French soil, and transport him to sea by Civita Vecchia. {68} It will be shown later that, at least in the autumn of 1749, this ignorance was probably feigned.

What is really known of the movements of the Prince in 1749? Curiously enough, Mr. Ewald does not seem to have consulted the 'Stuart Papers' at Windsor, while the extracts in Browne's 'History of the Highland Clans' are meagre. To these papers then we turn for information. The most useful portions are *not* Charles's letters to James. These are brief and scanty. Thus he writes from Avignon (January 15, 1749), 'We are enjoying here the finest weather ever was seen.' He always remarks that his health 'is perfect.' He orders patterns for his servants' liveries and a button, blue and yellow, still remains in a letter from Edgar! The button outlasts the dynasty. Our intelligence must be extracted from ill–spelled, closely scrawled, and much erased sheets of brown paper, on which Charles has scribbled drafts for letters to his household, to Waters, his banker in Paris, to adherents in Paris or London, and to ladies. The notes are almost, and in places are quite, illegible. The Prince practised a disguised hand, and used pseudonyms instead of names. Many letters have been written in sympathetic ink, and then exposed to fire or the action of acids. However, something can be made out, but not why he concealed his movements even from his banker, even from his household, Oxburgh, Kelly, Harrington, and Graeme. It is certain that he started, with a marriage in his eye, from Avignon on February 28, 1749, accompanied by Henry Goring, of the Austrian service. There had already been a correspondence, vaguely hinted at by James's secretary, Edgar, between Charles and the Duke and a Princess of Hesse–Darmstadt. On February 24, 1749, Charles drafted, at Avignon, a proposal for the hand of the Duke's daughter. He also drafted (undated) a request to the King of Poland for leave to bring his wife, the Princess of Hesse–Darmstadt, into Polish territory. {69} We may imagine His Polish Majesty's answer. Of course, the marriage did not take place.

Charles had other secrets. On February 3, 1749, he wrote to Waters about the care to be taken with certain letters. These were a correspondence with 'Thomas Newton,' (Major

Kennedy), at Mr. Alexander Macarty's, in Gray's Inn, London. Newton was in relations with Cluny Macpherson, through a friend in Northumberland. Cluny, skulking on his Highland estates, was transmitting or was desired to transmit a part of the treasure of 40,000 *louis d'or*, buried soon after Culloden at the head of Loch Arkaig. {70a} Of this fatal treasure we shall hear much. A percentage of the coin was found to be false money, a very characteristic circumstance. Moreover, Cluny seems to have held out hopes, always deferred, of a rising in the Highlands. Charles had to be ready in secrecy, to put himself at the head of this movement. There was also to be an English movement, which was frowned on by official Jacobitism. On February 3, 1749, Charles writes from Avignon to 'Thomas Newton' (Kennedy) about the money sent south by Cluny. He repeated his remarks on March 6, giving no place of residence. But probably he was approaching Paris, dangerous as such a visit was, for in a note of March 6 to Waters, he says that he will 'soon call for letters.' {70b} His *noms de guerre* at this time were 'Williams' and 'Benn'; later he chose 'John Douglas.' He was also Smith, Mildmay, Burton, and so forth.

There should have been no difficulty in discovering Charles. Modern police, in search of a person who is 'wanted,' spy on his mistress. Now the Princesse de Talmond, when out of favour at Versailles, went to certain lands in Lorraine, near her exiled king, Stanislas. In Lorraine, therefore, at Lunéville, the Court of the ex–king of Poland, or at Commercy, Bar–le–Duc, or wherever the Princesse de Talmond might be, Charles was sure to be heard of by an intelligent spy, if permitted to enter the country. Consequently, we are not surprised to find Charles drafting on April 3, at Lunéville (where he resided at the house of one Mittie, physician of the ex–king of Poland), a 'Project for My arrival in Paris. Mr. Benn [himself] must go straight to Dijon, and his companion, Mr. Smith [Goring], to Paris. Mr. Smith will need a chaise, which he must buy at Lunéville. Next he will take up the servant of C. P. [Prince Charles] at Ligny, but on leaving that place Mr. Smith must ride on horseback, and the chaise can go there as if for his return to Paris; the person in it seeming to profit by this opportunity. Mr. Benn [the Prince] must remain for some days, as if he wanted to buy a trunk, and will give his own as if in friendship to Mr. Smith; all this seeming mere chance work. Next, Mr. Smith will go his way and his friend will go his, after waiting a few days, and on arriving at Dijon must write to nobody, except the letter to W–[Waters]. The Chevalier Graeme, whom he must see (and to whom he may mention having been at Dijon on the Prince's business, without naming his companion, but as if alone), knows nothing, and Graeme must be left in the dark as if he (Mr. Smith) [Goring] were in the same case, and were waiting new orders in total ignorance, not having seen me for a long time.' {71}

There follow a few private addresses in Paris; and the name, to be remarked, of 'Mademoiselle Ferrand.'

All this is very puzzling; we only make out that, by some confusion of the personalities of 'Benn' (the Prince) and 'Mr. Smith' (Goring), Charles hoped to enter Paris undetected. Yet he *was* seen 'entering a gate of Paris in disguise.' Doubtless he had lady allies, but a certain Mademoiselle Ferrand, to whom he wrote, he seems not to have known personally. We shall find that she was later of use to him, and indeed his most valuable friend and ally.

Next, we find this letter of April 10 to Madame Henrietta Drummond, doubtless of the family of Macgregor, called Drummond, of Balhaldie. Charles appears to have had enough of Paris, and is going to Venice. He is anxious to meet the Earl Marischal.

'April 10, 1749.

'I have been very impatient to be able to give you nuse of me as I am fully persuaded of yr Friendship, and concern for everything that regards me; I send you here enclosed a Letter for Ld Marishal, be pleased to enclose it, and forward it without loss of time; the Bearer (he is neither known by you or me), is charged to receive at any time what Letters you want to send me, and you may be shure of their arriving safe. Iff Lord Marishal agrees with my Desier when you give his Packet to yr Bearer, you must put over it *en Dilligence*, iff otherwise, direct by my Name as I sign it here. I flatter myself of the Continuation of your Friendship, as I hope you will never doubt of mine which shall be constant. I remain yr moste obedient humble Servant

'JOHN DOUGLAS.

'P.S.—Tell ye Bearer when to comback for the answer of ye enclosed or any other Letters you want to send me.

'P.S. to Lord Marischal.—Whatever party you take, be pleased to keep my writing secret, and address to me at Venise to the Sig. Ignazio Testori to Mr. de Villelongue under cover to a Banquier of that town, and it will come safe to me.

'To Md. Henrietta Drummond.'

Charles, on April 20, wrote another letter to the Lord Marischal, imploring for an interview, at some place to be fixed. But the old Lord was not likely to go from Berlin to Venice, whither Charles was hastening.

It is perfectly plain that, leaving Avignon on February 28, Charles was making for Paris on March 6 by a circuitous route through Lorraine (where he doubtless met Madame de Talmond), and a double back on Burgundy. What he did or desired in Paris we do not know. He is said to have visited Lally Tollendal, and he must have seen Waters, his banker. By April 10 he is starting for Venice, where he had, as a boy, been royally received. But, in 1744, the Republic of Venice had resumed relations with England, interrupted by Charles's too kind reception in 1737. The whole romance, therefore, of Henry Goring's letter, and all the voyages to Stockholm, Berlin, Lithuania, and so forth, are visions. Charles probably saw some friends in Paris, was tolerated in Lorraine (where his father was protected before 1715), and he vainly looked for a home in any secular State of Europe. This was all, or nearly all, that occurred between March and May 1749. Europe was fluttered, secret service money was poured out like water, diplomatists caballed and scribbled despatches, all for very little. The best place to have hunted for Charles was really at Lunéville, near the gay Court of his kinsman, the Duke Stanislas Leczinski, the father of the Queen of France. There Charles's sometime admirer, Voltaire, was a welcome guest; thither too (as we saw) went his elderly cousin, people said his mistress, the Princesse de Talmond. But the English diplomatists appear to have neglected Lunéville. D'Argenson was better informed.

On April 26 Charles was at Strasbourg. Here, D'Argenson says, he was seen, and warned to go, by an *écuyer* of the late Cardinal Rohan. Hence he wrote again to the Earl Marischal at Berlin. From this note it is plain that he had sent Goring ('Mr. Smith') to the Earl; Goring, indeed, had carried his letters of April 10–20. He again proposes a meeting with the Earl Marischal at Venice. He will 'answer for the expenses,' and apologises for 'such a long and fatiguing journey.' He wrote to Waters, 'You may let Mr. Newton know that whenever he has thoroly finished his Business, Mr. Williams [the Prince] will make him very wellcum in all his Cuntrihouses.'

The 'business' of 'Mr. Newton' was to collect remittances from Cluny.

On April 30, the Prince, as 'Mr. Williams,' expresses 'his surprise and impatience for the delay of the horses [money] and other goods promised by Mr. Newton.'

On May 3, Charles wrote, without address, to Goring, 'I go strete to Venice, and would willingly avoid your Garrison Towns, as much as possible: *id est*, of France. I believe to compass that by goin by Ruffach to Pfirt: there to wate for me. The Chese [chaise] you may either leve it in consine to your post–master of Belfort, or, what is still better, to give it to the bearer.'

Goring and Harrington were to meet the bearer at Belfort, but Harrington seems to have been mystified, and to have failed in effecting a junction. The poor gentleman, we learn, from letters of Stafford and Sheridan, Charles's retainers at Avignon, could scarcely raise money to leave that town. Sir James Harrington was next to meet Charles at Venice. He was to carry a letter for Charles to a Venetian banker. 'Nota bene, that same banquier, though he will deliver to me your letter, knows nothing about me, nor who I am. . . . Change your name, and, in fine, keep as private as possible, till I tell you what is to be done.' Harrington failed, and lay for months in pawn at Venice, pouring out his griefs in letters to Goring. He was a lachrymose conspirator.

These weary affairs are complicated by mysterious letters to ladies: for example to Mademoiselle Lalasse, 'Je vous prie, Mademoiselle, de rendre justice à mon inviolable attachement . . .' (May 3). He gives her examples of his natural and of his disguised handwriting; probably she helped him in forwarding his correspondence. Charles's chief anxiety was to secure the Lord Marischal. Bulkeley and the official English Jacobites kept insisting that he should have a man with him who was trusted by the party. Kelly was distrusted, though Bulkeley defends him, and was cashiered in autumn. Charles's friends also kept urging that he must 'appear in public,' but where? Bulkeley suggested Bologna. The Earl Marischal, later (July 5), was for Fribourg. No place was really both convenient and possible. On May 17 Charles wrote from Venice to the Earl Marischal, 'I am just arrived, but will not be able for some days, to know what reception to meet with.'

He fears he 'may be chased from hence,' and his fears were justified. On the same day (May 17) he wrote to Edgar in Rome, 'Venice, next to France, is the best for my interest, and the only one in Italy.'

Venice ejected the Prince. On May 26 he wrote to his father:

'Sir,—I received last night from ye Nuntio a definitive answer about my project, which is quite contrary to my expectation; as I have nothing further to do here, and would not run the least risk of being found out, I depart this very evening, having left a direction to the said Nuntio how to forward my letters for me.' On the same day he wrote to Chioseul de Stainville, the minister at Versailles of the Empress, 'Could an anonymous exiled Prince be received by the Kaiser and the Queen of Hungary? He would remain incognito.'

On June 3 Charles wrote to James, without address or news, and to Bulkeley. 'Now my friend must skulk to the perfect dishonour and glory of his worthy relations, until he finds a reception fitting at home or abroad.' On the back of the draft he writes:

'What can a bird do that has not found a right nest? He must flit from bough to bough—*ainsi use les Irondel.*'

Probably Charles, after a visit, perhaps, to Ferrara, returned to Paris and his Princess. We find a draft thus conceived and spelled:

'ARRENGEMENT.

'Goring to come here immediately, he to know nothing but that I am just arrived. I am not to go to Paris, but at the end of the month, as sooner no answer can be had, moreover perhaps obliged to wait another, which would oblige me to remain to long in P.' He also (June 3) wrote to Montesquieu, from whom (I think) there is an unsigned friendly letter. He sent compliments to the Duchesse d'Aiguillon, a lady much attached to Montesquieu. An unsigned English letter (June 5) advised him to appear publicly. People are coming to inquire into reports about his character, 'after which it is possible some proposals may be made to you.' The writer will say more when 'in a safer place.'

Newton (Kennedy), meanwhile, had been imprisoned and examined in London, but had been released, and was at Paris. He bought for the Prince 'a fine case of double barrill pistols, made by Barber,' and much admired 'on this side.' Charles expresses gratitude for the gift. Newton had been examined by the Duke of Newcastle about the 40,000 *louis d'or* buried at Loch Arkaig in 1740, but had given no information. On June 26 Charles again asks Bulkeley, 'What *can* a bird do that has found no right nest?'

On June 30 the Prince was probably in Paris, whither we have seen that he meant to go. He had 'found a right nest,' and a very curious nest he had found. The secret of the Prince's retreat became known, many years later, to Grimm, the Paris correspondent of Catherine the Great. Charles's biographers have overlooked or distrusted Grimm's gossip, but it is confirmed by Charles's accidentally writing two real names, in place of pseudonyms, in his correspondence. The history of his 'nest' was this. After her reign as favourite of Louis XIV., Madame de Montespan founded a convent of St. Joseph, in the Rue St. Dominique, in the Faubourg St. Germain. Attached to the convent were rooms in which ladies of rank might make a retreat, or practically occupy chambers. {79}

About this convent and its inmates, Grimm writes as follows:

'The unfortunate Prince Charles, after leaving the Bastille [really Vincennes] lay hidden for three years in Paris, in the rooms of Madame de Vassé, who then resided with her friend, the celebrated Mademoiselle Ferrand, at the convent of St. Joseph. To Mademoiselle de Ferrand the Abbé Condillac owed the ingenious idea of the statue, which he has developed so well in his treatise on "The Sensations." The Princesse de Talmond, with whom Prince Charles was always much in love, inhabited the same house. All day he was shut up in a little *garderobe* of Madame de Vassé's, whence, by a secret staircase, he made his way at night to the chambers of the Princesse. In the evening he lurked behind an alcove in the rooms of Mademoiselle Ferrand. Thus, unseen and unknown, he enjoyed every day the conversation of the most distinguished society, and heard much good and much evil spoken of himself.

'The existence of the Prince in this retreat, and the profound mystery which so long hid him from the knowledge of the world, by a secret which three women shared, and in a house where the flower of the city and the Court used to meet, seems almost miraculous. M. de Choiseul, who heard the story several years after the departure of the Prince, could not believe it. When Minister of Foreign Affairs he wrote to Madame de Vassé and asked her for the particulars of the adventure. She told him all, and did not conceal the fact that she had been obliged to get rid of the Prince, because of the too lively scenes between him and Madame de Talmond. They began in tender effusions, and often ended in a quarrel, or even in blows. This fact we learn from an intimate friend of Madame de Vassé.' {80}

There is exaggeration here. The Prince was not living a life 'fugitive and cloistered' for three whole unbroken years. But the convent of St. Joseph was one of his hiding–places from 1749 to 1752. Of Madame de Vassé I have been unable to learn much: a lady of that name was presented at Court in 1745, and the Duc de Luynes describes her as 'conveniently handsome.' She is always alluded to as 'La Grandemain' in Charles's correspondence, but once he lets her real name slip out in a memorandum. Mademoiselle Ferrand's father is apparently described by d'Hozier as 'Ferrand, Ecuyer, Sieur des Marres et de Ronville en Normandie.' Many of Charles's letters are addressed to 'Mademoiselle Luci,' *sister* of 'La Grandemain.' Now Madame de Vassé seems, from a passage in the Duc de Luynes's 'Mémoires,' to have been the only daughter of her father, M. de Pezé. But once, Charles, writing to 'Mademoiselle Luci,' addresses the letter to 'Mademoiselle La Marre,' for 'Marres.' Now, as *Marres* was an estate of the Ferrands, this address seems to identify 'Mademoiselle Luci' with Mademoiselle Ferrand, the intimate friend, not really the sister, of Madame de Vassé. Mademoiselle Ferrand, as Grimm shows, had a taste for philosophy. We shall remark the same taste in the Prince's friend, 'Mademoiselle Luci.'

Thus the secret which puzzled Europe is revealed. The Prince, sought vainly in Poland, Prussia, Italy, Silesia, and Staffordshire, was really lurking in a fashionable Parisian convent. Better had he been 'where the wind blows over seven glens, and seven Bens, and seven mountain moors,' like the Prince in the Gaelic fairy stories.

We return to details. On June 30, 1749, the Prince, still homeless, writes a curious letter to Mademoiselle Ferrand:

'The confidence, Mademoiselle, which I propose to place in you may seem singular, as I have not the good fortune to know you. The Comtesse de Routh, however, will be less surprised.' This lady was the wife of an Irishman commanding a regiment in the French service, one of those stationed on the frontier of Flanders. 'You [Mademoiselle Ferrand], who have made a *Relation de Cartouche* [the famous robber], may consent to be the depositary of my letter. I pray you to give this letter to the Comtesse de Routh, and to receive from her all the packets addressed to Monsieur Douglas.' He then requests Madame de Routh not to let the Waterses know that she is the intermediary.

The reason for all this secrecy is obvious. D'Argenson (not the *Bête*, but his brother) had threatened Waters with the loss of his head if he would not tell where the Prince was concealed {82}. The banker did not want to know the dangerous fact, and was able to deny his knowledge with a clear conscience.

On July 23 Charles again wrote to Mademoiselle Ferrand: 'It is very bold of Cartouche to write once more, without knowing whether you wish to be concerned with him, but people of our profession are usually impudent, indeed we must be, if we are to earn our bread. . . . I pray you to have some confidence in this handwriting, and to believe that Cartouche, though he be Cartouche, is a true friend. As for his smuggling business, even if it does not succeed as he hopes, he will be none the less grateful to all who carry his flag, as he will be certain that, if he fails, it is because success is impossible.' {83}

This letter was likely to please a romantic girl, as we may suppose Mademoiselle Ferrand to have been, despite her philosophy.

Stafford and Sheridan now kept writing pitiful appeals for money from Avignon. Charles answers (July 31, 1749):

'I wish I were in a situation at present to relive them I estime, in an exotick cuntry that desiers nothing else but to exercise their arbitrary power in distressing all honest men, even them that [are] most allies to their own Soverain.'

Charles, in fact, was himself very poor: when money came in, either from English adherents or from the Loch Arkaig hoard, he sent large remittances to Avignon.

Money did come in, partly, no doubt, from English adherents. We find the following orders from the Prince to Colonel Goring.

From the Prince to Goring.

'Ye 31st July, 1749.

'I gave you Lately a proof of my Confidence, by our parting together from Avignion, so that you will not be surprized of a New Instance. You are to repair on Receipt of this to London, there to Let know to such friends as you can see, my situation, and Resolutions; all tending to nothing else but the good and relieve of our Poor Country which ever was, and shall be my only thoughts. Take Care of yr.Self, do not think to be on a detachement, but only a simple Minister that is to comback with a distinct account from them parts, and remain assured of my Constant friendship and esteem.

'C. P. R. For GORING.

'P.S.—Cypher.

'I. S h a l. C o n q u e r.

'3 w k y p t d b q x m f.

'My name shall be John Douglas.

'Jean Noé D'Orville & fils. A Frankfort sur Maine, a Banquier of that Town.'

The Prince may have been at Frankfort, but, as a rule, he was hiding in Lorraine when not in Paris or near it, and, as we have seen, was under the protection of various French and fashionable Flora Macdonalds. Of these ladies, 'Madame de Beauregard' and the Princesse de Talmond are apparently the same person. With them, or her (she also appears as *la tante* and *la vieille*), Charles's relations were stormy. He wearied her, he broke with her, he scolded her, and returned to her again. Another protectress, Madame d'Aiguillon, was the mistress of the household most frequented by Montesquieu, *le filosophe*, as Charles calls him. Madame du Deffand has left to us portraits of both the Princesse de Talmond and Madame d'Aiguillon.

'Madame de Talmond has beauty and wit and vivacity; that turn for pleasantry which is our national inheritance seems natural to her. . . . But her wit deals only with pleasant frivolities; her ideas are the children of her memory rather than of her imagination. French in everything else, she is original in her vanity. Ours is more sociable, inspires the desire to please, and suggests the means. Hers is truly Sarmatian, artless and indolent; she cannot bring herself to flatter those whose admiration she covets. . . . She thinks herself perfect, says so, and expects to be believed. At this price alone does she yield a semblance of friendship: semblance, I say, for her affections are concentrated on herself . . . She is as jealous as she is vain, and so capricious as to make her at once the most unhappy and the most absurd of women. She never knows what she wants, what she fears, whom she loves, or whom she hates. There is no nature in her expression: with her chin in the air she poses eternally as tender or disdainful, absent or haughty; all is affectation. . . . She is feared and hated by all who live in her society. Yet she has truth, courage, and honesty, and is such a mixture of good and evil that no steadfast opinion about her can be entertained. She pleases, she provokes: we love, hate, seek, and avoid her. It is as if she communicated to others the eccentricity of her own caprice.'

Where a character like hers met a nature like the Prince's, peace and quiet were clearly out of the question.

Madame du Deffand is not more favourable to another friend of Charles, Madame d'Aiguillon. This lady gave a supper every Saturday night, where neither her husband, the lover of the Princesse de Conti, nor her son, later the successor of Choiseul as Minister of Louis XV., was expected to appear. 'The most brilliant men, French or foreign, were her guests, attracted by her abundant, active, impetuous, and original intellect, by her elevated conversation, and her kindness of manner.' {86} She was, according to Gustavus III., 'the living gazette of the Court, the town, the provinces, and the academy.' Voltaire wrote to her rhymed epistles. Says Madame du Deffand, 'Her mouth is fallen in, her nose crooked, her glance wild and bold, and in spite of all this she is beautiful. The brilliance of her complexion atones for the irregularity of her features. Her waist is thick, her bust and arms are enormous. yet she has not a heavy air: her energy gives her ease of movement. Her wit is like her face, brilliant and out of drawing. Profusion, activity, impetuosity are her ruling qualities . . . She is like a play which is all *spectacle*, all machines and decorations, applauded by the pit and hissed by the boxes. . . . '

Montesquieu was hardly a spectator in the pit, yet he habitually lived at Madame d'Aiguillon's; 'she is original,' he said, and she, with Madame Dupré de Saint–Maur, watched by the death–bed of the philosopher. {87}

In unravelling the hidden allusions of Charles's correspondence, I at first recognised Madame d'Aiguillon in Charles's friend 'La Grandemain.' The name seemed a suitable *sobriquet*, for a lady with *gros bras*, like Madame d'Aiguillon, might have large hands. The friendship of 'La Grandemain' with the *philosophe*, Montesquieu, also pointed to Madame d'Aiguillon. But Charles, at a later date, makes a memorandum that he has deposited his strong box, with money, at the rooms of La Comtesse de Vassé, in the Rue Saint Dominique, Faubourg St. Germain. That box, again, as he notes, was restored by 'La Grandemain.' This fact, with Grimm's anecdote, identifies 'La Grandemain,' not with Madame d'Aiguillon, but with Madame de Vassé, 'the Comtesse,' as Goring calls her, though Grimm makes her a Marquise. If Montesquieu's private papers and letters in MS. had been published in full, we should probably know more of this matter. His relations with Bulkeley were old and most intimate. Before he died he confessed to Father Routh, an Irish Jesuit, whom Voltaire denounces in 'Candide.' This Routh must have been connected with Colonel Routh, an Irish Jacobite in French service, husband of Charles's friend, 'la Comtesse de Routh.' Montesquieu himself, though he knew, as we shall show, the Prince's secret, was no conspirator. Unluckily, as we learn from M. Vian's life of the philosopher, his successors have been very chary of publishing details of his private existence. It is, of course, conceivable that Helvetius, who told Hume that his house had sheltered Charles, is the *philosophe* mentioned by Mademoiselle Luci and Madame de Vassé. But Charles's proved relations with Montesquieu, and Montesquieu's known habit of frequenting the society of his lady neighbours in the convent of St. Joseph, also his intimacy with Charles's friend Bulkeley, who attended his death–bed, all seem rather to point to the author of 'L'Esprit des Lois.' The *philosophes*, for a moment, seem to have expected to find in Prince Charlie the 'philosopher–king' of Plato's dream!

The Prince's distinguished friends unluckily did not succeed in inspiring him with common sense.

On August 16 he defends the conduct of *cette home, ou tête de fer* (himself), and he writes a few aphorisms, *Maximes d'un l'ome sauvage*! He aimed at resembling Charles XII., called 'Dener Bash' by the Turks, for his obstinacy, a nickname also given by Lord Marischal to the Prince. Like Balen, he was termed 'The Wild,' 'by knights whom kings and courts can tame.' He writes to the younger Waters,

To Waters, Junior.

'Ye 21st August, 1749.

'I receive yrs. of ye 8th. Current with yr two as mentioned and I heve send their Answers for Avignon, plese to Enclose in it a Credit for fifteen thousand Livers, to Relive my family there, at the disposal of Stafford and Sheridan. I am sorry to be obliged oftener to draw upon you, than to remit, and cannot help Reflection on this occasion, on the Misery of that poor Popish Town, and all their Inhabitants not being worth four hundred Louidors. Mr. B. [Bulkeley] Mistakes as to my taking amis anything of him, on the contrary I am charmed to heve the opinion of everybody, particularly them Like him, as I am shure say nothing but what they think: but as I am so much imbibed in ye English air, where My only Concerns are, I cannot help sometimes differing with ye inhabitants of forain Climats.

'I remain all yours.

'15,000 ff. Credit for Stafford and Sheridan at Avignon.'

'Newton' kept writing, meanwhile, that Cluny can do nothing till winter, 'on account of the sheilings,' the summer habitations of the pastoral Highlanders. There may have been sheilings near the hiding–places of the Loch Arkaig treasure. On September 30 we find Charles professing his *inébranlable amitié* for Madame de Talmond. He bids his courier stop at Lunéville, as she may be at the Court of Stanislas there.

The results of Goring's mission to England may be gleaned from a cypher letter of 'Malloch' (Balhaldie) to James. Balhaldie had been in London; he found the party staunch, 'but frighted out of their wits.' The usual names of the official Jacobites are given—Barrymore, Sir William Watkyns Wynne, and Beaufort. But they are all alarmed 'by Lord Traquair's silly indiscretion in blabbing to Murray of Broughton of their concerns, wherein he could be of no use.' They had summoned Balhaldie, and complained of the influence of Kelly, an adviser bequeathed to Charles by his old tutor,

Sir Thomas Sheridan, now dead. 'They saw well that the Insurrection Sir James Harrington was negotiating, to be begun at Litchfield Election and Races, in September '47, was incouraged, and when that failed, the Insurrection attempted by Lally's influence on one Wilson, a smuggler in Sussex, which could serve no end save the extinction of the unhappy men concerned in them; therefore they had taken pains to prevent any. They lamented the last steps the Prince had taken here as scarcely reparable.'

Goring had now been with them, and they had insisted on the Prince's procuring a reconciliation with the French Court. 'Goring's only business was to say that the Prince had parted with Kelly, Lally, Sir James Graeme, and Oxburgh, and the whole, and to assure friends in England that he would never more see any one of them.' Charles was, therefore, provided by his English friends with 15,000*l.*, and the King's timid party of men with much to lose won a temporary triumph. He sent 21,000 livres to his Avignon household, adding, 'I received yours with a list of my bookes: I find sumne missing of them. Particularly Fra Paulo [Sarpi] and Boccaccio, which are both rare. If you find any let me know it.'

Charles was more of a bibliophile than might be guessed from his orthography.

On November 22, 1749, Charles, from Lunéville, wrote a long letter to a lady, speaking of himself in the third person. All approaches to Avignon are guarded, to prevent his return thither. 'Despite the Guards, they assure me that he is in France, and not far from the capital. The Lieutenant of Police has been heard to say, by a person who informed me, that he knew for certain the Prince had come in secret to Paris, and had been at the house of Monsieur Lally. The King winks at all this, but it is said that M. de Puysieux and the Mistress (Madame de Pompadour) are as ill disposed as ever. I know from a good source that 15,000*l.* has been sent to the Prince from England, on condition of his dismissing his household.' {91}

The spelling of this letter is correct, and possibly the Prince did not write it, but copied it out. That Louis XV. winked at his movements is probable enough; secretive as he was, the King may have known what he concealed even from his Minister, de Puysieux.

On December 19, the Prince, who cannot have been far from Paris, sent Goring thither 'to get my big Muff and portfeul.' I do not know which lady he addressed, on December 10, as 'l'Adorable,' 'avec toute la tendresse possible.' On November 28, 'R. Jackson' writes from England. He saw Dr. King (of St. Mary Hall, Oxford), who had been at Lichfield races, 'and had a list of the 275 gentlemen who were there.' This Mr. Jackson was going to Jamaica, to Henry Dawkins, brother of Jemmy Dawkins, a rich and scholarly planter who played a great part, later, in Jacobite affairs.

In 1750, February found Charles still without a reply to his letter of May 26, in which he made an anonymous appeal for shelter in Imperial territories. Orders to Goring, who had been sent to Lally, bid him 'take care not to get benighted in the woods and dangerous places.' A good deal is said about a marble bust of the Prince at which Lemoine is working, the original, probably, of the plaster busts sold in autumn in Red Lion Square. 'Newton' (January 28) thinks Cluny wilfully dilatory about sending the Loch Arkaig treasure, and Æneas Macdonald, the banker, one of the Seven Men of Moidart, accuses 'Newton' (Kennedy) of losing 800*l*. of the money at Newmarket races! In fact, Young Glengarry and Archibald Cameron had been helping themselves freely to the treasure at this very time, whence came endless trouble and recriminations, as we shall see. {92}

On January 25 the Prince was embroiled with Madame de Talmond. He writes, obviously in answer to remonstrances:

'Nous nous prometons de suivre en tout les volontés et les arrangemens de notre fidèle amie et alliée, L. P. D. T.; nous retirer aux heures qu'il lui conviendra a la ditte P, soit de jour, soit de nuit, soit de ses états, en foy de quoi nous signons. C.'

He had begun to bore the capricious lady.

Important intrigues were in the air. The Prince resembled 'paper–sparing Pope' in his use of scraps of writing material. One piece bears notes both of February and June 1750. On February 16 Charles wrote to Mr. Dormer, an English Jacobite:

'I order you to go to Anvers, and there to execute my instructions without delay.'

Goring carried the letter. Then comes a despatch of June, which will be given under date.

Concerning the fatal hoard of Loch Arkaig, 'Newton' writes thus:–

Tho. Newton to ——

'March 18, 1750.

'You have on the other side the melancholy confirmation of what I apprehended. Dr. Cameron is no doubt the person here mentioned that carryd away the horses [money], for he is lately gone to Rome, as is also young Glengery, those and several others of them, have been very flush of money, so that it seems they took care of themselves. C. [Cluny] in my opinion is more to be blamed than any of them, for if he had a mind to act the honest part he certainly could have given up the whole long since. They will no doubt represent me not in the most advantageous light at Rome, for attempting to carry out of their country what they had to support them. I hope they will one day or other be obliged to give an acct. of this money, if so, least they shd. attempt to Impose upon you, you'l find my receipts to C. will exactly answer what I had already the honour of giving you an acct. of.'

Again 'Newton' writes:

(*Tho. Newton—From G. Waters's Letter.*)

'April 27, 1750.

'I am honored with yours of the 6th. Inst. and nothing could equal my surprize at the reception of the Letter I sent you. I did not expect C [Cluny] was capable of betraying the confidence you had in him, and he is the more culpable, as I frequently put it in his power to acquit himself of his duty without reproach of any side. Only Cameron is returned from Rome greatly pleased with the reception he met there. I have not seen him, but he has bragged of this to many people here since his return. I never owned to any man alive to have been employed in that affair.'

In spite of Newton, it is not to be credited that Cluny, lurking in many perils on Ben Alder, was unfaithful about the treasure.

Meanwhile, Young Glengarry (whose history we give later), Archibald Cameron (Lochiel's brother), Sir Hector Maclean, and other Jacobites, were in Rome, probably to explain their conduct about the Loch Arkaig treasure to James. He knew nothing about the matter, and what he said will find its proper place when we come to investigate the history of Young Glengarry. The Prince at this time corresponded a good deal with 'Mademoiselle Luci,' that fair philosophical recluse who did little commissions for him in Paris. On April 4 he wants a list of the books he left in Paris, and shows a kind heart.

'Pray take care of the young surgeon, M. Le Coq, and see that he wants for nothing. As the lad gets no money from his relations, he may be in need.' Charles, on March 28, writes thus to 'Madame de Beauregard,' which appears to be an alias of Madame de Talmond:

The Prince.

March 28, 1750.

'A Md. Bauregor. Je vois avec Chagrin que vous vous tourmentes et mois aussi bien innutillement, et en tout sans [sens]. Ou vous voules me servire, ou vous ne Le voules pas; ou vous voules me protege, ou non; Il n'y a acune autre alternative en raison qui puis etre. Si vous voules me servire il ne faut pas me soutenire toujours que Blan [blanc] est noire, dans Les Chose Les plus palpable: et jamais Avouer que vous aves tort meme quant vous Le santes. Si vous ne voules pas me servire, il est inutile que je vous parle de ce qui me regarde: si vous voules me protege, il ne faut pas me rendre La Vie plus malheureuse qu'il n'est. Si vous voules m'abandoner il faut me Le dire en bon Francois ou *Latin. Visus solum*' [sic].

Madame de Talmond sheltered the Prince both in Lorraine and in Paris. They were, unluckily, born to make each other's lives 'insupportable.'

Charles wrote this letter, probably to Madame d'Aiguillon, from Paris:

May 12, 1750.

'La Multitude d'affaire de toute Espèce dont j'ai été plus que surchargé, Madame, depuis plus de quatre Mois, Chose que votre Chancelier a du vous attester, ne m' avois permis de vous rappeller Le souvenir de vos Bontés pour Moi; qualque Long qu'ait ete Le Silance que j'ai gardé sur Le Desir que j'ai d'en mériter La Continuation j'espère qu'il ne m'en aura rien fait perdre: j'ose meme presumer Encore asses pour me flater qu'une Longue absence que je projette par raison et par une necessite absolue, ne m'efacera pas totalement de votre souvenir; Daigne Le Conserver, Madame a quelquun qui n'en est pas indigne et qui cherchera toujours a Le meriter par son tendre et respectueux attachement—a Paris Le 12 May, 1750.'

A quaint light is thrown on the Prince's private affairs (May 12) by Waters's note of his inability to get a packet of Scottish tartan, sent by Archibald Cameron, out of the hands of the Custom House. It was confiscated as 'of British manufacture.' Again, on May 18, Charles wrote to Mademoiselle Luci, in Paris. She is requested 'de faire avoire une ouvrage de Mr. Fildings, (auteur de Tom Jones) qui s'apel *Joseph Andrews*, dans sa langue naturelle, et la traduction aussi.' He also wants 'Tom Jones' in French, and we may infer that he is teaching to some fair pupil the language of Fielding. He asks, too, for a razor–case with four razors, a shaving mirror, and a strong pocket–book with a lock. His famous 'chese de post' (post–chaise) is to be painted and repaired.

Business of a graver kind is in view. 'Newton' (April 24) is to get ready to accompany the Prince on a long journey, really to England, it seems. Newton asked for a delay, on account of family affairs. He was only to be known to the bearer as 'Mr. Newton,' of course not his real name.

On May 28, Charles makes a mote about a mysterious lady, really Madame de Talmond.

Project.

'If ye lady abandons me at the last moment, to give her the letter here following for ye F. K. [French King], and even ye original, if she thinks it necessary, but with ye greatest secrecy; apearing to them already in our confidence that I will quit the country, if she does not return to me immediately.'

Drafts of letters to the French King, in connection with Madame de Talmond—to be delivered, apparently, if Charles died in England— will be given later. To England he was now bent on making his way. 'Ye Prince is determined to go over at any rate,' he wrote on a draft of May 3, 1750. {97} 'The person who makes the proposal of coming over assures that he will expose nobody but himself, supposing the worst.' Sir Charles Goring is to send a ship for his brother, Henry Goring, to Antwerp, early in August. 'To visit Mr. P. of D. [unknown] . . . and to agree where the arms &c. may be most conveniently landed, the grand affair of L. [London?] to be attempted at the same time.' There are notes on 'referring the Funds to a free Parliament,' 'The Tory landed interest wished to repudiate the National Debt,' 'To acquaint particular persons that the K. [King] will R—' (resign), which James had no intention of doing.

In preparation for the insurrection Charles, under extreme secrecy, deposited 186,000 *livres* ('livers!') with Waters. He also ordered little silver counters with his effigy, as the English Government came to know, for distribution, and he commanded a miniature of himself, by Le Brun, 'with all the Orders.' This miniature may have been a parting gift to Madame de Talmond, or one of the other protecting ladies, 'adorable' or quarrelsome. It is constantly spoken of in the correspondence.

The real business in hand is revealed in the following directions for Goring. The Prince certainly makes a large order on Dormer, and it is not probable, though (from the later revelations of James Mohr Macgregor) it is possible, that the weapons demanded were actually procured.

June 8.

Letter and Directions for Goring.—'Mr. Dutton will go directly to Anvers and there wait Mr. Barton's arrival and asoon as you have received his Directions you'l set out to join me, in the mean time you will concert with Dormer the properest means of procuring *the things* ['arms,' erased] I now order him, in the strictest secrecy, likewise how I could be concealed in case I came to him, and the safest way of travelling to that country?'

For Mr. Dormer. Same Date. Anvers.

'As you have already offered me by ye Bearer, Mr. Goring, to furnish me what Arms necessary for my service I hereby desire you to get me with all ye expedition possible Twenty Thousand Guns, Baionets, Ammunition proportioned, with four thousand sords and Pistols for horces [cavalry] in one ship which is to be ye first, and in ye second six thousand Guns without Baionets but sufficient Amunition and Six thouzand Brode sords; as Mr. Goring has my further Directions to you on them Affaires Leaves me nothing farther to add at present.'

On June 11, Charles remonstrated with Madame de Talmond: if she is tired of him, he will go to 'le Lorain.' 'Enfin, si vous voulez ma vie, il faut changer de tout.' On June 27, Newton repeated his expressions of suspicion about Cluny, and spoke of 'disputes and broils' among the Scotch as to the seizure of the Loch Arkaig money.

On July 2, Charles, in cypher, asked James for a renewal of his commission as Regent. Goring, or Newton, was apparently sent at least as far as Avignon with this despatch. He travelled as Monsieur Fritz, a German, with complicated precautions of secrecy. James sent the warrant to be Regent on parchment—it is in the Queen's Library—but he added that Charles was 'a continual heartbreak,' and warned his son not to expect 'friendship and favours from people, while you do all that is necessary to disgust them.' He 'could not in decency' see Charles's envoy (August 4). On the following day Edgar wrote in a more friendly style, for this excellent man was of an amazing loyalty.

From James Edgar.

'August 5, 1750: Rome.

'Your Royal Highness does me the greatest pleasure in mentioning the desire you have to have the King's head in an intaglio. There is nobody can serve you as well in that respect as I, so I send you by the bearers two, one on a stone like a ruby, but it is a fine *Granata*, and H.M.'s hair and the first letters of his name are on the inside of it. The other head is on an emerald, a big one, but not of a fine colour; it is only set in lead, so you may either set it in a ring, a seal, or a locket, as you please: they are both cut by Costanzia, and very well done.'

These intagli would be interesting relics for collectors of such flotsam and jetsam of a ruined dynasty. On August 25, Charles answered Edgar. He is 'sorry that His Majesty is prevented against the most dutiful of sons.' He sends thanks for the engraved stones and the powers of Regency. This might well have been James's last news of Charles, for he was on his way to London, a perilous expedition. {101}

CHAPTER V—THE PRINCE IN LONDON; AND AFTER.— MADEMOISELLE LUCI (SEPTEMBER 1750–JULY 1751)

The Prince goes to London—Futility of this tour—English Jacobites described by Æneas Macdonald—No chance but in Tearlach—Credentials to Madame de Talmond—Notes of visit to London—Doings in London— Gratifying conversion—Gems and medals—Report by Hanbury Williams— Hume's legend—Report by a spy— *Billets* to

Madame de Talmond— Quarrel—Disappearance—'The old aunt'—Letters to Mademoiselle Luci —Charles in Germany—Happy thought of Hanbury Williams—Marshal Keith's mistress—Failure of this plan—The English 'have a clue'—Books for the Prince—Mademoiselle Luci as a critic—Jealousy of Madame de Talmond—Her letter to Mademoiselle Luci—The young lady replies—Her bad health—Charles's reflections—Frederick 'a clever man'—A new adventure.

The Prince went to London in the middle of September 1750; and why did he run such a terrible risk? Though he had ordered great quantities of arms in June, no real preparations had been made for a rising. His Highlanders—Glengarry, Lochgarry, Archy Cameron, Clanranald—did not know where he was. Scotland was not warned. As for England, we learn the condition of the Jacobite party there from a letter by Æneas Macdonald, the banker, to Sir Hector Maclean—Sir Hector whom, in his examination, he had spoken of as 'too fond of the bottle.' {103} Æneas now wrote from Boulogne, in September 1750. He makes it clear that peace, luxury, and constitutionalism had eaten the very heart out of the grandsons of the cavaliers. There was grumbling enough at debt, taxes, a Hanoverian King who at this very hour was in Hanover. Welsh and Cheshire squires and London aldermen drank Jacobite toasts in private. 'But,' says Æneas, 'there are not in England three persons of distinction of the same sentiments as to the method of restoring the Royal family, some being for one way, some for another.' They have neither heart nor money for an armed assertion of their ideas. In 1745, Sir William Watkins Wynne (who stayed at home in Wales) had not 200*l.* by him in ready money, and money cannot be raised on lands at such moments. Yet this very man was believed to have spent 120,000 *l.* in contested elections. 'It is very probable that six times as much money has been thrown away upon these elections'—he means in the country generally—'as would have restored the King.' Æneas knew another gentleman who had wasted 40,000*l.* in these constitutional diversions. 'The present scheme,' he goes on, 'is equally weak.' The English Jacobites were to seem to side with Frederick, the Prince of Wales, in opposition, and force him, when crowned, 'to call a free Parliament.' That Parliament would proclaim a glorious Restoration. In fact, the English Jacobites were devoured by luxury, pacific habits, and a desire to save their estates by pursuing 'constitutional methods.' These, as we shall see, Charles despised. If a foreign force cannot be landed (if landed it would scarcely be opposed), then 'there is no method so good as an attempt such as *Terloch* [Tearlach] made: if there be arms and money: men, I am sure, he will find enough. . . . One thing you may take for granted, that Terloch's appearance again would be worth 5,000 men, and that without him every attempt will be vain and fruitless.' Æneas, in his examination, talked to a different tune, as the poor timid banker, distrusted and insulted by ferocious chieftains.

'Terloch' was only too eager to 'show himself again'; money and arms he seems to have procured (d'Argenson says 4,000,000 francs!), but why go over secretly to London, where he had no fighting partisans? There are no traces of a serious organised plan, and the Prince probably crossed the water, partly to see how matters really stood, partly from restlessness and the weariness of a tedious solitude in hiding, broken only by daily quarrels and reconciliations with the Princesse de Talmond and other ladies.

We find a curious draft of his written on the eve of starting.

'Credentials given ye 1st. Sept, 1750. *to ye P. T.*' (Princesse de Talmond).

'Je me flate que S.M.T.C. [Sa Majesté Très Chrétien] voudra bien avoire tout foi et credi à Madame La P. de T., ma chere Cousine, come si s'etoit mois–meme; particulierement en l'assurant de nouveau come quois j'ai ses veritable interest plus a cour que ses Ministres, etant toujours avec une attachemen veritable et sincere pour sa sacre persone. C. P. R.' (Charles, Prince Regent).

Again,

A Mr. Le Duc de Richelieu.

'Je comte sur votre Amitié, Monsieur, je vous prie d'être persuade de la mienne et de ma reconnaissance.

'All these are deponed, not to be given till farther orders.'

What use the Princesse de Talmond was to make of these documents, on what occasion, is not at all obvious. That the Prince actually went to London, we know from a memorandum in his own hand. 'My full powers and commission of Regency renewed, when I went to England in 1750, and nothing to be said at Rome, for every thing there is known, and my brother, who has got no confidence of my Father, has always acted, as far as his power, against my interest.' {105}

Of Charles's doings in London, no record survives in the Stuart Papers of 1750. We merely find this jotting:

'Parted ye 2d. Sep. Arrived to A. [Antwerp] ye 6th. Parted from thence ye 12th. Sept. E. [England] ye 14th, and at L. [London] ye 16th. Parted from L. ye 22d. and arrived at P. ye 24th. From P. parted ye 28th. Arrived here ye 30th Sept. If she [Madame de Talmond, probably] does not come, and ye M. [messenger] agreed on to send back for ye Letters and Procuration [to] ye house here of P. C. and her being either a tretor or a hour, to chuse which, [then] not to send to P. even after her coming unless absolute necessity order, requiring it then at her dor.'

On the back of the paper is:

'The letter to Godie [Gaudie?] retarded a post; ye Lady's being arrived, or her retard to be little, if she is true stille.'

Then follow some jottings, apparently of the lady's movements. 'N.S. [New style] ye 16th. Sept. Either ill counselled or she has made a confidence. M. Lorain's being here [the Duke of Lorraine, ex–King of Poland, probably, a friend of Madame de Talmond] ye 12th. Sept. To go ye same day with ye King, speaking to W. [Waters?] ye last day, Madame A. here this last six weeks.'

These scrawls appear to indicate some communication between Madame de Talmond, the Duke of Lorraine, and Louis XV. {106}

In London Charles did little but espouse the Anglican religion. Dr. King, in his 'Anecdotes,' tells how the Prince took the refreshment of tea with him, and how his servant detected a resemblance to the busts sold in Red Lion Square. He also appeared at a party at Lady Primrose's, much to her alarm. {107} He prowled about the Tower with Colonel Brett, and thought a gate might be damaged by a petard. His friends, including Beaufort and Westmoreland, held a meeting in Pall Mall, to no purpose. The tour had no results, except in the harmless region of the fine arts. A medal was struck, by Charles's orders, and we have the following information for collectors of Jacobite trinkets. The English Government, never dreaming that the Prince was in Pall Mall, was well informed about cheap treasonable jewellery.

'Paris: August 31, 1750.

'The Artist who makes the seals with the head of the Pretender's eldest Son, is called le Sieur Malapert, his direction is hereunder, he sells them at 3 Livres apiece, but by the Dozen he takes less.

'It is one Tate, who got the engraving made on metal, from which the Artist takes the impression on his Composition in imitation of fine Stones of all colours. This Tate was a Jeweller at Edinborough, where he went into the Rebellion and having made his escape, has since settled here, but has left his wife and Family at Edinborough. He is put upon the list of the French King's Bounty for eight hundred Livres yearly, the same as is allowed to those that had a Captain's Commission in the Pretender's Service and are fled hither. It is Sullivan and Ferguson who employ Tate to get the 1,500 Seals done, he being a man that does still Jeweller's business and follows it. The Artist has actually done four dozen of seals, which are disposed of, having but half a dozen left. He expects daily an order for the said quantity more—As there are no Letters or Inscription about it, the Artist may always pretend that it is only a fancy head, though it is in reality very like the Pretender's Eldest Son.' {108}

Oddly enough, we find Waters sealing, with this very intaglio of the Prince, a letter to Edgar, in 1750. It is a capital likeness.

Wise after the event, Hanbury Williams wrote from Berlin (October 13, 1750) that Charles was in England, 'in the heart of the kingdom, in the county of Stafford.' By October 20, Williams knows that the Prince is in Suffolk. All this is probably a mere echo of Charles's actual visit to London, reverberated from the French Embassy at Berlin, and arriving at Hanbury Williams, he says, through an Irishman, who knew a lacquey of the French Ambassador's. In English official circles no more than this was known. Troops were concentrated near Stafford after Charles had returned to Lorraine. Hume told Sir John Pringle a story of how Charles was in London in 1753, how George II. told the fact to Lord Holdernesse, and how the King expressed his good–humoured indifference. But Lord Holdernesse contradicted the tale, as we have already observed.

If Hume meant 1750 by 1733 he was certainly wrong. George was then in Hanover. In 1753 I have no proof that Charles was in London, though Young Glengarry told James that the Prince was 'on the coast' in November 1752. If Charles did come to London in 1753, and if George knew it, the information came through Pickle to Henry Pelham, as will appear later. Hume gave the Earl Marischal as his original authority. The Earl was likely to be better informed about events of 1752–1753 than about those of September 1750.

After Charles's departure from London, the English Government received information from Paris (October 5, 1750) to the following effect:

'Paris: October 5, 1750.

'It is supposed that the Pretender's Son keeps at Montl'hery, six leagues from Paris, at Mr. Lumisden's, or at Villeneuve St. Georges, at a small distance from Town, at Lord Nairn's; Sometimes at Sens, with Col. Steward and Mr. Ferguson; when at Paris, at Madme. la Princesse de Talmont's, or the Scotch Seminary; nobody travels with him but Mr. Goring, and a Biscayan recommended to him by *Marshal Saxe*: the young Pretender is disguised in an Abbé's dress, with a black patch upon his eye, and his eyebrows black'd.

'An Officer of Ogilvie's Regimt. in this Service listed lately. An Irish Priest, who belonged to the Parish Church of S. Eustache at Paris, has left his Living, reckoned worth 80*l*. St. a year, and is very lately gone to London to be Chaplain to the Sardinian Minister: he has carried with him a quantity of coloured Glass Seals with the Pretender's Son's Effigy, as also small heads made of silver gilt about this bigness [example] to be set in rings, as also points for watch cases, with the same head, and this motto round "Look, Love, and follow."' {110}

On October 30, Walton wrote that James was much troubled by a letter from Charles, doubtless containing the news of his English failure; perhaps notifying his desertion of the Catholic faith. On January 15, 1751, Walton writes that James has confided to the Pope that Charles is at Boulogne–sur–Mer, which he very possibly was. On January 9 and 22, Horace Mann reports, on the information of Cardinal Albani, that James and the Duke of York are ill with grief. 'Something extraordinary has happened to the Pretender's eldest son.' He had turned Protestant, that was all. But Cardinal Albani withdraws his statement, and thinks that nothing unusual has really occurred. In fact, Charles, as we shall see, had absolutely vanished for three months.

Charles returned to France in September 1750, and renewed his *amantium irae* with Madame de Talmond. Among the Stuart Papers of 1750 are a number of tiny *billets*, easily concealed, and doubtless passed to the lady furtively. 'Si vous ne voulez, Reine de Maroc, pas cet faire, quelle plaisir mourir de chagrin et de desespoire!'

'Aiez de la Bonté et de confience pour celui qui vous aime et vous adore passionément.'

To some English person:

'Ask the Channoine where you can by hocks [buy hooks!] and lines for fishing, and by a few hocks and foure lines.' {111}

The Princess writes:

'Je partirai dimanche comme j'ai promis au Roy de Pologne' (Stanislas). 'Je vous embrasse bien tendrement, si vous êtes tel que vous devez être à mon égard.' She is leaving for Commercy. On the reverse the Prince has written, 'Judi. Je comance a ouvrire mes yeux a votre egar, Madame, vous ne voulez pas de mois, ce soire, malgre votre promes, et ma malheureuse situation.'

The quarrels grew more frequent and more embittered. We have marked his suspicious view of the lady's movements. On September 26, 1750, she had not returned, and he wrote to her in the following terms.

The Prince.

September 26, 1750.

'Je pars, Madame, dans L'instant, en Sorte que vous feriez reflection, et retourniez au plus vite, tout doit vous Engager, si vous avez de l'amitié pour mois, Car je ne puis pas me dispenser de vous repeter, Combien chaque jour de votre absence faira du tor a mes affaier outre Le desire d'avoire une Coinpagnie si agréable dans une si triste solitude, que ma malheureuse situation m'oblige indispensablement de tenire. J'ai cessé [?] des Ordres positive a Mlle. Luci, de ne me pas envoier La Moindre Chose meme une dilligence come aussi de mon cote je n'en veres rien, jusqu'a ce que vous soiez arrive.

'Quant vous partires alors Mdll. Luci vous remettera tout ce quil aura pour mois, vous rien de votre cote que votre personne.'

On the same paper Charles announces his intention of going instantly to 'Le Lorain.' There must have been a great quarrel with Madame de Talmond, outwearied by the exigencies of a Prince doomed to a *triste solitude* after a week of London. On September 30 he announces to Waters that there will be no news of him till January 15, 1751. For three months he disappears beyond even his agent's ken. On October 20 he writes to Mademoiselle Luci, styling himself 'Mademoiselle Chevalier,' and calling Madame de Talmond 'Madame Le Nord.' The Princesse de Talmond has left him, is threatening him, and may ruin him.

'Le October 20, 1750.

'A Mll. Luci: Mademoiselle Chevalier est tres affligee de voir le peu d'egard que Madame Lenord a pour ses Interest. La Miene du 12 auroit ete La derniere mais cette dame a ecrit une Letre en date du 18 a M. Le Lorrain qui a choqué cette Demoiselle [himself], Et je puis dire avec raison quelle agit come Le plus Grand de ses ennemis par son retard, elle ajoute encor a cela des menaces si on La presse d'avantage, et si l'on se plain de son indigne procedé. Md. Poulain seroit deja partit, et partiroit si cette dame lui en donnoit Les Moiens. Je ne puis trop vous faire connoitre Le Tort que Md. Lenord fait a cette demoiselle en abandonant sa société et La risque qu'elle fait courir a Md. de Lille qui par La pouroit faire banqueroute.

'A Mdll. La Marre.
Chez M. Lecuyer tapisse [Tapissier].
Grande Rue Garonne, Faubourg
St. Germain à Paris.

'Vous pouvez accuser La reception de cette Lettre par Le premier Ordinaire a M. Le Vieux [Old Waters].

'Adieu Mdll.

'Je vous embrace de tout mon Cour.'

On November 7 Charles writes again to Mademoiselle Luci: the Princesse de Talmond is here *la vieille tante*: now estranged and perhaps hostile. Madame de la Bruère is probably the wife of M. de la Bruère, whom Montesquieu speaks highly of when, in 1749, he was Chargé d'Affaires in Rome. {113}

'Le 7 Nov. 1750.

'Mdlle. Luci,—Je suis fort Etone Mademoiselle qu'une fame de cette Age qu'a notre Tante soi si deresonable. Elle se done tout La paine immaginable pour agire contre Les interets de sa niece par son retard du payment dont vous m'avez deja parlé.

'Voici une lettre que je vous prie de cachete, et d'y mettre son adress, et de l'envoier sur Le Champ a Madame de Labruière. Il est inutile d'hors en avant que vous communiquier aucune Chose de ce qui regard Mlle. Chevalier [himself], a Md. la Tante [Talmond] jusqu'a ce que Elle pense otrement, car, il n'est que trop cler ques es procedes sont separés et oposés à ce qui devroit etre son interet. Je vous embrace de tout mon Coeur.'

These embraces are from the supposed Mademoiselle Chevalier. There is no reason to suppose a tender passion between Charles and the girl who was now his Minister of Affairs, Foreign and Domestic. But Madame de Talmond, as we shall learn, became jealous of Mademoiselle Luci.

His deeper seclusion continues.

Madame de Talmond, in the following letter, is as before, *la tante*. The 'merchandise' is letters for the Prince, which have reached Mademoiselle Luci, and which she is to return to Waters, the banker.

'Le 16 Nov. 1750.

'A Mdll. Luci: Je vous ai écrit Mademoiselle, Le 7, avec une incluse pour Md. de La Bruière, je vous prie de m'en accuser la reception à l'adresse de M. Le Vieux [Old Waters], et de me donner des Nouvelles de M. de Lisle [unknown]; pour se que regarde Les Marchandises de modes que vous avez chez vous depuis que j'ai en Le plaisir de vous voire et que cette Tante [Madame de Talmond] veut avoire l'indignité d'en differer le paiement, il faut que vous les renvoiez au memes Marchands de qui vous Les avez reçu et leur dire que vous craignez ne pas avoir de longtems une occasion favorable pour Les débiter, ainsi qu'en attendant vous aimez mieux quelles soieut dans leurs mains que dans Les votres. Je vous embrasse de tout mon Coeur.'

By November 19, Charles is indignant even with Mademoiselle Luci, who has rather tactlessly shown the letter of November 7 to Madame de Talmond, *la tante*, *la vieille Femme*. Oh, the unworthy Prince!

Charles's epistle follows:

19th Nov.

'Je suis tres surprise, Mademoiselle, de votre Lettre du 15, par Laquelle vous dites avoire montres a la tante une Lettre touchant les Affaires de Mdlle. Chevalier, cependant la mienne du 7 dont vous m'accuses La reception vous marquoit positivement Le contraire, Mr. De Lisle ne voulant pas qu'on parlet a cette vieille Femme jesqu'a ce qu'elle changeat de sentiment, et qu'elle paix la somme si necessaire à son Commerce. Ne vous serriez vous pas trompée de l'adresse de l'incluse pour la jeune Marchande de Mdlle. La bruière—Vous devez peut ete La connoitre; si cela est, je vous prie de me le Marquer et d'y remedier au plutot. Enfin Mademoiselle vous me faites tomber des nues et les pauvrétés que vous me marquez sont a mépriser. Elles ne peuvent venir que de cette tante, ce sont des couleurs qui ne peuvent jaimais prendre.

'Adieu Mdlle., n'attendez plus de mes nouvelles jusqu'a ce que le paiement soit fait. Soiez Toujours assurée de ma sincere amitié.'

Charles's whole career, alas! after 1748, was a set of quarrels with his most faithful adherents. This break with his old mistress, Madame de Talmond, is only one of a fatal series. With Mademoiselle Luci he never broke: we shall see the reason for this constancy. His correspondence now includes that of 'John Dixon,' of London, a false name for an adherent who has much to say about 'Mr. Best' and 'Mr. Sadler.' The Prince was apparently at or near Worms; his letters went by Mayence. On December 30 he sends for 'L'Esprit des Lois' and 'Les Amours de Mlle. Fanfiche,' and other books of diversified character. On Decemuber 31, his birthday, he wrote to Waters, 'the indisposition of those I employ has occasioned this long silence.' Mr. Dormer was his chief medium of intelligence with England. 'Commerce with Germany' is mentioned; efforts, probably, to interest Frederick the Great. On January 27, 1751, Mademoiselle Luci is informed that *la tante* has paid (probably returned his letters), but with an ill grace. Cluny sends an account of the Loch Arkaig money (only 12,981*l.* is left) and of the loyal clans. Glengarry's contingent is estimated at 3,000 men. In England, 'Paxton' (Sir W. W. Wynne) is dead. On February 28, 1751, Charles is somewhat reconciled to his old mistress. 'Je me flatte qu'en cette Nouvelle Année vous vous corrigerez, en attendant je suis come je serois toujours, avec toutte la tendresse et amitié possible, C. P.'

It is, of course, just possible that, from October 1750 to February 1751, Charles was in Germany, trying to form relations with Frederick the Great. Goring, under the name of 'Stouf,' was certainly working in Germany. Sir Charles Hanbury Williams at Berlin wrote on February 6, 1751, to the Duke of Newcastle:

'Hitherto my labours have been in vain. But I think I have at present hit upon a method which may bring the whole to light. And I will here take the liberty humbly to lay my thoughts and proposals before Your Grace. Feldt Marshal Keith has long had a mistress who is a Livonian, and who has always had an incredible ascendant over the Feldt Marshal, for it was certainly upon her account that his brother, the late Lord Marshal, quitted his house, and that they now live separately. About a week ago (during Feldt Marshal Keith's present illness) the King of Prussia ordered that this woman should be immediately sent out of his dominions. Upon which she quitted Berlin, and is certainly gone directly to Riga, which is the place of her birth. Now, as I am well persuaded that she was in all the Feldt Marshal's secrets, I would humbly submit it to Your Grace, whether it might *not be proper for His Majesty* to order his Ministers at the Court of Petersburgh to make instance to the Empress of Russia, that this woman might be obliged to come to Petersburgh, where, *if proper measures were taken with her*, she may give much light into this, and perhaps into other affairs. The reason why I would have her brought to Petersburgh is, that if she is examined at Riga, that examination would probably be committed to the care of Feldt Marshal Lasci, who commands in Chief, and constantly resides there, and I am afraid, would not take quite so much pains to examine into the bottom of an affair of this nature, as I could wish . . .

'C. HANBURY WILLIAMS.

It is not hard to interpret the words 'proper measures' as understood in the land of the knout. The mistress of Field Marshal Keith could not be got at; she had gone to Sweden, and this chivalrous proposal failed. The woman was not tortured in Russia to discover a Prince who was in or near Paris. {118}

At the very moment when Williams, from Berlin, was making his manly suggestion, Lord Albemarle, from Paris (February 10, 1751), was reporting to his Government that Charles had been in Berlin, and had been received by Frederick 'with great civility.' The King, however, did not accede to Charles's demand for his sister's hand. This report is probably incorrect, for Charles's notes to Mademoiselle Luci at this time indicate no great absence from the French capital.

On February 17, 1751, the English Government, like the police, 'fancied they had a clue.' The Duke of Bedford wrote to Lord Albemarle, 'His Majesty would have your Excellency inform M. Puysieux that you have it now in your power to have the Young Pretender's motions watched, in such a manner as to be able to point out to him where he may be met with; and that his Majesty doth therefore insist that, in conformity to the treaties now subsisting between the two nations he be immediately obliged to leave France. . . . He must be sent by sea, either into the Ecclesiastical States, or to such other country at a distance from France, as may render it impossible for him to return with the same facility he did before.' {119}

These hopes of Charles's arrest were disappointed.

On March 4, young Waters heard of the Prince at the opera ball in Paris. He sent the Prince a watch from the Abbess of English nuns at Pontoise. Charles was always leaving his watches under his pillow. He certainly was not far from Paris. He scolded Madame de Talmond for returning thither (March 4), and sent to Mademoiselle Luci a commission for books, such as 'Attilie tragedie' ('Athalie') and 'Histoire de Miss Clarisse, Lettres Anglaises '(Richardson's 'Clarissa'), and 'La Chimie de Nicola' (*sic*). Mademoiselle Luci, writing on March 5, tells how the Philosophe (Montesquieu,), their friend, has heard a Monsieur Le Fort boast of knowing the Prince's hiding-place. 'The Philosophe turned the conversation.' The Prince answers that Le Fort is *très galant homme*, but a friend of *la tante* (Madame de Talmond), who must have been blabbing. He was in or near Paris, for he corresponded constantly with Mademoiselle Luci. The young lady assures him that some new philosophical books which he had ordered are worthless trash. 'L'Histoire des Passions' and 'Le Spectacle de l'Homme' are amateur rubbish; 'worse was never printed.'

The Prince now indulged in a new cypher. Walsh (his financial friend) is Legrand, Kennedy is Newton (as before), Dormer at Antwerp (his correspondent with England) is Mr. Blunt, 'Gorge in England' (Gorge!) is Mr. White, and so on. Owing to the death of Frederick, Prince of Wales, there was a good deal of correspondence with 'Dixon' and 'Miss Fines'—certainly Lady Primrose—while Dixon may be James Dawkins, or Dr. King, of St. Mary's Hall, Oxford. On May 16, Charles gave Goring instructions as to 'attempting the Court of Prussia, or any other except France, after their unworthy proceedings.' Goring did not set out till June 21, 1751. From Berlin the poor man was to go to Sweden. In April, Madame de Talmond was kind to Charles 'si malheureux et par votre position et par votre caractère.' Mademoiselle Luci was extremely ill in May and June, indeed till October; this led to a curious correspondence in October between her and *la vieille tante*. Madame de Talmond was jealous of Mademoiselle Luci, a girl whom one cannot help liking. Though out of the due chronological course, the letters of these ladies may be cited here.

From Madame de Beauregard (Madame de Talmond) to Mademoiselle Luci.

'October 19, 1751.

'The obstinacy of your taste for the country, Mademoiselle, in the most abominable weather, is only equalled by the persistence of your severity towards me. I have written to you from Paris, I have written from Versailles, with equal success—not a word of answer! Whether you want to imitate, or to pay court to our *amie* [the Prince] I know not, but would gladly know, that I may yield everything with a good grace, let it cost what it will. As a rule it would cost me much, nay, all, to sacrifice your friendship. But I have nothing to contest with old friends, who are more lovable than myself. On my side I have only the knowledge and the feeling of your worth, which require but discernment and justice. From such kinds of accomplishments as these, *you* are dispensed. So serious a letter might be tedious without being long, but it is saddened also by the weary weight of my own spirits. Will you kindly give me news of your health and of your return to town? I am sorry that Paris does not interest me; I am going to Fontainebleau at the end of the week.'

Mademoiselle Luci replies with dignity.

'October 22, 1751.

'Madame,—A fever, and many other troubles, have prevented me from answering the three letters with which you have honoured me. Permit me to mingle a few complaints with my thanks! Were I capable of the sentiments which you attribute to me, I could not deserve your flattering esteem. Its expressions I should be compelled to regard merely as an effort of extreme politeness on your side. Assuredly, Madame, I am strongly attached to Madame your friend [the Prince]; for her I would suffer and do everything short of stooping to an act of baseness. If, Madame, you have not found in me virtues which will assure you of this, at least trust my faults! My character is not supple. The one thing which makes my frankness endurable is, that it renders me incapable of conduct for which I should have to blush. Believe, then, Madame, that I can preserve my friendship for your friend, without falling, as you suspect, into the baseness of paying court to her [the Prince], in spite of the respect which I owe to *you*.'

The letters of the ladies (in French) are copied by the Prince's hand, nor has he improved the orthography. I therefore translate these epistles.

On July 10, 1751, after a tremendous quarrel with Madame de Talmond, Charles wrote out his political reflections. France must apologise to him before he can enter into any measures with her Court. 'I have nothing at heart but the interest of my country, and I am always ready to sacrifice everything for it, Life and rest, but the least reflection as to ye point of honour I can never pass over. There is nobody whatsoever I respect more as ye K. of Prussia; not as a K. but as I believe him to be a clever man. Has he intention to serve me? Proofs must be given, and ye only one convincive is his agreeing to a Marriage with his sister, and acknowledging me at Berlin for what I am.' He adds that he will not be a tool, 'like my ansisters.'

Such were Charles's lonely musings, such the hopeless dreams of an exile. He had now entered on his attempt to secure Prussian aid, and on a fresh chapter of extraordinary political and personal intrigues.

CHAPTER VI—INTRIGUES, POLITICAL AND AMATORY. DEATH OF MADEMOISELLE LUCI, 1752

Hopes from Prussia—The Murrays of Elibank—Imprisonment of Alexander Murray—Recommended to Charles—The Elibank plot—Prussia and the Earl Marischal—His early history—Ambassador of Frederick at Versailles—His odd household—Voltaire—The Duke of Newcastle's resentment—Charles's view of Frederick's policy—His alleged avarice —Lady Montagu—His money-box—Goring and the Earl Marischal—Secret meetings—The lace shop—Albemarle's information—Charles at Ghent— Hanbury Williams's mares' nests—Charles and 'La Grandemain'—She and Goring refuse to take his orders—Appearance of Miss Walkinshaw—Her history—Remonstrances of Goring—'Commissions for the worst of men' —'The little man'—Lady Primrose—Death of Mademoiselle Luci— November 10, date of postponed Elibank plot—Danger of dismissing an agent.

We have seen that Charles's hopes, in July 1751, were turned towards Prussia and Sweden. To these Courts he had sent Goring in June. Meanwhile a new and strange prospect was opening to him in England. On the right bank of Tweed, just above Ashiesteil, is the ruined shell of the old tower of Elibank, the home of the Murrays. A famous lady of that family was Muckle Mou'd Meg, whom young Harden, when caught while driving Elibank's kye, preferred to the gallows as a bride. In 1751 the owner of the tower on Tweed was Lord Elibank; to all appearance a douce, learned Scots laird, the friend of David Hume, and a customer for the wines of Montesquieu's vineyards at La Brède. He had a younger brother, Alexander Murray, and the politics of the pair, says Horace Walpole, were of the sort which at once kept the party alive, and made it incapable of succeeding. Their measures were so taken that they did not go out in the Forty–five, yet could have proved their loyalty had Charles reached St. James's in triumph. Walpole calls Lord Elibank 'a very prating, impertinent Jacobite.' {125} As for the younger brother, Alexander Murray, Sir Walter Scott writes, in his introduction to 'Redgauntlet,' 'a young Scotchman of rank is said to have stooped so low as to plot the surprisal of St. James's Palace and the assassination of the Royal family.'

This was the Elibank plot, which we shall elucidate later.

In the spring and summer of 1751, Alexander Murray had lain in Newgate, on a charge of brawling at the Westminster election. He was kept in durance because he would not beg the pardon of the House on his knees: he only kneeled to God, he said. He was released by the sheriffs at the close of the session, and was escorted by the populace to Lord Elibank's house in Henrietta Street. He then crossed to France, and, in July 1751, 'Dixon' (Dr. King?) thus reports of him to Charles:

'My lady [Lady Montagu or Lady Primrose?] says that M. [Murray] is most zealously attached to you, and that he is upon all occasions ready to obey your commands, and to meet you when and where you please . . . He assures my lady that he can raise five hundred men for your service in and about Westminster.'

These men were to be used in a plot for seizing the Royal family in London. This scheme went on simmering, blended with intrigues for Prussian and Swedish help, and, finally, with a plan for a simultaneous rising in the Highlands. And this combination was the last effort of Jacobitism before the general abandonment of Charles by his party.

The hopes, as regarded Prussia, were centred in Frederick's friend, the brother of Marshal Keith, the Earl Marischal. The Earl was by this time an old man. At Queen Anne's death he had held a command in the Guards, and if he had frankly backed Atterbury when the bishop proposed to proclaim King James, the history of England might have been altered, and the Duke of Argyll's regiment, at Kensington, would have had to fight for the Crown. {126} The Earl missed his chance. He fought at Shirramuir (1715), and he with his brother, later Marshal Keith, was in the unlucky Glensheil expedition from Spain (1719). That endeavour failed, leaving hardly a trace, save the ghost of a foreign colonel which haunts the roadside of Glensheil. From that date the Earl was a cheery, contented, philosophic exile, with no high opinion of kings. Spain was often his abode, where he found, as he said, 'his old friend, the sun.' In 1744 he declined to accompany the Prince, in a herring–boat, to Scotland. In the Forty–five he did not cross the Channel, but, as we have seen, endeavoured to wring men and money from d'Argenson. In 1747 the Earl, then at Treviso, declined to be Charles's minister on the score of 'broken health.' {127a} Charles, as we saw, vainly asked the Earl for a meeting at Venice in 1749. Indeed,

Charles got nothing from his adherent but a mother–of–pearl snuff–box, with the portrait of the old gentleman. {127b} The Earl dwelt, not always on the best terms, with his brother, Marshal Keith, at Berlin, and was treated as a real friend, for a marvel, by Frederick.

On July 20 the Earl had seen Goring at Berlin, and wrote to Charles. Nothing, he said, could be done by Swedish aid. If Sweden moved, Russia would attack her, nor could Frederick, in his turn, assail Russia, for Russia and the Empress Maria Theresa would have him between two fires. {127c} Frederick now (August 1751) took a step decidedly unfriendly as regarded his uncle of England. He sent the Earl Marischal as his ambassador to the Court of Versailles. This was precisely as if the United States were to send a banished Fenian as their Minister to Paris. The Earl was proscribed for treason in England, and, as we shall see, his house in Paris became the centre of truly Fenian intrigues. On these the worthy Earl was wont to give the opinion of an impartial friend. All this was known to the English Government, as we shall show, through Pickle, and the knowledge must have strained the relations between George II. and 'our Nephew,' as Horace Walpole calls Frederick of Prussia.

The Earl's household, when he left Potzdam in August 1751 for Paris, is thus described by Voltaire: 'You will see a very pretty little Turkess, whom he carries with him: they took her at the siege of Oczakow, and made a present of her to our Scot, who seems to have no great need of her. She is an excellent Mussalwoman: her master allows her perfect freedom of conscience. He has also a sort of Tartar *Valet de chambre* [Stepan was his name], who has the honour to be a Pagan.' {128a} On October 29, Voltaire writes that he has had a letter from the Earl in Paris. 'He tells me that his Turk girl, whom he took to the play to see *Mahomet* [Voltaire's drama] was much scandalised.'

Voltaire was to receive less agreeable news from the friend of Frederick. 'Some big Prussian will box your ears,' said the Earl Marischal, after Voltaire's famous quarrel with his Royal pupil.

The appointment of an attainted rebel to be Ambassador at Versailles naturally offended England. The Duke of Newcastle wrote to Lord Hardwicke: {128b}

'One may easily see the views with which the King of Prussia has taken this offensive step: first, for the sake of doing an impertinence to the King; then to deter us from going on with our negotiations in the Empire, for the election of a King of the Romans, and to encourage the Jacobite party, that we may apprehend disturbances from them, if a rupture should ensue in consequence of the measures we are taking abroad.' He therefore proposes a subsidy to Russia, to overawe Frederick.

At Paris, Yorke remonstrated. Hardwicke writes on September 10, 1751:

'I am glad Joe ventured to say what he did to M. Puysieux,' but 'Joe' spoke to no purpose.

James was pleased by the Earl Marischal's promotion and presence in Paris. Charles, at first, was aggrieved. He wrote:

'L. M. coming to Paris is a piece of French politics, on the one side to bully the people of England; on the other hand to hinder our friends from doing the thing by themselves, bambouseling them with hopes. . . . They mean to sell us as usual. . . . The Doctor [Dr. King] is to be informed that Goring saw Lord Marischal, but nothing to be got from him.'

The Prince mentions his 'distress for money,' and sends compliments to Dawkins, 'Jemmy Dawkins,' of whom we shall hear plenty. He sends 'a watch for the lady' (Lady Montagu?).

I venture a guess at Lady Montagu, because Dr. King tells, as a proof of Charles's avarice, that he took money from a lady in Paris when he had plenty of his own. {130a}

Now, on September 15, 1751, Charles sent to Dormer a receipt for 'One Thousand pounds, which he paid me by orders for account of the Right Honourable Vicecountess of Montagu,' signed 'C. P. R.' {130b} Again, on quitting Paris on December 1, 1751, he left, in a coffer, '2,250 *Louidors*, besides what there is in a little bag above, amounting to about 130 guines, and od Zequins or ducats.' These, with 'a big box of books,' were locked up in the house of the Comtesse de Vassé, Rue St. Dominique, Faubourg de St. Germain, in which street Montesquieu lived. The deposit was restored later to Charles by 'Madame La Grandemain,' 'sister' of Mademoiselle Luci. In truth, Charles, for a Prince with an ambition to conquer England, was extremely poor, and a loyal lady did not throw away her guineas, as Dr. King states, on a merely avaricious adventurer. Charles (August 25, 1751) was in correspondence with 'Daniel Macnamara, Esq., at the Grecian Coffee–house, Temple, London,' who later plays a fatal part in the Prince's career.

This is a private interlude: we return to practical politics.

No sooner was the Earl Marischal in Paris than Charles made advances to the old adherent of his family. He sent Goring post–haste to the French capital. Goring, who already knew the Earl, writes (September 20, 1731): 'My instructions are not to let myself be seen by anybody whatever but your Lordship.' The Earl answers on the same day: 'If you yourself know any safe way for both of us, tell it me. There was a garden belonging to a Mousquetaire, famous for fruit, by Pique–price, beyond it some way. I could go there as out of curiosity to see the garden, and meet you to–morrow towards five o'clock; but if you know a better place, let me know it. Remember, I must go with the footmen, and remain in coach as usual, so that the garden is best, because I can say, if it came possibly to be known, that it was by chance I met you.'

'An ambassador,' as Sir Henry Wotton remarked, 'is an honest man sent to lie abroad for his country,' an observation taken very ill by Gentle King Jamie. {131}

Goring replied that the garden was too public. The night would be the surest time. Goring could wear livery, or dress as an Abbé. The Tuileries, when 'literally dark,' might serve. On September 23, the Earl answers, 'One of my servants knows you since Vienna.' Goring, as we know, had been in the Austrian service. 'I will go to the Tuileries when it begins to grow dark, if it does not rain, for it would seem too od that I had choose to walk in rain, and my footman would suspect, and perhaps spye. I shall walk along the step or terrace before the house in the garden.' {132a}

So difficult is it for an ambassador to dabble in treasonable intrigue, especially when old, and when the weather is wet. Let us suppose that Goring and the Earl met. Goring's business was to ask if the Earl 'has leave to disclose the secret that was not in his power to do, last time you saw him. I am ready to come myself, and meet him where he pleases.'

Meetings were difficult to arrange. We read, in the Prince's hand:

To Lord M. from Goring.

'18th Oct. 1751.

'Saying he had received an express from the Prince with orders to tell him [Lord M.] his place of residence, and making a suggestion of meeting at Waters's House.

'Answer made 18th. Oct. by Lord M.

'You may go to look for Lace as a Hamborough Merchant. I go as recommended to a Lace Shop by Mr. Waters and shall be there as it grows dark, for a pretence of staying some time in the house you may also say you are recommended by Waters.

'Mr Vignier Marchand de Doreure rue du Route, au Soleil D'or. Paris.'

(*Overleaf.*)

'18th Oct 1751.

'I shall be glad to see you when you can find a fit place, but to know where your friend is is necessary unfit. Would Waters's house be a good place? Would Md Talmont's, mine is not, neither can I go privately in a hackney coach, my own footman would dogg me, here Stepan knows you well since Vienna.' (Stepan was the Tartar valet.)

It is clear that Charles was now near Paris, and that the Ambassador of Prussia was in communication with him. What did the English Government know of this from their regular agents?

On October 9, Albemarle wrote from Paris that Charles was believed to have visited the town. His 'disguises make it very difficult' to discover him. Albemarle gives orders to stop a Dr. Kincade at Dover, and seize his papers. He sends a list of traffickers between England and the Prince, including Lochgarry, 'formerly in the King's service, and very well known; *is now in Scotland*.' 'The Young Pretender has travelled through Spain and Italy in the habit of a Dominican Fryar. He is expected soon at Avignon. He was last at Berlin and Dantzich, and has nobody with him but Mr. Goring.' This valuable information is marked 'Secret!' {133a}

On October 10, Albemarle writes that Foley, a Jacobite, is much with the Earl Marischal. On October 30, Dr. Kincaid had not yet set out. But (December 1) Dr. Kincaid did start, and at Dover 'was culled like a flower.' On St. Andrew's Day (November 30) there was a Jacobite meeting at St. Germains. Albemarle had a spy present, who was told by Sullivan, the Prince's Irish friend, that Charles was expected at St. Germains by the New Year. The Earl Marischal would have kept St. Andrew's Day with them, but had to go to Versailles. Later we learn that no papers were found on Dr. Kincaid. On January 5, 1752, Albemarle mentions traffickings with Ireland. On August 4, 1752, Mann learns from a spy of some consequence in Rome that the Prince is in Ireland. His household in Avignon is broken up—which, by accident, is true. 'Something is in agitation'—valuable news!

The English Government, it is plain, was still in the dark. But matters were going ill for Charles. In February 1752, Waters, respectfully but firmly, declined to advance money. Charles dismissed in March all his French servants at Avignon, and sold the coach in which Sheridan and Strafford were wont to take the air. Madame de Talmond was still jealous of Mademoiselle Luci. Money came in by mere driblets. 'Alexander' provided 300*l*., and 'Dixon,' in England, twice sends a humble ten pounds. Charles transferred his quarters to the Netherlands, residing chiefly at Ghent, where he was known as the Chevalier William Johnson.

The English Government remained unenlightened. The Duke of Newcastle, on January 29, 1752, had 'advice that the Pretender's son is certainly in Silesia,' and requests Sir Charles Hanbury Williams to make inquiries. {135}

On April 23, 1752, when Charles was establishing himself at Ghent, and trying to raise loans in every direction, the egregious Sir Charles hears that the Prince is in Lithuania, with the Radzivils. On April 27, Williams, at Leipzig, is convinced of this, and again proposes to waylay and seize the papers of a certain Bishop Lascaris, as he passes through Austrian territory on his way to Rome. In Lithuania the Prince might safely have been left. He could do the Elector of Hanover no harm anywhere, except by such Fenian enterprises as that which Pickle was presently to reveal. The anxious and always helpless curiosity of George II. and his agents about the Prince seems especially absurd, when they look in the ends of the earth for a man who is in the Netherlands.

At Ghent, May 1752, Charles to all appearances was much less busied with political conspiracies than with efforts to raise the wind. Dormer, at Antwerp, often protests against being drawn upon for money which he does not possess, and Charles treated a certain sum of 200*l.* as if it were the purse of Fortunatus, and inexhaustible. 'Madame La Grandemain' writes on May 5 that she cannot assist him, and *le Philosophe* (Montesquieu), she says, is out of town. On May 12 the Prince partly explains the cause of his need of money. He has taken, at Ghent, 'a preti house, and room in it to lodge a friend,' and he invites Dormer to be his guest. The house was near the Place de l'Empereur, in 'La Rue des Varnsopele' (?). He asks Dormer to send 'two keces of Books:' indeed, literature was his most respectable consolation. Old Waters had died, and young Waters was requested to be careful of Charles's portrait by La Tour, of his 'marble bousto' by Lemoine, and of his 'silver sheald.' To Madame La Grandemain he writes in a peremptory style: 'Malgré toute votre repugnance je vous ordonne d'éxecuter avec toutes les precautions possibles ce dont je vous ai chargé.' What was this commission? It concerned 'la demoiselle.' 'You must overcome your repugnance, and tell a certain person [Goring] that I cannot see him, and that, if he wishes to be in my good graces, he must show you the best and most efficacious and rapid means of arriving at the end for which I sent him to you. I hope that this letter will not find you in Paris.'

I have little doubt that the 'repugnances' of 'Madame La Grandemain' were concerned with the bringing of Miss Walkinshaw to the Prince. The person who is in danger of losing the Prince's favour is clearly Goring, figuring under the name of 'Stouf,' and, at this moment, with 'Madame La Grandemain' in the country.

The facts about this Miss Walkinshaw, daughter of John Walkinshaw of Barowfield, have long been obscure. We can now offer her own account of her adventures, from the archives of the French Foreign Office. {137} In 1746 (according to a memoir presented to the French Court in 1774 by Miss Walkinshaw's daughter, Charlotte) the Prince first met Clementina Walkinshaw at the house of her uncle, Sir Hugh Paterson, near Bannockburn. The lady was then aged twenty: she was named after Charles's mother, and was a Catholic. The Prince conceived a passion for her, and obtained from her a promise to follow him 'wherever providence might lead him, if he failed in his attempt.' At a date not specified, her uncle, 'General Graeme,' obtained for her a nomination as *chanoinesse* in a *chapitre noble* of the Netherlands. But 'Prince Charles was then incognito in the Low Countries, and a person in his confidence [Sullivan, tradition says] warmly urged Miss Walkinshaw to go and join him, as she had promised, pointing out that in the dreadful state of his affairs, nothing could better soothe his regrets than the presence of the lady whom he most loved. Moved by her passion and her promise given to a hero admired by all Europe, Miss Walkinshaw betook herself to Douay. The Prince, at Ghent, heard news so interesting to his heart, and bade her go to Paris, where he presently joined her. They renewed their promises and returned to Ghent, where she took his name [Johnson], was treated and regarded as his wife, later travelled with him in Germany, and afterwards was domiciled with him at Liege, where she bore a daughter, Charlotte, baptized on October 29, 1753.' {138}

So runs the memoir presented to the French Court by the Prince's daughter, Charlotte, in 1774. Though no date is assigned, Miss Walkinshaw certainly joined Charles in the summer of 1752. 'Madame La Grandemain' and Goring were very properly indisposed to aid in bringing the lady to Charles. The Prince this replies to the remonstrances of Goring ('Stouf').

To M. Stouf.

'June 6, 1752.

'It is not surprising that I should not care to have one in my Family that pretends to give me Laws in everything I do, you know how you already threatened to quit me If I did not do your will and pleasure. What is passed I shall forget, provided you continue to do yr. Duty, so that there is nothing to be altered as to what was settled. Do not go to Lisle, but stay at Coutray for my farther orders. As to ye little man [an agent of Charles] he need never expect to see me unless he executes ye Orders I gave him. I send you 50 Louisdors so that you may give ye Frenchman what is necessary.

'The little man' is, probably, Beson, who was also recalcitrant. Goring replies in the following very interesting letter. He considered his errand unworthy of a man of honour.

From Stouf.

'I did not apprehend the money you sent by Dormer was for me, but thought, as you write in yours, to furnish the little man for the journey to Cambray, and that very reasonably, for with what he had of me he could not do it. On his refusing to go I sent it back. He says he has done what lays in his power, as Sullivan's letter testifies, that his desires to serve you were sincere, for which you abused him in a severe manner. Believe me, Sir, such commissions are for the worst of men, and such you will find enough for money, but they will likewise betray you for more. Virtue deserves reward and you treat it ill, I can only lament this unfortunate affair, which if possible to prevent, I would give my life with pleasure.

'You say nothing is to be altered in regard to the plan. Pray Sir reflect on Lady P. [Primrose] who will expect the little man. {139} He was introduced to her, and told her name. What frights will she and all friends be in, when they know you sent him away, for fear he should come over [to England] and betray them! I assure you all honest men will act as we have done, and should you propose to all who will enter into yr. service to do such work, they will rather lose their service than consent. Do you believe Sir that Lrd. Marischal, Mr. Campbell, G. Kelly, and others would consent to do it? Why should you think me less virtuous? My family is as ancient, my honour as entire. . . . I from my heart am sorry you do not taste these reasons, and must submit to my bad fortune . . for as to my going to Courtray nobody will know it, and if any accident should happen to you by the young lady's means [Miss Walkinshaw], I shall be detested and become the horrour of Mankind, but if you are determined to have her, let Mr. Sullivan bring her to you here, or any where himself. The little man will carry your letter to him, as he has done it already I suppose he wont refuse you.

'You sent a message for the pistols yourself, and as you had not given him the watch, he sent it, lest he should be accused of a design to keep it. We have no other Messages to send, since you have forbid us coming near you . . . for God's sake Sir let me have an audience of you; I can say more than I can write.'

Thus, from the beginning, Charles's friends foreboded danger in his *liaison*. Miss Walkinshaw had a sister, 'good Mrs. Catherine Walkinshaw, the Princess dowager's bed–chamber woman.' Lady Louisa Stuart knew her, and described to Scott 'the portly figure with her long lace ruffles, her gold snuff–box, and her double chin.' {141} The English Jacobites believed that Clementina was sent as a spy on Charles, communicating with her sister in London. In fact, Pickle was the spy, but Charles's refusal to desert his mistress broke up the party, and sealed his ruin. So much Goring had anticipated. The 'Lady P.' referred to as 'in a fright' is Lady Primrose. An English note of May 1752 represents 'Miss Fines' as about to go to France, where 'Lady P.' or 'Lady P. R.' actually arrived in June. The Prince answered Goring thus:

The Prince to Stouf in reply.

'I hereby order you to go to Lisle there to see a Certain person in case she has something new to say, and Let her know that Everything is to be as agreed on, except that, on reflection, I think it much better not to send ye French man over, for that will avoid any writing, and Macnamara can be sent, to whom one can say by word of mouth many things further. As I told you already nothing is to be chenged, on your Side, and you are to be anywhere in my Neiborod for to be ready when wanted. . . . Make many kinde Compliments from me to her and all her dear family.

'Burn this after reading.'

Charles also wrote to 'Lady P. R.' in a conciliatory manner. Goring met 'the Lady' at Lens: she was indignant at the dismissal of 'the little Frenchman,' merely because he was no Englishman. 'It would be unjust to refuse that name to one who had served you so faithfully.' Goring was still (June 18) 'at Madame La Grandemain's.' 'The Lady' in this correspondence may be Miss Walkinshaw or may be Lady Primrose, probably the latter. Indeed, it is by no means absolutely certain that the errand which Goring considered so dishonourable was connected with Miss Walkinshaw alone. The Elibank plot must have been maturing, though no light is thrown on it by the papers of the summer of 1752. Did Goring regard that plot as 'wicked,' or did he object to escorting Miss Walkinshaw?

There were clearly two difficulties. One concerned Miss Walkinshaw, the other, Lady Primrose. She, as a Jacobite conspirator, had been used to seeing 'the little man,' a Frenchman, whom Charles threatens to dismiss. If dismissed, he would be dangerous. Charles's hatred and distrust of the French now extended to 'the little man.' It is barely conceivable that Miss Walkinshaw had left England under Lady Primrose's escort, of course under the pretext of going to join her chapter of canonesses in the Low Countries. If she announced, when once in France, her desire to go to Charles as his mistress, Lady Primrose's position would be most painful, and Goring might well decline to convoy Miss Walkinshaw. But the political and the amatory plot are here inextricably entangled. As to the wickedness of the Elibank plot, if Goring hesitated over that, Forsyth, in his 'Letters from Italy,' tells a curious tale accepted by Lord Stanhope. Charles, on some occasion, went to England in disguise, and was introduced into a room full of conspirators. They proposed some such night attack on the palace as Murray's, but Charles declined to be concerned in it, unless the personal safety of George II. and his family was guaranteed. Charles certainly always did discountenance schemes of assassination; we shall see a later example. But, if Pickle does not lie, in a letter to be cited later, Lord Elibank, a most reputable man, saw no moral harm in his family plot. Was Goring more sensitive? All this must be left to the judgment of the reader.

In October 1752 a very sad event occurred. 'Madame La Grandemain' had to announce the death of her 'sister:' the Prince, in a note to a pseudonymous correspondent, expresses his concern for 'poor Mademoiselle Luci.' And so this girl, with her girlish mystery and romance, passes into the darkness from which she had scarcely emerged, carrying our regrets, for indeed she is the most sympathetic, of the women who, in these melancholy years, helped or hindered Prince Charles. 'As long as I have a Bit of Bred,' Charles writes to an unknown adherent, 'you know that I am always ready to shere it with a friend.' In this generous light we may fancy that Mademoiselle Luci regarded the homeless exile whom Goring was obliged to reprove in such uncourtly strains.

Madame La Grandemain, writing on November 5, 1752, expresses her inconsolable sorrow for her 'sister's' death, and says that she has made arrangements, as regards the Prince's affairs, in case of her own decease. The Prince, on *November* 10, 1752, sends his condolences, and this date is well worth remembering. For, according to Young Glengarry, in a letter to James cited later, November 10 was either the day appointed for the bursting of the Elibank plot, or was the day on which the date of the explosion was settled. As to that plot, the papers of Prince Charles contain no information. Documents so compromising, if they ever existed, have been destroyed. {144}

CHAPTER VII—YOUNG GLENGARRY

Pickle the spy—Not James Mohr Macgregor or Drummond—Pickle was the young chief of Glengarry—Proofs of this—His family history— His part in the Forty–five—Misfortunes of his family—In the Tower of London—Letters to James III.—No cheque!—Barren honours—In London in 1749—His poverty—Mrs. Murray of Broughton's watch— Steals from the Loch Arkaig hoard—Charges by him against Archy Cameron—Is accused of forgery—Cameron of Torcastle—Glengarry sees James III. in Rome—Was he sold to Cumberland?—Anonymous charges against Glengarry—A friend of Murray of Broughton—His spelling in evidence against him—Mrs. Cameron's accusation against Young Glengarry—Henry Pelham and Campbell of Lochnell—Pickle gives his real name and address—Note on Glengarry family—Highlanders among the Turks.

In November 1752, if not earlier, a new fountain of information becomes open to us, namely, the communications made by Pickle the spy to the English Government. His undated letters to his employers are not always easily attributed to a given month or year, but there can be mo mistake in assigning his first *dated* letter to November 2, 1752. {145}

The spy called Pickle was a descendant of Somerled and the Lords of the Isles. In her roll–call of the clans, Flora MacIvor summons the Macdonalds:

'O sprung from the kings who in Islay held state,
Proud chiefs of *Glengarry*, Clanranald, and Sleat,

Combine like three streams from one mountain of snow,
And resistless in union rush down on the foe!'

Pickle was the heir to the chieftainship of *Glengarry*; he was *Alastair Ruadh Macdonnell* (or Mackdonnell, as he often writes it), son of John Macdonnell, twelfth of Glengarry. Pickle himself, till his father's death in 1754, is always spoken of as 'Young Glengarry.' We shall trace the steps by which Young Glengarry, the high–born chief of the most important Catholic Jacobite clan, became *Pickle*, the treacherous correspondent of the English Government. On first reading his letters in the Additional MSS. of the British Museum, I conceived Pickle to be a traitorous servant in the household of some exiled Jacobite. I then found him asserting his rank as eldest son of the chief of a great clan; and I thought he must be personating his master, for I could not believe in such villainy as the treason of a Highland chief. Next, I met allusions to the death of his father, and the date (September 1, 1754) corresponded with that of the decease of Old Glengarry. Presently I observed the suspicions entertained about Young Glengarry, and the denunciation of him in 1754 by Mrs. Cameron, the widow of the last Jacobite martyr, Archibald Cameron. I also perceived that Pickle and Young Glengarry both invariably spell 'who' as 'how.' Next, in Pickle's last extant epistle to the English Government (1760), he directs his letters to be sent to 'Alexander Macdonnell, Glengarry, Fort William.' Finally, I compared Pickle's handwriting, where he gives the name 'Alexander Macdonnell,' with examples of Young Glengarry's signature in legal documents in the library of Edinburgh University. The writing, in my opinion, was the same in both sets of papers. Thus this hideous charge of treachery is not brought heedlessly against a gentleman of ancient, loyal, and honourable family. Young Glengarry died unarmed, at home, on December 23, 1761, leaving directions that his political papers should be burned, and the present representatives of a distinguished House are not the lineal descendants of a traitor.

The grandfather of Alastair Ruadh Macdonnell (*alias* Pickle, *alias* Roderick Random—he was fond of Dr. Smollett's new novels— *alias* Alexander Jeanson, that is, Alastair, son of Ian), was Alastair Dubh, Black Alister, 'who, with his ponderous two–handed sword, mowed down two men at every stroke' at Killiecrankie, and also fought at Shirramuir. At Killiecrankie he lost his brother, and his son Donald Gorm (Donald of the Blue Eyes), who is said to have slain eighteen of the enemy. At Shirramuir, when Clanranald fell, Glengarry tossed his bonnet in the air, crying in Gaelic,

'Revenge! Revenge! Revenge to–day, and mourning to–morrow.' He then led a charge, and drove the regular British troops in rout. He received a warrant of a peerage from the King over the water.

This hero seems a strange ancestor for a spy and a traitor, like Pickle. Yet we may trace an element of 'heredity.' About 1735 a member of the Balhaldie family, chief of Clan Alpin or Macgregor, wrote the Memoirs of the great Lochiel, published in 1842 for the Abbotsford Club. Balhaldie draws rather in Clarendon's manner a portrait of the Alastair Macdonnell of 1689 and of 1715. Among other things he writes:

'Most of his actions might well admitt of a double construction, and what he appeared generally to be was seldome what he really was. . . . Though he was ingaged in every attempt that was made for the Restoration of King James and his family, yet he managed matters so that he lossed nothing in the event. . . . The concerts and ingagements he entered into with his neighbours . . . he observed only in so far as suited with his own particular interest, but still he had the address to make them bear the blame, while he carried the profits and honour. To conclude, he was brave, loyal, and wonderfully sagacious and long–sighted; and was possessed of a great many shineing qualities, blended with a few vices, which, like patches on a beautifull face, seemed to give the greater *éclat* to his character.'

Pickle, it will be discovered, inherited the ancestral 'vices.' 'What he appeared generally to be was seldome what he really was.' His portrait, {149a} in Highland dress, displays a handsome, fair, athletic young chief, with a haughty expression. Behind him stands a dark, dubious–looking retainer, like an evil genius.

Alastair Dubh Macdonnell died in 1724, and was succeeded by his son John, twelfth of Glengarry. This John had, by two wives, four sons, of whom the eldest, Alastair Ruadh, was Pickle. Alastair held a captain's commission in the Scots brigade in the French service. In March 1744, he and the Earl Marischal were at Gravelines, meaning to sail with the futile French expedition from Dunkirk. In June 1745, Glengarry went to France with a letter from the Scotch Jacobites, bidding Charles *not* to come without adequate French support. Old Glengarry, in January 1745, had 'disponed' his lands to Alastair his son, for weighty reasons to him known. {149b} Such deeds were common in the Highlands, especially before a rising.

From this point the movements of Young Glengarry become rather difficult to trace. If we could believe the information received from Rob Roy's son, James Mohr Macgregor, by Craigie, the Lord Advocate, Young Glengarry came over to Scotland in *La Doutelle*, when Charles landed in Moidart in July 1745. {150a} This was not true. Old Glengarry, with Lord George Murray, waited on Cope at Crieff in August, when Cope marched north. Cope writes, 'I saw Glengarry the father at Crieff with the Duke of Athol; 'tis said that none of his followers are yet out, tho' there is some doubt of his youngest son; the eldest, as Glengarry told me, is in France.' {150b} On September 14, Forbes of Culloden congratulated Old Glengarry on his return home, and regretted that so many of his clan were out under Lochgarry, a kinsman. {150c} Old Glengarry had written to Forbes 'lamenting the folly of his friends.' He, like Lovat, was really 'sitting on the fence.' His clan was out; his second son Æneas led it at Falkirk. Alastair was in France. At the close of 1745, Alastair, conveying a detachment of the Royal Scots, in French service, and a piquet of the Irish brigade to Scotland, was captured on the seas and imprisoned in the Tower of London. {150d} In January 1746 we find him writing from the Tower to Waters, the banker in Paris, asking for money. Almost at this very time Young Glengarry's younger brother, Æneas, who led the clan, was accidentally shot in the streets of Falkirk by a Macdonald of Clanranald's regiment. The poor Macdonald was executed, and the Glengarry leader, by Charles's desire, was buried in the grave of Wallace's companion, Sir John the Graeme, as the only worthy resting–place. Many Macdonalds deserted. {151a}

After Culloden (April 1746), an extraordinary event took place in the Glengarry family. Colonel Warren, who, in October 1746, carried off Charles safely to France, arrested, in Scotland, Macdonell of Barrisdale, on charges of treason to King James. {151b} Barrisdale had been taken by the English, but was almost instantly released after Culloden. One charge against him, on the Jacobite side, was that he had made several gentlemen of Glengarry's clan believe that their chief meant to deliver them up to the English. Thereon 'information was laid' (by the gentlemen?) against Old Glengarry. Old Glengarry's letters in favour of the Prince were discovered; he was seized, and was only released from Edinburgh Castle in October 1749.

Here then, in 1746, were Old Glengarry in prison, Young Glengarry in the Tower, and Lucas lying in the grave of Sir John the Graeme. Though only nineteen, Æneas was married, and left issue. The family was now in desperate straits, and already a *sough* of treason to the cause was abroad. Young Glengarry says that he lay in the Tower for twenty–two months; he was released in July 1747. The Rev. James Leslie, writing to defend himself against a charge of treachery (Paris, May 27, 1752), quotes a letter, undated, from Glengarry. 'One needs not be a wizard to see that mentioning you was only a feint, and the whole was aimed at me.' {152a} If this, like Leslie's letter, was written in 1752, Glengarry was then not unsuspected. We shall now see how he turned his coat.

On January 22, 1748, he writes to James from Paris, protesting loyalty. But 'since I arrived here, after my tedious confinement in the Tower in London, I have not mett with any suitable encouragement.' Glengarry, even as Pickle, constantly complains that his services are not recognised. Both sides were ungrateful! In the list of gratuities to the Scotch from France, *Glengarry l'Ainé* gets 1,800 livres; Young Glengarry is not mentioned. {152b} From Amiens, September 20, 1748, Young Glengarry again wrote to James. He means 'to wait any opportunity of going safely to Britain' on his private affairs. These journeys were usually notified by the exiles; their mutual suspicions had to be guarded against. In December, Young Glengarry hoped to succeed to the Colonelcy in the Scoto–French regiment of Albany, vacated by the death of the Gentle Lochiel. Archibald Cameron had also applied for it, as *locum tenens* of his nephew, Lochiel's son, a boy of sixteen. James replied, through Edgar, that he was unable to interfere and assist Glengarry, as he had recommended young Lochiel. What follows explains, perhaps, the circumstance that changed Young Glengarry into Pickle.

'His Majesty is sorry to find you so low in your circumstances, and reduced to such straits at present as you mention, and he is the more sorry that his own situation, as to money matters, never being so bad as it now is, he is not in a condition to relieve you, as he would incline. But His Majesty being at the same time desirous to do what depends on him for your satisfaction, he, upon your request, sends you here enclosed a duplicate of your grandfather's warrant to be a Peer. You will see that it is signed by H. M. and I can assure you it is an exact duplicate copie out of the book of entrys of such like papers.' {153a}

It is easy to conceive the feelings and to imagine the florid eloquence of Young Glengarry, when he expected a cheque and got a duplicate copy of a warrant (though he had asked for it) to be a Peer— over the water! As he was not without a sense of humour, the absurdity of the Stuart cause must now have become vividly present to his fancy. He must starve or 'conform,' that is, take tests and swallow oaths. But it was not necessary that he should sell himself. Many loyal gentlemen were in his position of poverty, but perhaps only James Mohr Macgregor and Samuel Cameron vended themselves as Glengarry presently did.

Glengarry loitered in Paris. On June 9, 1749, he wrote to the Cardinal Duke of York. He explained that, while he was in the Tower, the Court of France had sent him 'unlimited credit' as a Highland chief. He understood that he was intended to supply the wants of the poor prisoners, 'Several of whom, had it not been our timely assistance [Sir Hector Maclean was with him] had starved.' Sir Hector tells the same tale. From Sir James Graeme, Glengarry learned that the Duke of York had procured for him this assistance. But now the French War Office demanded repayment of the advance, and detained four years of his pay in the French service. He 'can't receive his ordinary supply from home, his father being in prison, and his lands entirely destroyed.' To James's agent, Lismore, he tells the same story, and adds, 'I shall be obliged to leave this country, if not relieved.' {154} Later, in 1749, we learn from Leslie that he accompanied Glengarry to London, where Glengarry 'did not intend to appear publicly,' but 'to have the advice of some counsellors about an act of the Privy Council against his returning to Great Britain.' At this time Leslie pledged a gold repeater, the property of Mrs. Murray, wife of that other traitor, Murray of Broughton. 'Glengarry, after selling his sword and shoe–buckles to my certain knowledge was reduced to such straits, that I pledged the repeater for a small sum to relieve him, and wrote to Mr. Murray that I had done so.' He pledged it to Clanranald. Mrs. Murray was angry, for (contrary to the usual story that she fled after the Prince to France) she was living with her husband at this time. {155a}

Here then, in July or August 1749, is Young Glengarry in extreme distress at London. But Æneas Macdonald, writing to Edgar from Boulogne on October 12, 1751, says, 'I lent Young Glengarry 50*l.* when he was home in 1744, and I saw him in London just at the time I got out of gaol in 1749, and though in all appearance *he had plenty of cash*, yet' he never dreamed of paying Æneas his 50*l*! 'Nothing could have lost him but falling too soon into the hands of bad counsellors.'

I regret to say that the pious Æneas Macdonald was nearly as bad a traitor as any of these few evil Highland gentlemen. His examination in London was held on September 16, 1746. {155b} Herein he regaled his examiners with anecdotes of a tavern keeper at Gravelines 'who threatened to beat the Pretender's son'; and of how he himself made Lord Sempil drunk, to worm his schemes out of him. It is only fair to add that, beyond tattle of this kind, next to nothing was got out of Æneas, who, in 1751, demands a Jacobite peerage for his family, that of Kinloch Moidart.

So much, at present, for Æneas. If we listen to Leslie, Young Glengarry was starving in July or August 1749; if we believe Æneas, he had 'plenty of cash' in December of the same year. Whence came this change from poverty to affluence? We need not assume it to be certain that Glengarry's gold came out of English secret service money. His father had been released from prison in October 1749, and may have had resources. We have already seen, too, that Young Glengarry was accused of getting, in the winter of 1749, his share of the buried hoard of Loch Arkaig. Lord Elcho, in Paris, puts the money taken by Young Glengarry and Lochgarry (an honest man) at 1,200 louis d'or. We have heard the laments of 'Thomas Newton' (Kennedy), who himself is accused of peculation by Æneas Macdonald, and of losing 800*l*. of the Prince's money at Newmarket. {156} We do not know for certain, then, that Young Glengarry vended his honour when in London in autumn 1749. That he made overtures to England, whether they were accepted or not, will soon be made to seem highly probable. We return to his own letters. In June 1749 he had written, as we saw, from Paris, also to Lismore, and to the Cardinal Duke of York. On September 23, 1749, he again wrote to Lismore from Boulogne. He says he has been in London (as we know from Leslie), where his friends wished him to 'conform' to the Hanoverian interest. This he disdains. He has sent a vassal to the North, and finds that the clans are ready to rise. If not relieved from his debt to the French War Office he must return to England.

He did return in the winter of 1749, and he accompanied his cousin, Lochgarry (a truly loyal man), to Scotland, where he helped himself to some of the hoard of gold. On January 16, 1750, he writes to Edgar from Boulogne, reports his Scotch journey, and adds that he is now sent by the clans to lay their sentiments before James, in Rome. He then declares that Archibald Cameron has been damping all hearts in the Highlands. 'I have prevented the bad consequences that might ensue from such notions; but one thing I could not prevent was his taking 6,000 louis d'ors of the money left in the country by his Royal Highness, which he did without any opposition, as he was privy to where the money was laid, only Cluny Macpherson obliged him to give a receipt for it. . . . I am credibly informed he designs to lay this money in the hands of a merchant in Dunkirk, and enter partners with him. . . .' He hopes that James will detain Archibald Cameron in Rome, till his own arrival. He protests that it is 'very disagreeable to him' to give this information. {157}

As we have already seen, 'Newton,' since 1748, had been in England, trying to procure the money from Cluny: we have seen that Archibald Cameron, Young Glengarry, and others, had obtained a large share of the gold in the winter of 1749. Charges of dishonesty were made on all sides, and we have already narrated how Archibald Cameron, Sir Hector Maclean, Lochgarry, and Young Glengarry carried themselves and their disputes to Rome (in the spring of 1750), and how James declined to interfere. The matter, he said, was personal to the Prince. But the following letter of James to Charles deserves attention.

The King to the Prince.

'March 17, 1750.

'You will remark that at the end of Archy's paper, it is mentioned as if a certain person should have made use of my name in S—-d, *and have even produced a letter supposed to be mine* to prove that he was acting by commission from me: what there may be in the bottom of all this I know not, but I think it necessary you should know that since your return from S—-d I never either employed or authorized the person, or anybody else, to carry any commissions on politick affairs to any of the three kingdoms.'

Now this certain person, accused by 'Archy' (Archibald Cameron) of forging a letter from James, with a commission to take part of the hidden hoard, is Young Glengarry. In his letter of October 12, 1751, Æneas Macdonald mentions a report 'too audacious to be believed; that Glengarry had counterfeited his Majesty's signature to gett the money that he gott in Scotland.' Glengarry 'was very capable of having it happen to him,' but *he* accused Archibald Cameron, and the charge still clings to his name. Even now Cameron is not wholly cleared. On November 21, 1753, his uncle, Ludovic Cameron of Torcastle, wrote to the Prince from Paris:

'My nephew, Dr. Cameron, had the misfortune to take away a round sum of your highness's money, and I was told lately that it was thought I should have shared with him in that base and mean undertaking. I declare, on my honour and conscience, that I knew nothing of the taking of the money, until he told it himself in Rome, where I happened to be at the time, and that I never touched one farthing of it, or ever will.' {159}

Cluny, as well as Cameron, was this gentleman's nephew. The character of Archibald Cameron is so deservedly high, the praises given to him by Horace Walpole are so disinterested, that any imputation on him lacks credibility. One is inclined to believe that there is a misunderstanding, and that what money Cameron took was for the Prince's service. Yet we find no proof of this, and Torcastle's letter is difficult to explain on the hypothesis of Cameron's innocence. Glengarry tried to secure himself by a mysterious interview with the King. On May 23, at Rome, he wrote to Edgar. 'As His Majesty comes into town next week, and that I can't, in your absence, have an audience with such safety, not choising to confide myself on that particular to any but you; I beg you'l be so good as contrive, if His Majesty judges it proper, that I have the honour of meeting him, in the duskish, for a few moments.'

No doubt Glengarry was brought to the secret cellar, whence a dark stair led to James's furtive audience chamber.

We must repeat the question, Was Young Glengarry, while with James in Rome, actually sold to the English Government at this time? We have seen that he was in London in the summer of 1749. On August 2 of that year, the Duke of Cumberland wrote to the Duke of Bedford, who, of all men in England, is said by Jacobite tradition to have most frequently climbed James's cellar stair! Cumberland speaks of 'the goodness of the intelligence' now offered to the Government. 'On my part, I bear it witness, for I never knew it fail me in the least trifle, and have had very material and early notices from it. How far the price may agree with our present saving schemes I don't know, but good intelligence ought not to be lightly thrown away.' {160}

Was Glengarry (starving in August 1749) the source of the intelligence which, in that month, Cumberland had already found useful? The first breath of suspicion against Glengarry, not as a forger or thief (these minor charges were in the air), but as a traitor, is met in an anonymous letter forwarded by John Holker to young Waters. {161} A copy had also been sent to Edgar at Rome. Already, on November 30, 1751, some one, sealing with a stag's head gorged, and a stag under a tree in the shield, had written to Waters, denouncing Glengarry's suspected friend, Leslie the priest, as 'to my private knowledge an arrant rogue.' Leslie has been in London, and is now off to Lorraine. 'He is going to discover if he can have any news of the Prince in a country which, it is strongly suspected, His Royal Highness has crossed or bordered on more than once.' In the later anonymous letter we are told of 'a regular correspondence between John Murray [of Broughton, the traitor] and Samuel Cameron'—a spy of whom we shall hear again. 'What surprises people still more is that Mr. Macdonald of Glengarrie, who says that he is charged with the affaires of his Majesty, is known to be in great intimacy with Murray, and to put Confidence in one Leslie, a priest, well known for a very infamous character, and who, I'm authorised to say, imposed upon one of the first personages in England by forging the Prince's name.'

The anonymous accusers were Blair and Holker, men known to Edgar and Waters, but not listened to by Charles. Glengarry, according to his anonymous accuser of February 1752, was in London nominally 'on the King's affaires.' On July (or, as he spells it, 'Jully') 15, 1751, Young Glengarry wrote from London to James and to Edgar. He says, to James, that the English want a Restoration, but have 'lost all martial spirit.' To Edgar he gave warning that, if measures were not promptly taken, the Loch Arkaig hoard would be embezzled to the last six–pence. 'I must drop the politicall,' he says; he will no longer negotiate for James, but 'my sword will be always drawn amongst the first.'

The letter to James is printed by Browne; {162a} that to Edgar is not printed. And now appears the value of original documents. In the manuscript Glengarry spells 'who' as 'how': in the printed version the spelling is tacitly corrected. Now Pickle, writing to his English employers, always spells 'who as 'how,' an eccentricity not marked by me in any other writer of the period. This is a valuable trifle of evidence, connecting Pickle with Young Glengarry. In an undated letter to Charles, certainly of 1751, Glengarry announces his approaching marriage with a lady of 'a very Honourable and loyall familie in England,' after which he will pay his share of the Loch Arkaig gold. He ends with pious expressions. When at Rome he had been 'an ardent suitor' to the Cardinal Duke 'for a relick of the precious wood of the Holy Cross, in obtaining which I shall think myself most happy.' {162b}

In 1754, two years after the anonymous denunciation, we find a repetition of the charge of treachery against Glengarry. On January 25, 1754, Mrs. Cameron, by that time widow of Archibald, sends to Edgar, in Rome, what she has just told Balhaldie about Young Glengarry. Her letter is most amazing. 'I was telling him [Balhaldie] what character I heard of Young Glengarry in England,' where she had vainly thrown herself at the feet of

George II., praying for her husband's life. 'Particularly Sir Duncan Campbell of Lochnell [Mrs. Cameron was a Campbell] told me, and others whom he could trust, that in the year 1748, or 1749, I don't remember which, as he, Sir Duncan, was going out of the House of Commons, Mr. Henry Pelham, brother to the Duke of Newcastle, and Secretary of State, called on him, and asked if he knew Glengarry? Sir Duncan answered he knew the old man, but not the young. Pelham replied, it was Young Glengarry he spoke of; for that he came to him offering his most faithful and loyal services to the Government in any shape they thought proper, as he came from feeling the folly of any further concern with the ungrateful family of Stuart, to whom he and his family had been too long attached, to the absolute ruin of themselves and country.'

It is difficult to marvel enough at the folly of Pelham in thus giving away a secret of the most mortal moment. Mrs. Cameron did not hear Lochnell's report till after the mischief was wrought, the great scheme baffled, and her husband traduced, betrayed, and executed. By January 1754, Pickle had done the most of his business, as will appear when we come to study his letters. In these Henry Pelham is always 'my great friend,' with him Pickle communicates till Pelham's death (March 1754), and his letters are marked by the Duke of Newcastle, 'My Brother's Papers.'

All this may be called mere circumstantial evidence. The anonymous denouncer may have been prejudiced. Mrs. Cameron's evidence is not at firsthand. Perhaps other Highland gentlemen spelled 'who' as 'how.' Leslie was not condemned by his ecclesiastical superiors, but sent back to his mission in Scotland. {164} But Pickle, writing as Pickle, describes himself, we shall see, in terms which apply to Young Glengarry, and to Young Glengarry alone. And, in his last letter (1760), Pickle begs that his letters may be addressed 'To Alexander Macdonnell of Glengarry by Fort Augustus.' It has been absurdly alleged that Pickle was James Mohr Macgregor. In 1760, James Mohr had long been dead, and at no time was he addressed as Alexander Macdonnell of Glengarry. Additional evidence of Pickle's identity will occur in his communications with his English employers. He was not likely to adopt the name of Pickle before the publication of Smollett's 'Peregrine Pickle' in 1751, though he may have earlier played his infamous part as spy, traitor, and informer.

* * * * *

NOTE.

The Family of Glengarry.

ALASTAIR RUADH MACDONELL, *alias* Pickle, Jeanson, Roderick Random, and so forth, died, as we saw, in 1761. He was succeeded by his nephew Duncan, son of Æneas, accidentally shot. at Falkirk in 1746. Duncan was followed by Alastair, Scott's friend; it was he who gave Maida to Sir Walter. Alastair, the last Glengarry who held the lands of the House, died in January 1828. Scott devotes a few lines of his journal to the chief (January 21, 1828), who shot a grandson of Flora Macdonald in a duel, and disputed with Clanranald the supremacy of the Macdonalds. Scott says 'he seems to have lived a century too late, and to exist, in a state of complete law and order, like a Glengarry of old, whose will was law to his Sept. Warm–hearted, generous, friendly, he is beloved by those who knew him . . . To me he is a treasure . . . ' {165} He married a daughter of Sir William Forbes, a strong claim on Scott's affection. He left sons who died without offspring; his daughter Helen married Cunninghame of Balgownie, and is represented by her son, J. Alastair Erskine–Cunninghame, Esq., of Balgownie. If Charles, half brother of Alastair Ruadh (Pickle), who died in America, left no offspring, the House of Glengarry is represented by Æneas Ranald Westrop Macdonnell, Esq., of the Scotus branch of Glengarry. According to a letter written to the Old Chevalier in 1751, by Will Henderson in Moidart, young Scotus had extraordinary adventures after Culloden. The letter follows. I published it first in the *Illustrated London News.*

To the King. From W. Henderson in Moydart.

'October 5, 1750.

'Sir,—After making offer to you of my kind compliments, I thought it my indispensable duty to inform you that one Governor Stewart of the Isle of Lemnos on the coast of Ethiopia in ye year 1748 wrot to Scotland a letter for Stewart of Glenbucky concerning

Donald McDonell of Scothouse younger, and John Stewart with 20 other prisoners of our countrymen there, to see, if by moyen of ransome they could be relieved. The substance of the Letter, as it came with an Irish Ship this year to Clyde, is as follows:

'That Donald McDonell of Scothouse, younger, and first cousin german to John McDonell of Glengarry, and with John Stewart of Acharn and other 20 persons mortally wounded in the Battle of Culloden, were by providence preserved, altho without mercy cast aboard of a ship in Cromarty Bay the very night of the Battle, and sailed next morning for Portsmouth, where they were cast again aboard of an Indiaman to be carried, or transported without doom or law to some of the british plantations, but they had the fate to be taken prisoners by a Salle Rover or a Turkish Privatir or Pirat, who, after strangling the captain and crew, keeped the 22 highlanders in their native garb to be admired by the Turks, since they never seed their habit, nor heard their languadgue befor, and as providence would have it, the Turks and Governor Stewart came to see the Rarysho, and being a South country hiland man, that went over on the Darien expedition, and yet extant, being but a very young boy when he went off, seeing his countrymen, spok to them with surprize in their native tong or language, and by comoning but a short time in galick, found in whose's army they served, and how they suffered by the fate of war and disaster, after which he ordered them ashoar, and mitigated their confinement as far as lay'd in his power, but on them landing, by the Turks' gelosie [jealousy?] they were deprived of all writting instroments, for fear they sho'd give their friends information of the place they were in, and so it would probably happen them during life: if John Stewart of Acharn had not got his remot cousin Governor Stewart to writt a letter and inclosed one from himself giving particular information of Scothouse, wishing and begging all frinds concerned to procure written orders from the King of France to his Ambassador at Constantinopol for to make all intercession for the relesement of the forsaid Two Gentlemen and other 20 British christians in the King His Majesty's Name, or to recommend their condition to his holyness to see if by ransome they might be relived. And they'll always be gratefull to their Deliverurs, to this pious end. I make chuse of you to inform your Master, who's the capablest person under God to do for them, which will with other infinit titles endear you to your fast friends in Scotland, and especially to your Will Henderson, who lives there 13 years past among the MacDonalds of Clanranald, so I hope you'll make use of what I have wrot, to the end I intend, and God will give the due reward . . . I remain, etc.'

In fact, the younger Scotus was not taken prisoner at Culloden, but remained in the Highlands, and is mentioned by Murray of Broughton, in his account of his expenditure, and of the Loch Arkaig treasure, published by Robert Chambers as an Appendix to his 'History of the Rising of 1745.'

CHAPTER VIII—PICKLE AND THE ELIBANK PLOT

The Elibank plot—George II. to be kidnapped—Murray and Young Glengarry—As Pickle, Glengarry betrays the plot—His revelations— Pickle and Lord Elibank—Pickle meets Charles—Charles has been in Berlin—Glengarry writes to James's secretary—Regrets failure of plot—Speaks of his illness—Laments for Archy Cameron—Hanbury Williams seeks Charles in Silesia—Pickle's 'fit of sickness'—His dealings with the Earl Marischal—Meets the Prince at the masked ball —'A little piqued'—Marischal criticises the plot to kidnap George II.—'A night attack'—Other schemes—Charles's poverty—'The prophet's clothes'—Mr. Carlyle on Frederick the Great—Alleges his innocence of Jacobite intrigues—Contradicts statesmen—Mr. Carlyle in error—Correspondence of Frederick with Earl Marischal—The Earl's account of English plotters—Frederick's advice—Encouragement underhand—Arrest of Archy Cameron—His early history—Plea for clemency—Cameron is hanged—His testimony to Charles's virtues—His forgiveness of his enemies—Samuel Cameron the spy—His fate—Young Edgar on the hidden treasure—The last of the treasure—A *salmo ferox.*

The Stuart Papers, we have said, contain no hints as to the Elibank plot of November 1752, unless Goring's scruples were aroused by it. It was suggested and arranged by Alexander Murray, younger brother of Lord Elibank, whom young Edgar describes as 'having a very light head; he has drunk deep of the Garron' (Garonne?). {169} With a set of officers in the French service, aided by Young Glengarry (who had betrayed the scheme) and 400 Highlanders, Murray was to attack St. James's Palace, and seize the

King. If we may believe Young Glengarry (writing to Edgar in Rome), Charles was 'on the coast,' but *not* in London. Pickle's letters to his English employers show that the design was abandoned, much to his chagrin. As Glengarry, he expresses the same regret in a letter to Edgar. We now offer Pickle's letters. He is at Boulogne, November 2, 1752.

Add. B.M. MSS. 32,730.

'Boulogne: November 2, 1752.

My dear Sir,—My friends will be most certainly greatly surprised at my silence, but I have such reasons that I can clear all at meeting. I have been so hurried, what with posting, what with Drinking, and other matters of greater weight than they dream of, that I have not had a moment, as the french says, *Sans temoigne*, till now; thus rendered my writing impracticable. Next Post brings a letter to my friend, and I hope he will not grudge to send Credit to this place, for I am to take a trip for ten days, the Jurny is of importance, it's likewise very expencive, and I must give mony. After this trip, my stay here will be short, for I dare not be explicite on a certain point. I can answer for myself—but how soon my letter is received, I beg remittance. You'll think all this very strange, and confus'd, but I assure you, *there you'l soon hear of a hurly Burly*; but I will see my friend or that can happen. I wish I had the Highland pistoles. If Donald wants mony, pray give him. He is to come with a Shoot of Close to me, when I receive Credit. *I will run at least tow Hundred leagues post.* You'l hear from me when I write to my friend. Aquent them of what I write, and ever believe me

'Yours unalterable
'JEANSON. {171}

'Don't proceed in your jurney, till you have further advice—Direct for me as Johnny directs you.

To the Provost.

Add. 32,730.

'Boulogne: November 4, 1752.

'Dear Sir—By this post I write to my great friend [Henry Pelham], I hope what I say will prove agreeable, and as I am sure what I write will be communicated to Grand Papa [Gwynne Vaughan] I beg he excuses my not writing. Besides it would be both dangerous and precarious, as I have not a moment to write but after 12 at night, being hurried at all other hours with company. If the credit I demand be sent, I will immediately proceed to Paris—If not, I will return directly. Without a trip to Paris, I can't come at the bottom of matters. I wish I had the Pistoles. I beg you'l give my servt. any little thing he wants, and let him come off by the first ship without faile. Let me hear from you upon recet, and derect for me simply to this place in french or English. I have told friends here that I expect a considerable remittance from Baron Kenady [Newcastle], and that how soon I receve it, I go for a trip to Paris. This admits of no delay. My kind respects to Grand papa and allways believe me, Dr. Sir,

'Your sincere and affte. friend

'ALEXR. JEANSON.

'To Mr. William Blair, at Mr. Brodie's in Lille Street, Near Leister fields—London.

(marked) 'PICKLE.' {172}

The following letter of November 4 is apparently to Henry Pelham. If Charles was in Berlin, as Pickle says here, about August 1752, the Stuart Papers throw no light on the matter. What we know of Frederick's intrigues with the Jacobites will find its place in the record of the following year, 1753. Pickle here confesses that his knowledge of future intrigues is derived from Frederick's ambassador at Versailles, the Earl Marischal.

The letter to Pelham follows:

'Bologne: November 4, 1752.

'Sir—Tho' I delayd till now aquenting you of my arrival this side of the watter, yet I hope you will not attribute my silence either to neglect or forgetfulness of my friends. I mostly pass my time in company of my old aquentences how [who] have each in theire turn entertaind me handsomely. I am now returning the compliment.

'Notwithstanding my endeavours, I have lost sight of 6 [Goring]—I took a trip in hopes to meet him, at which time I had a long chatt with 69 [Sir James Harrington], how [who] is in top spirits, and assures me that very soon a scene will be opend that will astonish most of Envoys. Whatever may be in this, I can for certain assure you, that 51 [King of Prussia] will countenance it, for three months ago 80 [Pretender's Son] was well received there. He has left that part, for he was within these twenty days not the distance of thirty leagues from this town. This depend upon, and was you to credit all he says, it would be justly termd what the french term *Merveille*; whatever is in it they keep all very hush from 8 [Pretender] tho I have some reason to believe that 72 [Sir John Graeme] was dispatched to him leatly, for he disappear'd from Paris four days ago. Whatever tune they intend to play of this, Battery 66 [Scotland] is not desir'd to mouve, untill his neibour [London] pulls off the mask. If 01—2d [French Ministry] countenances 80 [Pretender's Son], its thro the influence of 51 [King of Prussia]. I have some reason to believe they dow, for 80 [Pretender's Son] is accompanied by one of that faction. I suspect its 59 [Count Maillebois] but I cant be positive untill I go to Paris, which I think a most necessary chant [jaunt] in this juncture, for if 2 [Lord Marshall] has no finger in the piy, I lost my host of all. When I am a few days at Paris, I take a trip sixty leagues farther South to meet 71 [Sir J. Graemne or Sir James Harrington] and some other friends, when I will be able to judge of matters by my reception from them and 01–2d [French Ministry], {174} and if the last are concerned I must beg leave not to write upon these topicks, for no precaution can prevent a discovery in this country; should this be the case, and that anything particular cast up, I will make the quickest dispatch to lay before you *in person* all I can learn of these affairs—I only wait here for your orders, and be assur'd whatever they be they will be obeyd with pleasure. I have not had time to write to my worthy old friend [Gwynne Vaughan], so I beg you'l aquent him that the place he visits ought [to] be looked after with a watchful eye—I doubt not but D. B. [Bruce, an English official] has inform'd you of his receving a few lines from me by last post, in which I aquented him that I was necessitated to thro a way some mony, and be at a very considerable expence. I dow not pretend to make a particular demand yet I assure you

200*l.* St. is necessary, and I intirely reffer to yourself to diminish or augment, only I beg you be convinced that no selfish interesting view occasions my making this demand, but only that I would be vext want of cash would disapoint either of us in our expectations, since I dow assure you that I dont look upon anything I tuch upon such journeys as solid, for it does not long stick in my pockets. I will drop this point, being fully perswaded if my correspondence proves anything amusing, such Bagatelle will not be grudged, but if I go forward, I beg credit be sent me either upon this place or Paris, any mony I receve passes for being remitted by the order of Baron Kenady {175} [Newcastle]. All this is fully submitted to your better judgement, only I beg you'l be fully perswaded how much I have the honour to remain, Sir,

'Your most obedient and most humble Servt.,

'ALEXR. JEANSON.

P.S. Lord Strathallan left this a few days ago, to meet Lord George [Murray] some says at the Hague, others at his house near Claves (?).

'(PICKLE.)'

The following undated 'Information' appears to have been written by Pickle on his return from France, early in December. It is amazing to find that, if we can believe a spy, Lord Elibank himself was in the plot. The scene between the political economist and the swaggering Celt, when Pickle probably blustered about the weakness of deferring the attack which he had already betrayed, may be imagined.

Information.

'December 1752.

'The Young Pretender about the latter end of September [1752] sent Mr. Murray [of Elibank] for Lochgary and Doctor *Archabald Cameron.* They meet him at Menin. He informed them that he hoped he had brought matters to such a bearing, particularly at the King of Prussia's Court, whom he expected in a short time to have a strong alliance with—that he did not desire the Highlanders to rise in Arms untill General Keith was landed in the North of Scotland with some Swedish troops. He likewise assur'd them that some of the greatest weight in England, tho' formerly great opposers to his family, were engaged in this attempt, and that he expected to meet with very little opposition. In consequence of this he gave Lochgary, Doctor Cameron, Blairfety, Robertson of Wood Streat, Skalleter, mony; and sent them to Scotland, so as to meet several highland gentlemen at the Crief Market for Black Cattel. Cameron Cassifairn and Glenevegh were those how [who] were to carry on the Correspondence twixt the Southern Jakobits and Clunie Mackpherson. Lochgary was after the general meeting at Menin with the Young Pretender, for two nights at *Gent* in Flanders. I was at Boulogne when Sir James Harrinton gave me directions to go to Gent, but to my great surprize as I lighted of horseback at Furnes was tipt upon the shoulder by one Morison [Charles's valet] how [who] desir'd me to stop for a little at the Inn. I was not long there when the Young Pretender enter'd my room. The discourse chiefly turn'd upon the Scheme in England, when he repeated the same assurances as to Lochgary, but in stronger terms, and with the adition that the Swedes were to embark at Gattenburgh [Göthenburg], and that Mr. Murray was sent with commissions for me, and full instructions how I was to act in Scotland. The Young Chevalier was so positive of his schemes succeeding, that he told me he expected to be in London very soon himself, and that he was determin'd to give the present Government no quiet until he succeeded or dyed in the attempt. I came over here [to England] by his express orders; I waited of Lord Elibank who, after the strong assurances of the Young Pretender, surprised me to the greatest degree, by telling me that all was put off for some time, and that his Brother [Murray] had repassd the seas in order to aquent the Young Pretender of it, and from him he was to go streight for Paris to Lord Marishal. Its not above nine days since I left the Young Pretender at Furnes. When he was at Menin a French gentleman attended him. Goren [Goring] has been within these two months twice in England, and Mr. Murray three times since he first went over. Its not above five days since Mr. Murray left London. Probably the landing for England was to be from France, as there is 12,000 troops in Flanders more than the ordinary compliment. This the Comon French takes notice off. But I can say nothing of this with certainty. The Young Chevalier has more than once seen the King of Prussia, but none other of his Court, that I ever could learn, but General Keith.

'Sir John Douglas, Mr. Charteris, {178} and Heparn of Keith, are in the secret. The Young Chevalier has been in close correspondence with England for a year and a halph past. Mr. Carte the Historian has carried frequent messages. They *never commit anything to writing*. Elderman Hethcot is a principall Manager. The very words the Young Pretender told me was that all this schemne was laid and transacted by Whiggers, that no Roman Catholick was concerned, and oblidged me to give my word and honour that I would write nothing concerning him or his plan to Rome. After what I said last night this is all that occurs to me for the present. I will lose no time in my transactions, and I will take care they will allways be conforme to your directions, and as I have throwen myself entirely upon you, I am determined to run all hazards upon this occasion, which I hope will entittle me to your favour and his Majestys protection. Dec. 1752.'

Pickle, of course, broke his 'word and honour' about not writing to Rome. In April 1753, to anticipate a little, he indited the following epistle to Edgar. He can have had no motive, except that of alarming James by the knowledge that his son had been on the eve of a secret and perilous enterprise, in which he was still engaged. Glengarry here confirms the evidence against himself by allusions to his dangerous illness in the spring of 1753. To this he often refers when he corresponds, as Pickle, with his English employers.

MackDonell to Edgar.

'Arras: April 5, 1753.

'Sir, I frequently Intended since my coming to this Country to renew our former corespondence. But as I had nothing to say worth your notice, that I could with prudence comitt to writing, I choise rather to be silent than to trouble you with my Letters: yet I cant perswad myself to leave this Country without returning you many thanks for your former friendship and good offices, and at same time assuring you of the great Value and Estime I allways had, and still have for you.

'I would gladly comunicate to his Majesty the leate Schemes, and those still persuid, upon the same fondation. But as I am hopfull that his Majesty is fully Informed of all that is past, and what is now a Transacting, I will not trouble his Majesty with a repetition of facts, which I am hopfull he has been Informed off from the fountaine head. All I will say is that for my owne parte I will allways make very great difference t'wixt English promasis and Action, and am more fully confirmed in this opinion *since the tenth of Nov. last*, when the Day was fixt; But when matters come to the puish, some frivolous excuses retarded this great and Glorious blow; Thank God the Prince did not venture himself then at London, {180} tho he was upon the Coast ready at a Call to put himself at their head. I wish he may not be brought to venture sow far, upon the stress laid upon a suden blow, to be done by the English; we will see if the Month of May or June will produce something more effective than Novr., and I am sorry to aquent you that the sow great stress laid upon those projects is lick to prove fatal to some, for Lochgary, and Doctor Archibald Cameron, were sent to the Highlands to prepair the Clans to be in readiness: thire beeing sent was much against my opinion, as I allways ensisted, and will allways persist, that no stirr should be done there untill the English would be so farr engaged that they could not draw back. I hope his Majesty will aprove of my Conduct in this. Doctor Cameron was taken by a party of soldiers in Boruder [?], and is now actually secured in the Castel of Edinr. Loch still remains but what his fate will be is very precarious. The concert in Novr. was that I was to remain in London, as I had above four hundred Brave Highlanders ready at my call, and after matters had broke out there to sett off directly for Scotland as no raising would be made amongst the Clans without my presence. Now I beg in laying this before the King, you'l at same time assure his Majesty of my constant resolution to venture my owne person, let the consequence be what it will and dow everything that can convince his Majesty of my Dutifull attachmt to his sacred person and Royal Cause, for which I am ready to Venture my all, and nothing but the hand I had in those leate and present Schemes and the frequent jants I was oblidged to take in Consequence, Has hindered me from beeing settled in a very advantagious and honorable way, being affraid that Matrimony might Incline me to a less active life than my Prince's affairs now requires. I belive in a few days that I will take a private start to London, tho I am still so weake after my leate Illness at Paris {181} that I am scarse yet able to undergo much fatigue. I have left directions with Mr. Gordon, principal of the Scots Colledge, to forward any letters for me to a friend at Boulogne, *how* [who] has a secure way of forwarding by trading ships any Letters for me.

'I will be very glad to hear from you particularly as I Expect to return in a few weeks back to France. I have one favour to ask of you, and I hope it wont displeace his Majesty; Its, that whatever I write upon this topick, be neither shown or comunicated to any other person, as there are reports that people with you comumicate their Intelligence too freely to the Court of france, which von know may go farther, and prove of dangerous consequence. I hope the freedom with which I express myself will be wholly attributed to the warmth of my zeall for the good of the cause, and it beg you'l forgive the hurry I am in writing this, and I rely upon your friendship to Excuse the same towards his Majesty in case you think Proper to lay this hurried scrawle before him, for what with the fatigue of posting and Other Affairs, I am so Tumbled. I wish with all my heart you may conceve the sincer true and reale sentiments which Induced me to write so freely, and as the Gentilman with whom I send this to Paris is just ready to set off, I beg you'll allow me to conclude, and I hope you'll not faile to lay me at his Majesty's and Royal Emmency's feet and at same time to Believe me Sir

'Your most obedient and most humble Servt

'MACKDONELL.'

Edgar probably did not reply directly. John Gordon, of the Scots College in Paris, writes to Edgar:

'Paris: 19th August.

'I had the favour of yours of the 17th. July in Course. I found an opportunity lately to acquaint Glengarie of what you wrot me on his account some time ago in answer to his from Arras; he desires me to thank you for what you say obliging to him, and begs youll accept of his best compliments.'

It will be remarked that Pickle, who had informed the English Government of Archy Cameron's and Lochgarry's mission to Scotland in September 1752, in his letter to Edgar laments Archy's capture! Hypocrisy was never carried so far. To Cameron and his fate we return later.

The Stuart Papers contain nothing of interest about Charles for some time after Mademoiselle Luci's death and the postponement of the Elibank plot. The news of the Prince's conversion was spread by himself, in October 1752. Sir James Harrison was charged to inform Lord Denbigh, who thought the change 'the best and happiest thing.' Lady Denbigh, 'a most zealous smart woman,' saw Mr. Hay at Sens, and received from him some of the Prince's hair, wherewith 'she would regale three or four of her acquaintances, and each of them set in heart–form, encircled with diamonds.' {183a} Cardinal Tencin also heard of the conversion. In January 1753, Charles was in Paris. His creditors were clamorous, and he deplores his 'sad situation.' {183b} On January 24 he was more in funds, thanks to a remittance from Rome. Hanbury Williams, meanwhile, was diligently hunting for him in Silesia! On January 17 and February 11, 1753, Williams wrote long letters from Dresden. He had sent an honest fellow of a spy into Silesia, where the spy got on the tracks of a tall, thin, fair gentleman, a little deaf, travelling with a single servant, who took coffee with him. The master spoke no German, the servant had a little German, and the pair were well provided with gold. As Charles was a little deaf, this enigmatic pair must be the Prince and Goring. Hanbury Williams was energetic, but not well informed. {184} By February 18, 1753, the excellent Williams learned from Count Brühl that Charles was *dead*, 'in one of the seaports of France.' Meanwhile the English Government knew, though they did not tell Williams, all that they needed to know, through their friend Pickle. Williams they kept in the dark.

In March 1753, Charles was trafficking with Hussey, lieutenant–colonel of a regiment stationed in Luxembourg. He conceived a plan for sending Goring to Spain, and he put some boxes of his, long kept by 'La Grandemain,' into the hands of Waters. He wrote a mutilated letter to Alexander Murray in Flanders, and there our information, as far as the Stuart Papers go, fails us. But Pickle steps in with the following letter. He describes the illness about which, as we saw, he wrote to Edgar in April of this year. Here follows his letter:

Add. 32,843.

'17th March, 1753.

Dr. Sir,—I receved some time ago your kind favour, and no doubt you'll be greatly surprised at my long silence which nothing could have occasiond but a violent fitt of sickness, which began with a stich that seasd me as I was coming from the Town of Sence, in fine it threw me into a violent fever that confin'd me to my bed twenty days. I was let blood ten times, which has so reduc'd me, that I am but in a very weake situation still. This with my long stay here, has quite exausted my finances, and oblidg'd me to contract 300 Livres, tow of which I am bound to pay in the month of Aprile, and if I am not suplay'd, I am for ever undon. I beg you'l represent this to Grandpapa, upon whose friendship, I allways relay. The inclosed is for him, and I hope to see him soon in person, tho. I am to make a little tour which will still augment my Debts and think myself very lucky to find credit. Let me heare from you after you see Grandpapa, for there is no time to be lost, but pray don't sign that fellow's name you made use of to my Correspondent. It occasions —-'s [the Prince's?] speculations, you know he is sharp. I don't comprehend what you would be at in your last. What regards my cusins I don't comprehend. I will soon remouve my dr. mistres jelousies, if she has any . . . The old woman you mention is a great tatteler, but knows nothing solid but what regards Court amours and little intrigues. I hope to overtake her in your City, as I believe she will not incline to come so soon over as she leatly recev'd the news of her son's being kill'd in a dowell by one of the petit masters of this Capitall. The Deer hunting will be dangerous without a good set of hounds which will prove expencive and very trubelsome. If I don't hear upon recet I will conclude I am entirely neglected and dropt. I beg you'l offer my dutiful respects to Grandpapa, and all friends, and still believe me, Dear Sir,

'Your sincere and affte. friend

'ALEXR. PICKLE.

'To Mr. William Blair, at Mr. Brodie's in Lille Street, near Leister fields—London.'

This illness of Pickle's was troublesome: it is to be feared the poor gentleman never quite recovered his health. As usual, he is in straits for money. England was already ungrateful. Here follows another despatch

Add. 32,843.

'Paris: March 15, 1753.

Dr. Sir,—I had a long letter leatly from Mr. Cromwell [Bruce] contining in chief tow Artickles by way of charge; the first complaining of my long silence—t'other for not keeping a due and regular correspondence . . .What I beg you assure my mistress of, is, that had there been any new mode worth her notice invented since I gave her one exact patron of the last [the Elibank plot], I would not have neglected to have sent her due patrons. Please aquent my mistress that of leate they have comenced some new fashions in the head dresses, very little varying from the former one, yet they estime it is a masterpiece in its kind, for my part, I have but a slight idea of it, though they bost the people of the first rank of our country will use it. I would have wrot of this sooner, but my illness occasiond my not knowing anything of the matter till very leatly, and I was so very ill, that it was impossible for me to write, as you may see by Mr. Cromwell's letter. You may remember, dr. Papa, that I was always very desirous that my love intrigues should be secret from all mortalls but those agreed upon, and that my letters might be perus'd by non, but by my mistress and you, now if you have people how [who] were, and a few that still are, at the helme, that don't act honourably, I can't be possitive, neither will I mention them at this distance, beeing myself a little credulous, as I have but one under architect's word for it. Were I to credit some of the managers, some of the fundation stones are pleacd upon a very sandy ground, but our little thin friend, the Embassador [Earl Marischal?], gives it little or no credit, it may be but a puff in hopes to create suspicion, and make one of each other mistrustfull. In consequence of all this the managers have derected our Northern friends [Lochgarry and the clans] to keep their posts. I can answer for such as regards me, and I beg least the Company [Jacobites] make banckrout that you proteck my parte of them. I am now pretty well recover'd of my leate illness, tho' I have been very much afraid of a relapse, having catch'd a violent cold at the Masquerad ball of Lundi Gras, beeing over perswaded to accompany our worthy friend Mr. Murray to that diversion, where I was greatly astonish'd to find Mr. *Strange*

[Prince Charles] whom I imagin'd to be all this time in Germanie, for I took it for granted that he went for Berlin when I meet him at Furnes. I know not how long his stay was at Paris, for I was *a little pickt that he did not inquire after me during my illness.* He left this early Tuesday morning, and our friend Mr. Murray gave him the convoie for some days, and yesterday he returnd to town. I am to dine with him this day, and you may be sure, we will not forget to drink a bumper to our British friends and your health and prosperity in particular.

'I leave this in a cuple of days, and I must, tho, with reluctance, aquent you, my dear Papa, that my long stay here, together with my illness, has runn me quite aground, which forct me to borow very near 150*l*. St. and Mr. Woulf, Banquier, has my note payable the 5th of Aprile to his correspondent at Boulogne. As for the remaining 50, its not so pressing, as I had it from my Collegian friends [Scots College], now if I'm not enabled to pay this triffle, my credit, which was always good in this country, will be blown . . . I beg you ly me at my charming Mistress' feet [Pelham], and assure her how ardent my desires are to preserve her love and affections, which I hope very soon to assure her personally.

'I ever remain, my dear Papa

'Your most obedient, and most oblidged humble servt

'ALEXR. JACKSON.'

'P.S. Tho' I am still very weake, I will endeavour to leave this upon the 18th. Instant, and I stear my course for Imperiall Flanders.'

The following communication is undated, but, from the reference to Pickle's illness, it must be of March or April 1753. In April, Glengarry informed Edgar, as we saw, that he was going to England from Arras. He apparently went over, and handed in this intelligence. If he speaks truth, the Earl Marischal criticised the Elibank plot as a candid friend. There exists evidence of a spy on a spy, who tracked Glengarry to the Earl Marischal's house. 'Swem–rs M. P.' is a Mr. Swymmer.

Add. 33,050.

'Pickle remaind about ten days at Boulogne, where he was frequently in company with Sir J. Harrington who at that instant knew as little as Pickle of the P. Destination. Sir J. H–a–r–t–n was much cast down at the grand affair's [Elibank plot] being retarded. He wrote to Ld. S–t–ln [Strathallan] aquenting him therewith, for Ld. S–t–ln and Young Ga [Glengarry?] had been sent some time before to sound Ld. George Murray, not knowing how he stood affected, as he [Prince Charles] had once greatly disoblidgd him. S. J. H–a–r–t–n aquenting them of the disappointment in England, stopt further proceedings, so they return'd back to Boulogne. Pickle went streight from Boulogne to Paris, where he was very intimate with Ld. Marischal; few days past but Pickle was at his lodgings or M–r–l– at Pickle's. Ld. M–r–l– was first aquented with the intended insurrection in England by Goring who waited of him by his master's [Charles's] particular order, a person of distinction spoke very seriously to M–r–l– upon this head. Pickle does not know how [who] this was, M–r–l– declining to mention names, yet he estem'd this person as a man of weight, and good judgement, this person was publick at Paris, but waited of M–r–l at night—Carte has been several times over, he is trusted, and it is by his means chiefly, that the P. turn'd off Kelly, as Mr. Carte inform'd the P. that persons of note would enter upon no scheme with him whilst that fellow shar'd his confidence. Sir Jo: A–s–ly [?] was over, and Pickle believes he met the P. at Paris. The pretence of Mr. Swem–rs, Memr. of Pt. traveling abroad with his lady, was to settle the English Scheme. Ld. M–r–l has not seen the P. but twice, before Pickle went over. He never saw him at Berlin, *tho' he believed that he had taken several trips to that Court.* He saw Goring twice at Berlin. M–r–l knew nothing of a foreign Invation, and did not believe there could be any in time of peace. Pickle one day asking his opinion of their affairs, he answer'd that he could say nothing upon the head with certainty, he kept his mind to himself, that when they ask'd his Opinion, he told them he *could not judge so well as they, since he was quite a stranger to London, and to the different posts, and manner of placing their Guards, but that if they executed according to their plan laid before him, he doubted not but they might succeed,* but Pickle making some objections as to the veracity of this plan, told him that he could not positively contradick them, and tell the P. that they impost upon him, for, says he, "what Opinion, Mr. Pickle, can I entertain of people that propos'd that I should abandon my Embassy, and embark headlong with them? what can I answer, when they assure me that B–d–rl, S–dh G–me–ele [?] with others of that party have agreed when once matters break out, to declare themselves? But you need not, Mr. Pickle, be apprehensive, you may safely waite the event, as you are not desir'd to make any appearance [in Scotland] untill London and other parts of England pulls off the mask, or untill there is a foreign landing." This, and matters much of the same nature were the ordinary topicks of Mrl and Pickle's conversation.

'Pickle was not above six weeks in France, when he was determin'd to return, but was prevented by M–r–y [Count Murray, Elibank's brother] aquenting him that he would soon see the P. personally. Of this he at once aquented Mr. Cromwell [Bruce, English official] and that it was the only thing that detain'd him, but as Pickle in the interim went to Sens, in his return to Paris, *he was seased with a fluxion de Poitrine* which had very near tript up his hiells. Pickle, when he recover'd, went to the Opera Ball, here to his great surprise he met the P. who received him very kindly, and he still insisted upon foreign assistance, and the great assurances he had from England, and that he expected matters would go well in a very little time, he often mentioned foreign assistance by the Court of Berlin's influence, from Swedland. His conversation with Pickle was in general terms. Pickle told him that he intended returning to Britain. "Well then," says he, "I hope soon to send you an agreeable message, as you'l be amongest the very first aquented when matters coms to a Crisis: for my parte I hope to have one bold puish for all;" then after assurances of his friendship, he went off, and Pickle has not seen him since; this was upon Lundie Gras. He left Paris that very morning, and Capt. Murray gave him the Convoy, and was absent four days. A few days after this, Pickle met, by meare accident, Goring going to Ld. Mrl. Gor was then upon his way to England where he did not tarry above six days. D.K–ns [Dawkins] went leatly over, and brought mony for the P. Pickle believes upwards of 4,000*l*. St. There is few weeks but Sir J. H–a–r–t–n leeves messages by means of the Smugglers. *Eldermen Blastus Heth* [Heathcote] *B–n J–r–n–d* Black, with many others, are mannagers in the City. *If anything is to be attempted, its to be executed by a set of resolute daring young fellows, laid on by a set of young Gentlemen, conducted by a few regular Officers.* If ever any attempt is made, it's to be a Night onset, and if they succeed in 'scaping the Guards then all will declare. The P. has been tampering with the Scots Dutch, he saw some of them. Pickle cant condescent who they were, his Agents spoke to many of them. No Officers are fitter for such attempts, as they are both brave and experienced. The P. depends upon having many friends in the Army, there being not a few added to their number by the [Duke of Cumberland's] conduct towards many gallant gentlemen and men of property, but whatever steps they have been taking, to sound or gaine over either Officers of the Land or Sea Service, they still keep a dead secret. As for B–r [Beaufort?], Ld. W–r–d [Westmoreland] Sir Jo–s–ps with other of the Cohelric [choleric?] and [Bould?] Pickle is very ready, as he is not accustom'd to such Surnames and titles, to forget them, but assemblys of that nature are pretty publick, members of such meetings can't escape the vigilancy of the Ministry: Murray, when he came over in Novr. last, brought over several manefestos to England, with a very ample comission for —– [Glengarry?] to raise the Clans and command in Chief untill an Expressd Generall Officer landed, and even then the Clans were to have a particular Commander (a Highlander) this they insisted upon, knowing what tools they have been in times past to Low Country Commanders, no more experienced than the most ordinary amongest themselves. —– [?] was pitched upon, as the P. believed he would readily comploy with any reasonable plan that would be concerted by the Commander in Chief, what Pickle asserts as to this, will probably be known by others. *Neith. Drum. Heb*, were pitched upon to try the pulse of D. H. [Hamilton?] and other nobelmen and gentlemen of the South. Aber–ny with some of the excepted Skulkers were to manadge and concert matters with the North Country Lowlanders, and Menzy of Cul–d–re was to be agent betwixt the Lowlands and bordering Highlands. Several were sent to Scotland by the P. and mony given them in order to prepaire the people.

'—– [Glengarry] can fully answer for the Highlands, for nothing can be transacted there without his knowledge, as his Clan must begin the play, or they can come to no head there. What Pickle knows of English schemes he can't be so positive, as he was not designed to be an actor upon that Stage, yet in time he may perhaps be more initiated in those misterys, as they now believe that Pickle could have a number of Highlanders even in London to follow him, but whatever may happen, you may always rely upon Pickle's attachment.'

To be 'pick't' (piqued) by the Prince's neglect to inquire about Pickle's precious health is very characteristic of Glengarry. His vanity and pride are alluded to by men of all parties.

Pickle's remarks on Charles's receipt of 4,000*l.* must be erroneous. His Royal Highness was in the very lowest water, and could not afford a new suit of clothes for his servant Daniel, 'the profet,' as he once calls him. This we learn from the following letter to Avignon:

To Sheridan and Stafford. From the Prince.

'April 10, 1753.

'This is to let you know that as I am extremely necessitous for money, it engages me out of economi to send for Daniell's Close which you are to Pack up in his own trunc, and to send it adresed to Mr. Woulfe to Paris, but let there be in ye trunc none of Daniel's Papers or anything else except his Close.'

Meanwhile, on March 20, 1753, Archy Cameron had been arrested. His adventure and his death, with the rumours which flew about in society, bring us into collision with a great authority, that of Mr. Carlyle.

'If you, who have never been in rich Cyrene, know it better than I, who *have*, I much admire your cleverness,' said the Delphian Oracle to an inquiring colonist. Mr. Carlyle had never lived in the Courts of Europe about 1753; none the less, he fancied he knew more of them, and of their secrets, than did their actual inhabitants, kings, courtiers, and diplomatists. We saw that, in September 1752, according to Pickle, Prince Charles sent Archibald Cameron and Lochgarry to Scotland, with a mission to his representative, Cluny Macpherson, and the clans. The English Government, knowing this and a great deal more through Pickle, hanged Cameron, in June 1753, on no new charge, but on the old crime of being out in the Forty–five. Sir Walter Scott was well aware of the circumstances. We have already quoted his remark. 'The ministers thought it prudent to leave Dr. Cameron's new schemes in concealment, lest by divulging them they had indicated the channel of communication which, it is well known, they possessed to all the plots of Charles Edward.'

Mr. Carlyle, however, knew better. After giving a lucid account of the differences which, in 1752–1753, menaced the peaceful relations between England and Prussia; after charging heavily in favour of his hero Frederick, Mr. Carlyle refers to Archibald Cameron. Cameron, he says, was 'a very mild species of Jacobite rebel. . . . I believe he had some vague Jacobite errands withal, never would have harmed anybody in the rebel way, and might with all safety have been let live. . . . ' But 'His Grace the Duke of Newcastle and the English had got the strangest notion into their head; . . . what is certain, though now well nigh inconceivable, it was then, in the upper classes and political circles, universally believed that this Dr. Cameron was properly an emissary of the King of Prussia, that Cameron's errand here was to rally the Jacobite embers into a flame, . . . ' and that Frederick would send 15,000 men to aid the clans. These ideas of the political circles Mr. Carlyle thinks 'about as likely as that the Cham of Tartary had interfered in the Bangorian Controversy.' {196a} Now, Horace Walpole says {196b} 'intelligence had been received some time before [through Pickle] of Cameron's intended journey to Britain, with a commission from Prussia to offer arms to the disaffected Highlanders . . . . That Prussia, who opened her inhospitable doors to every British rebel, should have tampered in such a business, was by no means improbable. . . . Two sloops were stationed to watch, yet Cameron landed.' Writing to Mann (April 27, 1753), Horace Walpole remarks: 'What you say you have heard of strange conspiracies fomented by *our nephew* [Frederick] is not entirely groundless.' He adds that Cameron has been taken while 'feeling the ground.'

Information as to Frederick's 'tampering' with Jacobitism came to the English Government not only through Pickle, but through Count Kaunitz, the Austrian minister. On December 30, 1753, Mr. Keith wrote to the Duke of Newcastle from the Imperial Court. He had thanked Count Kaunitz for his intelligence, and had expressed the wish of George II. for news as to 'the place of the Young Pretender's abode.' He commented on Frederick's 'ill faith and ambition,' which 'could not fail to set the English nation against his interest, by showing the dangerous effects of any increase of force, or power, in a Prince capable of such horrid designs.' {197}

As between Mr. Carlyle in 1853, and the diplomatists of Europe in 1753, the game is unequal. The upper classes and political circles knew more of their own business than the sage of Ecclefechan. Frederick, as Walpole said, *was* 'tampering' with the Jacobites. He as good as announced his intention of doing so when he sent the Earl Marischal to Paris, where, however, the Earl could *not* wear James's Green Ribbon of the Thistle! But, to Frederick, the Jacobites were mere cards in his game. If England would not meet his views on a vexed question of Prussian merchant ships seized by British privateers, then he saw that a hand full of Jacobite trumps might be useful. The Earl Marischal had suggested this plan. {198a} The Earl wrote from Paris, February 10, 1753: 'The King of England shows his ill–will in his pretensions on East Frisia, in the affairs of the Empire, and in revoking the guarantee of Silesia. Your Majesty, therefore, may be pleased to know the strength of the party hostile to him at home, in which, and in the person of

Prince Edouard [Charles] you may find him plenty to do, if he pushes you too far.' The Earl then suggests sending a rich English gentleman to Frederick; this was Mr. James Dawkins, of the Over Norton family, the explorer of Palmyra. Pickle mentions him as 'D–k–ns.'

Frederick did not expect a rupture with England, but condescended to see the Earl's friend, Mr. Dawkins. On May 7 the Earl announces his friend's readiness to go to Berlin, and says that there is a project maturing in England. The leaders are Dawkins, Dr. King of Oxford, ' *homme d'esprit, vif, agissant*,' and the Earl of Westmoreland, '*homme sage, prudent, d'une bonne tête, bon citoyen, respectable, et respecté*.' {198b} They will communicate with Frederick through the Earl Marischal, if at all. 'The Prince knows less of the affair than Dawkins does. The Prince's position, coupled with an intrepidity which never lets him doubt where he desires, causes others to form projects for him, which he is always ready to execute. I have no direct communication with him, not wishing to know his place of concealment: we correspond through others.'

Frederick (May 29, 1753) thinks the plot still crude, and advises the Jacobites to tamper with the British army and navy. 'It will be for my interest to encourage them in their design underhand, and without being observed. You will agree with me that the state of European affairs does not permit me to declare myself openly. If the English throne were vacant, a well conceived scheme might succeed under a Regency.'

Such is the attitude of Frederick. He receives a Jacobite envoy; he listens to tales of conspiracies against his uncle; he offers suggestions; he will encourage treason *sous main*. In fact, Frederick behaves with his usual cold, curious, unscrupulous skill.

Frederick's letters have brought us to May 1753, when Archy Cameron, in the Tower of London, lay expecting his doom. While kings, princes, ambassadors, statesmen, and highland chiefs were shuffling, conspiring, peeping, lying and spying, the sole burden of danger fell on Archibald Cameron, Lochgarry, and Cluny. They were in the Elector's domains; their heads were in the lion's mouth. We have heard Young Glengarry accuse both Archy Cameron and Cluny of embezzling the Prince's money in the Loch Arkaig hoard, but Glengarry's accusations can scarcely have been credited by Charles, otherwise he would not have entrusted the Doctor with an important mission. Cluny's own character, except by Kennedy and Young Glengarry, is unimpeached, and Lochgarry bore the stoutest testimony to his honour.

The early biography of Archibald Cameron is interesting. As the youngest son of old Lochiel, he, with his famous brother 'the gentle Lochiel,' set about reforming the predatory habits of their clan, with considerable success. Archibald went to Glasgow University, and read Moral Philosophy 'under the ingenious Dr. Hutchinson.' He studied Medicine in Edinburgh and in France; then settled in Lochaber, and married a lady of the clan of Campbell. He was remarked for the sweetness of his manners, and was so far from being a violent Jacobite that he dissuaded his brother, Lochiel, from going to see the Prince at his first landing in 1745. This account of his conversion, from 'The Gentleman's Magazine' (June 1753), is *naïf.* 'Dr. Cameron was at last brought to engage by the regard due to a benefactor and a brother, who was besides his Chief as head of his Clan, *and threatened to pistol him if he did not comply.*' Wounded at Falkirk (the ball was never extracted), he served at Culloden, escaped to France with Lochiel, was surgeon in his regiment, and later in Lord Ogilivie's, was guardian of Lochiel's son, and, as we know, came and went from Scotland with Lochgarry and Young Glengarry. His last trip to Scotland was undertaken in September 1752. Of his adventures there in concerting a rising we know nothing. On March 20 he was detected near Inversnaid (possibly through a scoundrel of his own name), and was hunted by a detachment of the Inversnaid garrison. They were long baffled by children set as sentinels, who uttered loud cries as the soldiers approached. At last they caught a boy who had hurt his foot, and from him discovered that Cameron was in a house in a wood. Thence he escaped, but was caught among the bushes and carried to Edinburgh by Bland's dragoons. On April 17 he was examined by the Council at the Cockpit in Whitehall. He was condemned on his attainder for being out in 1745, {201} and his wife in vain besieged George II. and the Royal Family with petitions for his life. 'The Scots Magazine' of May 1753 contains a bold and manly plea for clemency. 'In an age in which commiseration and beneficence is so very conspicuous among all ranks, and on every occasion, we have reason to hope that pity resides in that place where it has the highest opportunity of imitating the divine goodness in saving the distressed.'

They 'sought for grace at a graceless face.' Mrs. Cameron was shut up with her husband to prevent her troubling any of the Royal Family or nobility with petitions in his favour. On June 8, Cameron was hanged and disembowelled, but *not* while alive, as was the custom. A London letter of June 9 says 'he suffered like a brave man, a Christian, and a gentleman. . . . His merit is confessed by all parties, and his death can hardly be called untimely, as his behaviour rendered his last day worth an age of common life.'

'One crowded hour of glorious life
Is worth an age without a name!'

As Scott remarks, 'When he lost his hazardous game Dr. Cameron only paid the forfeit which he must have calculated upon.' The Government, knowing that plots against George II. and his family were hatching daily, desired to strike terror by severity. But Prince Charles, when in England and Scotland, more than once pardoned assassins who snapped pistols in his face, till his clemency excited the murmurs of his followers and the censures of the Cameronians. They wrote thus:

'We reckon it a great vice in Charles, his foolish pity and lenity in sparing these profane blasphemous Red Coats, that Providence put into his hand, when, by putting then to Death, this poor Land might have been eased of the heavy Burden of these Vermin of Hell.' {202}

Cameron was deprived in prison of writing materials, but he managed to secure a piece of pencil, with which on scraps of paper he wrote his last words to his friends. These were obtained by Mrs. Cameron, and are printed in the 'State Trials.' {203} Never was higher testimony borne to man than by Cameron to Prince Charles.

'As I had the honour from the time of the Royal youth's setting up his Father's standard, to be almost constantly about his person, till November 1748 . . . I became more and more captivated with his amiable and princely virtues, which are, indeed, in every instance so eminently great as I want words to describe.

'I can further affirm (and my present situation, and that of my dear Prince too, can leave no room to suspect me of flattery) that as I have been his companion in the lowest degree of adversity that ever prince was reduced to, so I have beheld him too, as it were, on the highest pinnacle of glory, amidst the continual applauses, and I had almost said, adorations, of the most brilliant Court in Europe; yet he was always the same, ever affable and courteous, giving constant proofs of his great humanity, and of his love for his friends and his country. . . . And as to his courage, none that have ever heard of his glorious attempt in 1745 can, I should think, call it in question.'

Cameron adds that if he himself *was* engaged in a new plot, 'neither the fear of the worst death their malice could invent, nor much less their flattering promises, could have extorted any discovery of it from me.' He forgives all his enemies, murderers, and false accusers, from 'the Elector of Hanover and his bloody son, down to Samuel Cameron, the basest of their spies.'

As to the Prince's religion, Cameron says (June 1753):

'I likewise declare, on the word of a dying man, that the last time I had the honour to see H.R.H. Charles, Prince of Wales, he told me from his own mouth, and bid me assure his friends from him, that he was a member of the Church of England.'

Who was this Samuel Cameron, who stained by treachery the glorious name of Lochiel's own clan? On this point the following letter, written after Archy's death, casts some light. We have already seen that Samuel Cameron was accused of being in communication with Murray of Broughton, as also was Young Glengarry. Young Edgar, in French service, writes thus to his uncle, James's secretary, from Lille:

'Samuel Cameron, whom Archy mentions in the end of his speech, is the same that Blair and Holker wrote to me about when at Rome, the end of 1751. He has been a constant correspondent of John Murray's, and all along suspected of being a spy. Cameron's remarks leave it without a doubt.' Samuel, Edgar adds, is now a half–pay lieutenant in French service, at Dunkirk. Lord Ogilvie and Lochiel mean to secure him, but Lord Lewis Drummond does not think the evidence sufficient. From 'The Scots Magazine' of September 1753, we learn that a court–martial of Scottish officers was held on Samuel at

Lille, and, in April 1754, we are told that, after seven months' detention, he was expelled from France, and was condemned to be shot if he returned. His sentence was read to him on board a ship at Calais, and we meet him no more. Dr. Cameron was buried in a vault of the Savoy Chapel, and, in 1846, her present Majesty, with her well–known sympathy for the brave men who died in the cause of her cousins, permitted a descendant of the Doctor to erect a monument to his memory. This was destroyed in a fire on July 7, 1864, but now a window in stained glass commemorates 'a brave man, a Christian, and a gentleman.'

The one stain on Cameron's memory, thrown, as on Cluny's, by Young Glengarry, may be reckoned as effaced. Whatever really occurred as to the Loch Arkaig treasure, it did not destroy the Prince's confidence in the last man who laid down his life for the White Rose.

Before Archy Cameron's death, young Edgar had written thus from Lille to old Edgar in Rome:

'May 2, 1753.

'We have no account of Cameron except by the Gazete. It is thought that all the others who have been apprehended either had of the Prince's money in their hands, or that the Government expects they can make some discoverys about it; I wish with all my heart the Gov. had got it in the beginning, for it has given the greatest stroke to the cause that can be imagined, it has divided the different clans more than ever, and even those of the same clan and family; so that they are ready to destroy and betray one another. Altho I have not altered my opinion about Mr. M—– [Murray] yet as he may on an occasion be of great use to the cause with the Londoners—I thought it not amiss to write him a line to let him know the regard you had for him, for as I know him to be vastly vain and full of himself I thought this might be a spur to his zeale.'

So practically closes the fatal history of the Loch Arkaig treasure. Cluny later bore back to France, it seems, the slender remains of the 40,000 louis d'or. But this accursed gold had set clan against clan, kinsman against kinsman, had stained honourable names, and, probably, had helped to convert Glengarry into Pickle.

The Highlanders yet remember the Prince's treasure. A few years ago, a Highland clergyman tells me, he was trolling with a long line in Loch Arkaig. He hooked something heavy, which came slowly to hand, with no resistance but that of weight. 'You have caught one of the Prince's money bags,' said the boatman, when suddenly the reel shrieked, and a large *salmo ferox* sped out into the loch. My friend landed him; he weighed fifteen pounds, and that is the latest news of Prince Charles's gold!

CHAPTER IX—DE PROFUNDIS

Charles fears for his own safety—Earl Marischal's advice—Letter from Goring—Charles's danger—Charles at Coblentz—His changes of abode—Information from Pickle—Charles as a friar—Pickle sends to England Lochgarry's memorial—Scottish advice to Charles—List of loyal clans—Pickle on Frederick—On English adherents—'They drink very hard'—Pickle declines to admit arms—Frederick receives Jemmy Dawkins—His threats against England—Albemarle on Dawkins—Dawkins an archæologist—Explores Palmyra—Charles at feud with Miss Walkinshaw—Goring's Illness—A mark to be put on Charles's daughter —Charles's *objets d'art*—Sells his pistols.

The ill news of Archy Cameron's arrest (March 20, 1753) soon reached Charles. On April 15 he wrote to 'Mr. Giffard' (the Earl Marischal) in Paris. He obviously feared that the intelligence which led to Cameron's capture might throw light on his own place of residence. His friends, at least, believed that if he were discovered his life would be in danger. He says:

To Mr. Giffard (Earl Marischal), from P.

'April 13, 1763.

'I am extremely unnesi by the accident that has hapened to a Certain person. you Now [know] how much I was against people in that Service. {208} My antipathi, iff possible, increses every day, which makes me absolutely determined whatever hapens never to aproch their Country, or have to do with anibody that comes with them. I have been on ye point of leaving this place,—but thought it better to differ it untill I here from you. My entention was to go to Francfor Sur Main and from thence to Bal in Swise, but without ever trespassing in ye F. Dominions, be pleased to send back by M. Dumon yr opinion of what Town in ye Queen of H. D. [Hungary's dominions] [Maria Theresa] would be ye best for me to go to.—would not D's Cuntry House be good: perhaps I may get it for six months . . .

'JOHN DOUGLAS.'

On April 29, misled it seems by a misapprehension of Lord Marischal's meaning, Charles had moved to Cologne, and notified the fact to Stouf (Goring). Goring replied:

From Stouf.

'Paris: May 8, 1753.

'The message delivered to you by Mr. Cambell has been falsely represented to you, or not rightly understood; the noble person Mr. Cambell mentions to have sent you a positive message to leave Gand and retire to Cologne, denies to have sent you any positive message at all on that account. He was indeed very anxious for your safety, and of opinion that since the taking of Mr. Cameron your person ran an inevitable danger, if you staid where you then were, and gave as his opinion only, that the dominions of the Elector of Cologne and the Palatinate appeared to be the safest, by reason of those princes being in interests opposite to the Court of Hanover, but was very far from saying you would be safe there, or indeed anywhere. How is it possible a man of his sense could think, much less a prince like you, who have so many powerfull enemies, that any place could guard you from them? No sir, he is of opinion that nothing can save your life but by yr taking just measures and prudent precautions to hyde yourself from them.

'These are the sentiments of the noble person you mention in yours of the 29th. whose name I do not put on paper, he having desired me never to do it till he gave me leave. He told me further that it would be more for your interest he should not know as yet where you were; and bid me advise you to have a care how you walked out of town near the Rhine, for in your taking such walks it would be easy for five or six men to seise your person and put you in a boat, and Carry you to Holland who have territories but one quarter of an hour distant from ye town. . . . '

The Elibank game can be played by two or more, and princes have been kidnapped in our own day. The Earl Marischal thought Charles's life in danger from the English.

On May 5, young Edgar noted the safe return of Lochgarry from Scotland. Charles went to Coblentz, but was anxious to return to Ghent. In June he tried Frankfort–on–the–Maine: his letters to 'La Grandemain' show him in correspondence with M. St. Germain, whether the General or the famous 'deathless charlatan' does not appear. In July he took a house in Liège. He asks Dormer for newspapers: 'I am a sedentary man: ye gazetes is en amusement to me.' On August 12 he desires an interview 'with G' (Glengarry), and here is Pickle's account of the interview:

'Before Pickle set out for France he writt to Loch Gairy, now Lieut. Col. of Lord Ogleby's Regiment in Garrison at Air, to meet him at Calais. Upon Pickle's arrivall at Calais, he met Loch Gairy there, and it was agreed between them that Loch Gairy should next morning set out to notify Pickle's arrivall to the Young Pretender, and that Pickle should move forward to see Sir James Harrington at *Simer* [?] near *Bulloighn*, and from thence to come to Ternan in about a week to meet Loch Gairy. Soon after Pickle arrived at Ternan, Loch Gairy came to him, and told him the youth [Prince Charles] would be there next morning, and he came accordingly without any servant, having with him only a French Gentleman, who has serv'd in the Army, but has of late travell'd about with the Young Pretender; Loch Gairy left them at Ternan and set out for Air. Soon after, the

Young Pretender, the French Gentleman, and Pickle set out for Paris, the Young Pretender being disguis'd with a *Capouch.* The Young Pretender shew'd Pickle Loch Gairy's report of his late Expedition with Dr. Cameron to Scotland, and also the List hereunto annex'd of the numbers of the disaffected Clans that Doctor Cameron and he had engaged in the Highlands, and also an Extract of a memorial or Scheme sent over to the Pretender from some of his friends in England. The Pretender seem'd fond of Loch Gairy's paper; [he said] that he had been of late hunted from place to place all over Flanders by a Jew sent out of England to watch him. The Pretender talked very freely with Pickle of affairs, but did not seem to like the Scheme sent him out of England about the Parliament, that it would be very expensive, and that he expected no good from the Parliament; that Loch Gairy was trusted by him with most of his motions, and how to send to him; that he has been a Rambling from one place to another about Flanders, generally from near Brussells towards Sens, and on the Borders of France down towards Air, except some small excursions he made; once he went to Hamburgh. He told Pickle that another rising in Scotland would not do untill a war broke out in the North, in that case he expected great things from Sweden would be done for him, by giving him Men, Arms and Ammunition: when Pickle talk'd to him of the King of Prussia, he said he expected nothing thence, as the King of Prussia is govern'd by his interest or resentment only—That he had sent Mr. Goring to Sweden, where he had found he had many friends—That Goring had also been at Berlin to propose a Match for the Young Pretender, with the King of Prussia's Sister, and that he had since sent for Sir John Graham to Berlin to make the same proposals, that they were both answer'd very civilly, that it was not a proper time, but they had no encouragement to speak further upon the Subject—The Pretender said that he beleiv'd he had many friends in England, but that he had no fighting friends; the best service his friends in England could do him at present was to supply him with money—The night they arriv'd at Paris, the Pretender went to a Bagnio—Pickle thinks it is call'd Gains' Bagno, and from thence to Sir John Graeme's House, as Pickle believes, but where he went, or how long he staid at Paris, he does not know. The Pretender said he should now get quit of the Jew, as he intended going to Lorain; he ask'd Pickle if he would go with him. Pickle says that Sir John Graeme, Sir James Harrington, and Goring, and Loch Gairy are the Pretender's chief Confidents and Agents, and know of his motions from place to place; that Goring is now ill, having been lately cut for a Fistula. Pickle kept himself as private as he could at Paris, went no where but to *Lord Marshall's*, and once to wait upon Madame Pier Cour, Monsr. D'Argenson's Mistress, who offer'd to recommend him to Monsr. D'Argenson if he inclin'd to return to the French Service. {213} Pickle believes Monsr. D'Argenson and Monsr. Paris Mont

Martell are the Pretenders chiefest friends at the Court of France; *he says that Mrs. Walkingshaw is now at Paris big with child*, that the Pretender keeps her well, and seems to be very fond of her—He told Pickle that he hath seen the Paper that was in Lord Marshall's hands, No. 2; which Lord Marshall return'd to Sir John Graeme, declaring that he would not meddle whatever his Brother [Marshal Keith] might do, that Lord Marshall would receive no papers from little people. Pickle believes that the paper was given to Lord Marshall by Mr. Swimmer, or a Knight that has lately been abroad, who is now in Parliament—Pickle has been told that the Pension lately given to the Cardinal out of the Abbey of St. Aman, 'twas for the Young Pretender's behoof, and that Mr. O'brien, commonly call'd Lord Lismore, and Mr. Edgar, are the chief people about the Old Pretender at Rome— Pickle says that all the disaffected people that come over from France call upon Sir James Harrington near Bulloign, but the Young Pretender has a Correspondence with England, by means of one Dormer, a Merchant at Antwerp, who Pickle believes is Brother to a Lord Dormer.'

Pickle, of course, forwarded to the English Government a copy of Lochgarry's report and list of clans. These follow.

'Partly extracted from Loch Gairy's Memorial to the Pretender after his return from Scotland, 1749 or 1750.

'It is the greatest consequence to your R.H. not to delay much longer making at attempt in Scotland. Otherwise it will be hardly possible to bring the Clans to any head, it would be no difficult matter at this instant to engage them once more to draw their swords.

'Because, besides their natural attachment to Your R.H. there is, most undoubtedly such a spirit of revenge still subsisting amongst the Clans who suffer'd, and such a general discontent amongst the others who have been scandalously slighted by the Government, that if made a right use of, before it extinguishes, must unavoidably produce great and good effects.

'In the present situation of your R.H. it is evident that the most simple scheme, and that in which the whole plan is seen at once is most proper for your R.H. to take in hand. It is without doubt that London would be the most proper place for the first scene of action, because it is the Fountain and Source of power, riches and influence. But the eye of the Government is so watchfull at the Fountain head that one can't easily comprehend, what they [the Jacobites] can be able to shew against six thousand of the best Troops in Britain which can be brought together against them upon the first alarm. That England will do nothing, or rather can do nothing without a foreign Force, or an appearance in Scotland, such as was in 45. In either of these cases there is all the reason to believe that England would do wonders. But am afraid its impossible for your R.H. to procure any Foreign assistance in the present situation of Europe, therefore the following Proposals are most humbly submitted to your R.H.

'That your R.H. emply such persons as will be judg'd most proper to negotiate a sum of money at Paris, London and Madrid, which is very practicable to be accomplish'd by known and skilfull persons, the sum may be suppos'd to be 200,000*l*., to be directly remitted to one centrical place (suppose Paris), this money to be lodg'd in the hands of Mons. De Montmartell, who can easily remitt any sum as demanded to any trading town in Europe. Sufficient quantity of Arms, Ammunition, etc. to be purchas'd, which can be done in some of the Hans Towns in the North, which can be done without giving any umbrage, supposing them bought for some Plantation, which is, now a common Transaction, especially in these Towns.

'Two stout ships to be purchas'd which is so common a transaction in Trade, more so now than ever, so much that I am told it might even be done at London, the Ships is absolutely necessary to batter down the small Forts on the Western Coast of the Highlands, which your R.H. knows greatly annoy'd us in 45, and prevented several Clans joining with their whole strength. When every thing is ready, your R.H. to pitch upon a competent number of choice Officers, of whom there are plenty, both in France, Holland, Germany and Spain, all Scots, or of Scots extraction, eminent for their loyalty and military capacity. Your R.H. to land where you landed before, or rather in Lochanuie. Your R.H. will have an army by the management and influence of yourself, and by their Concertion already agreed upon with me before you are twenty days landed, of at least six thousand Men, and there is actually but six Batallions of Foot, and two Regiments of Dragoons in Scotland, and your R.H. can have 2,000 good men ere you are eight and forty hours landed.

'If the enemy take the field they will make but a feint resistance against such a resolute determined set of men. Your R.H. has all advantages over the regular Troops in

Scotland, you can always attack them and force them to Battle without ever being forct but when its judg'd advantageous—this is certain you can move your Army across the Country in three or four days, which will take the regular Troops as many weeks. You can make them starve and rot with cold and fluxes, and make them dwindle away to nothing if they were triple your Number, and without striking a stroak, if we take the advantage the Countrey and Climate affords—the renown'd King Robert Bruce, Sir William Wallace, and the late Marquis of Montrose, of which your R.H. is a perfect model, made always use of this advantage with infallible success against their Enemys.

'It is a truth not disputed by any who knows the nature of the affair, that if your R.H. had oblig'd the regular forces in Scotland in 1746 to make one other Winter Campain without giving then battle (than which nothing was more easy) two thirds of them at least had been destroyed, whilst ten such Campains would have only more and more invigorated our R.H.'s Army. If this project be not long delayed, and that your R.H. persists in putting it into Execution, you will in all human probability drive your Enemys before you like a parcel of Sheep.'

There follows:

'A List of the Clans given by Loch Gairy to the Pretender in consequence of their agreement with him.

'Your R.H. arriving with money, Arms, and a few choice Officers, will find the following Clans ready to join, this Computation of them being very moderate, and most of them have been always ready to join the R. Strd under the most palpable disadvantages.

'The Mackdonells, as matters stand at present, by Young G—-[Glengarry's] concurrence only 2,600

By G—- Interest the Bearer [Lochgarry] can answer for the Mackleans at least 700

There is little doubt but the Mackkenzies would all join G—- as related to the most considerable Gentlemen of this Clan, and the Bearer can answer for at least 900

The Bearer having sounded several Gentlemen of the name of MacLeod over whom G—– as being nearly connected has great influence, the Bearer can answer for at least . . . 450

The Bearer answers for the MackInnans, MackLeods of Rasa—at least 300

The Bearer answers for the Chisolms . . . 200

The Bearer answers for the Robertsons . . . 250

Camerons . . . 500

Stuart of Alpin . . . 250

McNeals of Barra . . . 150

MackPhersons . . . 350

McIntoshes . . . 350

Frazers . . . 400

MackGregors . . . 200

Athol men, at least . . . 500

Out of Brodulbin 300

Duke of Gordon's Interest Glenlivat and Strathdon, at least . . . 500

M'Dugalls, McNobbs and McLouchlins . . . 250

The Bearer has tamper'd with the Grants, and if properly managed, at least . . . 500

Good men 9,660

'Besides the great Dependance on the Low Countreys and of other Clans that in all probability will join your R.H. the above mentioned Clans have not lost a thousand men during the transactions of 45 and 46, and by consequence are most certainly as numerous as they were then, and for the reasons already given they are readier and more capable for action at present than they were in 45. One reason in particular is worth your R.H.'s Observation, that since the end of the late War there has been by an exact Computation, between six and seven thousand men reform'd out of the British and Dutch Service, most of whom were of the Loyal Clans, and are now at home.'

We have provisionally dated this communication of Pickle's in August or September, when Charles wished to see 'G.' A date is given by the reference to Miss Walkinshaw's condition. Her child, born in Paris, was baptized at Liège in October 1753. So far, according to Pickle, Charles seemed 'very fond of her.' This did not last.

It may be observed that Lochgarry's Memorial shows how great was the influence of Young Glengarry. Nearly 5,000 men await his word. And Young Glengarry, as Pickle, was sending the Memorial to Henry Pelham!

On his return to London, Pickle gave the following information, in part a repetition of what he had already stated:

' . . . Pickle, since he has been in England, generally heard of the Young Pretender by Lochgary who requested him by directions from the Young Pretender, to make the last trip that he went upon to France, the intent of which was to communicate to Pickle the scheme that he [Lochgarry] and Dr. Cameron had concerted in the Highlands, and to offer him some arms to be landed at different times upon any part of his estate that he should appoint, but which Pickle absolutely refus'd to consent to, as he might be ruind by a discovery, and which could hardly be avoided, as the country was so full of Troops, and *nobody as yet knowing in what manner the forfeited estates would be settled* ;—Pickle believes that some friends of P. Charles of Lorraine in Hainault, often harbour the Young

Pretender, and favor him in his rambles;—that at the Court of France, Monsr. D'Argenson {219} is his chief friend in the Ministry, that Monsr. Puysieux was his enemy, as was also Monsr. St. Contest, who is a creature of Puysieux. Pickle looks upon the Duke of Richlieu, and all that are related to the family of Lorraine, to be friends of the Pretender's that Monsr. Paris Montmartell is the Pretender's great friend, and told Pickle he would contrive to raise 200,000*l*. for his Service, upon a proper occasion. Pickle was told by the Pretender himself, that Madame Pompadour was not his friend, for that she had been gaind over by considerable sums of money from England, and had taken offence at him, for his slighting two Billetts that had been sent by her to him, which he had done for fear of giving umbrage to the Queen of France and her relations; as to the French King, Pickle has had no opportunity of knowing much of his disposition, but does not look upon him as a well wisher to the Pretender's Cause, unless it be at any time to serve his own purpose.

'As to the King of Prussia, Pickle can say but little about him, having never been employd in that Quarter, and knows no more than what he has been told by the Young Pretender, which was, that he had sent Collonel Goring to Berlin to ask the K. of Prussia's Sister in marriage; that Goring had been received very cooly, and had had no favourable answer; that he afterwards had sent Sir John Graeme, whose reception was better, and that he soon went himself to Berlin, where he was well received, but the affair of the marriage was declin'd. That the K. of Prussia advised him to withdraw himself privately from Berlin, and retire to Silesia, and to keep himself conceal'd for some time, in some Convent there. That the K. of Prussia told the Pretender he would assist him in procuring him six thousand Swedes from Gottenburgh, with the Collusion of the Court of France, but Pickle understood that this was to take place in the Event only of a War breaking out.

'Pickle since his return to England, has been but once at a Club in the City, where they drink very hard, but at which, upon account of the expence, *he cannot be as frequently as he would wish to be*, nor can he afford to keep company with people of condition at this end of the Town. The Jacobites in England don't choose to communicate any of their schemes to any of the Irish or Scots, from the latter of whom all that they desire, is a rising upon a proper occasion;—That he does not personally know much of the heads of the Party in England—only as he has seen lists of their names in the Pretender's and Ld. Marishall's hands;—such as he knows of them would certainly introduce him to others were he in a condition of defraying the expence that this would be attended with, which he is not, being already endebted to several people in this Town and has hitherto had no more than his bare expences of going backwards and forwards for these three years past . . . '

It is needless to say that this piece deepens the evidence connecting Pickle with Glengarry. Poor James Mohr had no estates and no seaboard whereon to land arms. At the close of the letter, in autumn 1753, Pickle speaks of his three years' service. He had, therefore, been a spy since 1750, when he was in Rome. Now James Mohr, off and on, had been a spy since 1745, at least.

We may now pursue the course of intrigues with Prussia. Frederick, on June 6, 1753, the day before Cameron's execution, wrote to the Earl Marischal. He wished that Jemmy Dawkins's affair was better organised. But, 'in my present situation with the King of England, and considering his action against me, it would be for the good of my service that you should secretly aid by your good advice these people' (the Dawkins conspirators). {222a} So the Cham of Tartary *does* interfere in the Bangorian Controversy, despite Mr. Carlyle! It is easy to imagine how this cautious encouragement, *sous main*, would be exaggerated in the inflamed hopes of exiles. The Earl Marischal had in fact despatched Dawkins to Berlin on May 7, not letting him know that Frederick had consented to his coming. {222b} Dawkins was to communicate his ideas to Marshal Keith. The Earl did not believe in a scheme proposed by Dawkins, and was convinced that foreign assistance was necessary. This could only come from Prussia, Sweden, France, or Spain. Prussia has no ships, but few are needed, and merchant vessels could be obtained. The Earl would advise no Prussian movement without the concurrence of France. But France is unlikely to assent, and Sweden is divided by party hatreds. He doubts if France was ever well disposed to the House of Stuart. The Spanish have got the ships and got the men, but are hampered by engagements with Austria and Savoy.

Frederick saw Dawkins at Berlin, but did not think his plans well organised. He preferred, in fact, to await events, and to keep up Jacobite hopes by vague encouragement. On June 16, 1753, Frederick writes to his agent, Michell, in London. He does not believe that England will go to war with him for a matter of 150,000 crowns, 'which they refuse to pay to my subjects,' on account of captures made by English privateers. But, 'though the English King can do me much harm, *I can pay him back by means which perhaps he knows nothing of and does not yet believe in . . .* I command you to button yourself up on this head' (*de vous tenir tout boutonné*), 'because these people must not see my cards, nor know what, in certain events, I am determined to do.' {223} He was determined to use the Jacobites if he broke with England. On August 25, 1753, Frederick wrote to Klinggraeffen, at Vienna, that the English Ministry was now of milder mood, but in September relations were perilous again. On July 4, 1753, the Earl told Marshal Keith that a warrant was out against Dawkins. {224a} In fact, to anticipate dates a little, the English Government knew a good deal about Jemmy Dawkins, the explorer of Palmyra, and envoy to His Prussian Majesty. Albemarle writes from Paris to Lord Holdernesse (December 12, 1753): {224b}

'As yet my suspicions of an underhand favourer of their cause being come from England, and addressing himself to the late Lord Marshall, can only fall on one person, and that is Mr. Dawkins, who has a considerable property in one of our settlements in the West Indies. This is the gentleman who travelled in Syria with Mr. Bouverie (since dead) and Mr. Wood, who is now with the Duke of Bridgewater, and who are publishing an account of their view of the Antiquities of Palmeyra. Mr. Dawkins came from England to Paris early the last spring (1753), and was almost constantly with the late Lord Marshall. He used sometimes to come to my house too. In May he obtained a pass from this Court to go to Berlin, by the late Lord Marshall's means, as I have the greatest reason to believe, for he never applied to me to ask for any such, nor ever mentioned to me his intention of taking that journey, and by a mistake, Monsr. de St. Contest put that pass into my hands, as it was for an Englishman, which I have kept, and send it enclosed to your Lordship. But whether Mr. Dawkins never knew that it had been delivered to me, or was ashamed to ask it of me, as it had not been obtained through my Channell, or was afraid of my questioning him about it, or about his journey, I cannot say; however he went away without it, not long after its date, which is the 2d. of May. And he returned from thence to Compiègne, the latter end of July, which was a few days before the Court left that place.

'Since that he went to England, where, I believe, he now is, having had the Superintendency of the Publication of the work above mentioned [on Palmyra]. Mr. Dawkins, as well as his Uncle, who lives in Oxfordshire [near Chipping Norton], is warmly attached to the Pretender's interest, which with the circumstances I have related of him, which agree with most of those hinted at in Your Lordship's letter, particularly as to times, are very plausible grounds of my mistrusts of him. I shall make the strictest inquiries concerning him, as he is the only person of note, either British or Irish, who to my knowledge came here from England about the time your Lordship mentions —who frequented assiduously the late Lord Marshall [attainted, but alive!] who passed from thence to Berlin—and in short whose declared principles in the Jacobite Cause, and whose abilities, made him capable of the commission he may be supposed to be engaged in.

'I shall not be less attentive to get all the intelligence I can, of any other person under this description, who may at any time, frequent the late Lord Marshall, and to give Your Lordship an exact account of what shall come to my knowledge. If, on Your Lordship's part, you could come at any further discovery concerning Mr. Dawkins, I hope you will inform me of so much of it as may be of any service to me in my inquiries. The extreme caution and prudence with which, Your Lordship informs me, the late Lord Marshall conducts himself, for fear of risking the secret, will, I apprehend, make it impossible for me to penetrate into the instruction he may be charged with, in this respect, from his master, or how far he is intrusted with His Prussian Majesty's intentions. I have not the least doubt of the late Lord Marshall's being in correspondence with the Pretender's elder Son, who was lately (as I was informed some time after he left it) at the Abbaye of S. Amand, not far from Lisle, which is most convenient for him, his brother, the Cardinal, being, as I am assured, Abbot of that Monastery. As for the lady described under the character of *la bonne amie de Monsieur de Cambrai*, that is Mrs. Obrian, whosc husband is, by the Pretender's favour, the mock Earl of Lismore, a follower of his fortunes, and supposed to have a considerable share in his confidence.'

From the Same.

'Paris: Tuesday, December 18, 1753.

'. . . I must take this opportunity to rectify a small mistake in my last letter, relating to the Abbaye of St. Amand, of which I had been informed that the Pretender's younger Son, the Cardinal, was Abbot. It is the Abbaye of Aucline of which he is Commendatory, and which is at much about the same distance from Lille as the other. It is the more probable that the Pretender's Elder Son was there last autumn, as he might take that opportunity of seeing the Princess of Rohan [a relation of the Prince of Soubise], an ancient flame of his who went to Lille at the time of the encampment in Flanders, under that Prince's command.'

Apparently the warrant against Jemmy Dawkins was not executed. We shall meet him again. Meanwhile there were comings and goings between Goring and the Earl Marischal in July 1753. In September, Goring was ill, and one Beson was the Prince's messenger (July 2, September 5, 1753). On September 5, Charles made a memorandum for Beson's message to the Earl Marischal. 'I will neither leave this place, nor quit ye L. [the lady, Miss Walkinshaw]. I will not trust myself to any K. or P. I will never go to Paris, nor any of the French dominions.' The rest is confused, ill–spelled jottings about money, which Beson had failed to procure in London. {227} On September 12; Charles scrawls a despairing kind of note to Goring. He writes another, underscored, dismissing his Avignon household, that is, 'my Papist servants!' 'My mistress has behaved so unworthily that she has put me out of patience, and as she is a Papist too, I discard her also! . . . Daniel is charged to conduct her to Paris.'

This was on November 12. On October 29, Miss Walkinshaw's child, Charlotte, had been baptized at Liège. Charles's condition was evil. He knew he was being tracked, he knew not by whom. Hope deferred, as to Prussia, made his heart sick. Moreover, on August 19, 1752, Goring had written from Paris that he was paralysed on one side (Pickle says that his malady was a fistula). Goring expressed anxiety as to Charles's treatment of an invalided servant. 'You should know by what I have often expressed to you [Charles answered on November 3] that iff I had but one Lofe of Bred, I would share it with you. The little money that I have deposed on my good friend's hands you know was at your orders, and you would have been much in ye rong to have let yourself ever want in ye least.'

Again, on November 12, he writes to Goring:

To Mr. Stouf.

'November 12.

'I am extremely concerned for yr health, and you cannot do me a greater Cervice than in taking care of yrself for I am not able to spare any of my true friends.'

Dr. King, as we have said, accuses Charles of *avarice*. Charles II., in exile, would not, he says, have left a friend in want. Though distressed for money, the Prince does not display a niggardly temper in these letters to Goring. He had to defray the expenses of many retainers; he intended to dismiss his Popish servants, his household at Avignon, and to part with Dumont. We shall read Goring's remonstrances. But the affair of Daniel's 'close' proves how hardly Charles was pressed. On December 16, 1752, he indulged in a few books, including Wood and Dawkins's 'Ruins of Palmyra,' a stately folio. One extraordinary note he made at this time: 'A marque to be put on ye Child, iff i part with it.' The future 'Bonny Lass of Albanie' was to be marked, like a kelt returned to the river in spring. 'I am pushed to ye last point, and so won't be cagioled any more.' He collected his treasures left with Mittie, the surgeon of Stanislas at Lunéville. Among these was a *couteau de chasse*, with a double–barrelled pistol in a handle of jade. D'Argenson reports that the Prince was seen selling his pistols to an armourer in Paris. Who can wonder if he lost temper, and sought easy oblivion in wine!

CHAPTER X—JAMES MOHR MACGREGOR

Another spy—Rob Roy's son, James Mohr Macgregor—A spy in 1745— At Prestonpans and Culloden—Escape from Edinburgh Castle—Billy Marshall—Visit to Ireland—Balhaldie reports James's discovery of Irish Macgregors—Their loyalty—James Mohr and Lord Albemarle— James Mohr offers to sell himself—And to betray Alan Breck—His sense of honour—His long–winded report on Irish conspiracy—Balhaldie—Mrs. Macfarlane who shot the Captain—Her romance— Pitfirrane Papers—Balhaldie's snuff–boxes—James Mohr's confessions —Balhaldie and

Charles—Irish invasion—Arms in Moidart—Arms at the house of Tough—Pickle to play the spy in Ireland—Accompanied by a 'Court Trusty'—Letter from Pickle—Alan Breck spoils James Mohr— Takes his snuff-boxes—Death of James Mohr—Yet another spy—His wild information—Confirmation of Charles's visit to Ireland.

From the deliberate and rejoicing devilry of Glengarry, and from Charles's increasing distress and degradation, it is almost a relief to pass for a moment to the harmless mendacity of a contemporary spy, Rob Roy's son, James Mohr Macgregor, or Drummond. This highland gentleman, with his courage, his sentiment, and his ingrained falseness, is known to the readers of Mr. Stevenson's 'Catriona.' Though unacquainted with the documents which we shall cite, Mr. Stevenson divined James Mohr with the assured certainty of genius. From first to last James was a valiant, plausible, conscienceless, heartless liar, with a keen feeling for the point of honour, and a truly Celtic passion of affection for his native hand.

As early at least as the spring of 1745, James Mohr, while posing as a Jacobite, was in relations with the law officers of the Crown in Scotland. {231a} James's desire then was to obtain a commission in a Highland regiment, and as much ready money as possible. Either he was dissatisfied with his pay as a spy, or he expected better things from the Jacobites, for, after arranging his evidence to suit his schemes, he took up arms for the Prince. He captured with a handful of men the fortress of Inversnaid; he fell, severely wounded, at Prestonpans, and called out, as he lay on the ground, 'My lads, I am not dead! By God! I shall see if any of you does not do his duty.' Though he fought at Culloden, James appears to have patched up a peace with the Government, and probably eked out a livelihood by cattle-stealing and spying, till, on December 8, 1750, he helped his brother Robin to abduct a young widow of some property. {231b} Soon after he was arrested, tried, and lodged, first in the Tolbooth, next, for more security, in Edinburgh Castle.

On November 16, 1752, James, by aid of his daughter (Mr. Stevenson's Catriona), escaped from the Castle disguised as a cobbler. {232a} It has often been said that the Government connived at James's escape. If so, they acted rather meanly in sentencing 'two lieutenants' of his guard 'to be broke, the sergeant reduced to a private man, and the porter to be whipped.' {232b}

The adventures of James after his escape are narrated by a writer in 'Blackwood's Magazine' for December 1817. This writer was probably a Macgregor, and possessed some of James's familiar epistles. Overcoming a fond desire to see once more his native hills and his dear ones (fourteen in all), James, on leaving Edinburgh Castle, bent his course towards the Border. In a dark night, on a Cumberland moor, he met the famed Billy Marshall, the gipsy. Mr. Marshall, apologising for the poverty of his temporary abode, remarked that he would be better housed 'when some ill–will which he had got in Galloway for setting fire to a stackyard would blow over.' Three days later Billy despatched James in a fishing boat from Whitehaven, whence he reached the Isle of Man. He then made for Ireland, and my next information about James occurs in a letter of Balhaldie, dated August 10, 1753, to the King over the Water. {232c} Balhaldie's letter to Rome, partly in cypher, runs thus, and is creditable to James's invention:

'James Drummond Macgregor, Rob Roy's son, came here some days agoe, and informed me that, having made his escape from Scotland by Ireland, he was addressed to some namesakes of his there, who acquainted him that the clan Macgregor were very numerous in that country, under different names, the greatest bodies of them living together in little towns and villages opposite to the Scottish coast.' They had left Scotland some one hundred and fifty years before, when their clan was proscribed. James 'never saw men more zealously loyal and clanish, better looked, or seemingly more intrepid and hardy. . . . No Macgregors in the Scotch highlands are more willing or ready to joyn their clan in your Majesty's service than they were, and for that end to transport 3,000 of their name and followers to the coast of Argileshyre.' They will only require twenty–four hours 'to transport themselves in whirries of their own, even in face of the enemy's fleet, of which they are not affrayed.'

The King, in answer (September 11, 1753), expressed a tempered pleasure in Mr. Macgregor's information, which, he said, might interest the Prince. On September 6, 1753, Lord Strathallan, writing to Edgar from Boulogne, vouches only for James's courage. 'As to anything else, I would be sorry to answer for him, as he had but an indifferent character as to real honesty.' On September 20, James Mohr, in Paris, wrote to the Prince, anxious to know where he was, and to communicate important news from Ireland. Probably James got no reply, for on October 18, 1753, Lord Holdernesse wrote from Whitehall to Lord Albemarle, English ambassador in Paris, a letter marked 'Very secret,' acknowledging a note of Lord Albemarle's. Mr. Macgregor had visited Lord Albemarle on October 8th and 10th, with offers of information. Lord Holdernesse, therefore, sends a safe–conduct for Macgregor's return. {234} We now give Macgregor's letter of October 12, 1733, to Lord Albemarle, setting forth his sad case and honourably patriotic designs:

MS. Add. 32,733.

'Paris: October 12, 1753. Mr. James Drummond.

'My Lord,—Tho' I have not the Honour to be much acquainted with Your Lordship, I presume to give you the trouble of this to acquaint your lordship that by a false Information I was taken prisoner in Scotland in November 1751 and by the speat [spite] that a certain Faction in Dundas, Scotland, had at me, was trayd by the Justiciary Court at Edinburgh, when I had brought plenty of exculpation which might free any person whatever of what was alledged against me, yet such a Jurie as at Dundas was given me, thought proper to give in a special verdict, finding some parts of the Layable [libel] proven, and in other parts found it not proven. It was thought by my friends that I would undergo the Sentence of Banishment, which made me make my escape from Edinburgh Castle in Novr. 1752, and since was forced to come to France for my safety. *I always had in my vew if possable to be concerned in Government's service*, {235} and, *for that purpose*, thought it necessar ever since I came to France to be as much as possable in company with the Pretender's friends, so far as now I think I can be one useful Subject to my King and Country, upon giving me *proper Incouragement.*

'In the first place I think its in my power to bring Allan Breack Stewart, the suposd murdrer of Colin Campbell of Glenouir, late factor of the forfet Estate of Ardsheal, to England and to deliver him in safe custody so as he may be brought to justice, and in that event, I think the delivering of the said murderer merits the getting of a Remission from his Majesty the King, especially as I was not guilty of any acts of treason since the Year 1746, and providing your lordship procures my Remission upon delivering the said murderer, I hereby promise to discover a very grand plott on footing against the Government, which is more effectually carried on than any ever since the Family of Stewart was put off the Throne of Britain, and besides to do all the services that lays in my power to the Government.

'Only with this provision, that I shall be received into the Government's Service, and that I shall have such reward as my Service shall meritt, I am willing, if your lordship shall think it agreeable, to go to England privily and carry the murderer [Allan Breck] alongest with me, and deliver him at Dover to the Military, and after waite on such of the King's friends as your lordship shall appoint. If your lordship think this agreeable, I should wish General Campbell would be one of those present as he knows me and my family, and besides that, I think to have some Credit with the General, which I cannot expect with those whom I never had the Honour to know. Either the General or Lieutt. Colln. John Crawford of Poulteney's Regiment would be very agreeable to me, as I know both of these would trust me much, and at the same time, I could be more free to them than to any others there. Your lordship may depend [on] the motive that induces me to make this Offer at present to you, in the Government's name, is both honourable and just, {236} so that I hope no other constructions will be put on it, and for your lordship's further satisfaction, I say nothing in this letter, but what I am determined to perform, and as much more as in my power layes with that, and that all I have said is Trueth, and I shall answer to God.

'JAS. DRUMMOND.'

James was sent over to England, and we now offer the results of his examination in London, on November 6, 1753. The following document deals with the earlier part of Mr. Macgregor's appalling revelations, and describes his own conduct on landing in France, after a tour in the Isle of Man and Ireland, in December 1752. That he communicated his Irish mare's nest to Charles, as he says he did, is very improbable. Like Sir Francis Clavering, as described by the Chevalier Strong, James Mohr 'would rather he than not.' However, he certainly gave a version of his legend to the Old Chevalier in Rome.

Extract of the Examination of Mr. James Drummond.

'That about the 8th. of May following (vizt. May 1753) He (Mr. D.) did set out for France, and arrived at Boulogne on the 16th. where He met with Lord Strathalane, and as

He (Mr. D.) was asking after the Young Pretender, His Lordship told Him that He had seen a letter from Him (the Young Pretender) lately to Sir James Harrington, at which time he (the Young Pretender), was lodged at an Abbé's House, about a League and Half from Lisle, whereupon He (Mr. D.) communicated to his Lordship, in the presence of Capt. Wm. Drummond, and Mr. Charles Boyde, the Commission, with which He was charged. That thereupon His Lordship undertook to wait upon the Young Pretender with the Irish Proposal, and advised Him (Mr. D.) to go and stay at Bergue, till He (Lord Strathalane) came to Him there. That on the 20th. June following, His Lordship wrote Him (Mr. D.) a Letter (which is hereunto annexed) to this effect—"That he (Lord Strathalane) had laid Mr. Savage's Proposal before the Young Pretender, who desired, that he, (Mr. D.) would repair to Paris, and that He had sent Him (Mr. D.) a Bill upon Mr. Waters (the Banker) to pay His charges. {238} That He (Mr. D.) did accordingly go to Paris, and that upon His arrival there, He first waited upon Mr. Gordon, Principal of the Scot's College, but that nothing particular passed there. (N.B. There is not one word, in any of Mr. Drummond's papers, of His [the Prince's] intending to go to Berlin.) (Official Note.)'

Nobody, of course, can believe a word that James Mohr ever said, but his disclosures, in the following full report of his examination, could only have been made by a person pretty deep in Jacobite plans. For example, Balhaldie, chief of the Macgregors, did really live at Bièvre, as James Mohr says. There was in Edinburgh at this time a certain John Macfarlane, w.s., whose pretty wife, in 1716, shot dead an English captain, nobody ever knew why. She fled to the Swintons of Swinton, who concealed her in their house. One day Sir Walter Scott's aunt Margaret, then a child of eight, residing at Swinton, stayed at home when the family went to church. Peeping into a forbidden parlour she saw there a lovely lady, who fondled her, bade her speak only to her mother, and vanished while the little girl looked out of the window. This appearance was Mrs. Macfarlane, who shot Captain Cayley, and was now lying *perdue* at Swinton.

Now, in 1753 the pretty lady's husband, Mr. Macfarlane, was agent in Scotland for Balhaldie. To him Balhaldie wrote frequently on business, sent him also a 'most curious toy,' a tortoise-shell snuff-box, containing, in a secret receptacle, a portrait of King James VIII. Letters of his, in April 1753, show that James Mohr was so far right; Balhaldie *was* living at Bièvre, in a glen three leagues from Paris, and was amusing himself by the peaceful art of making loyal snuff–boxes in tortoise–shell. {239}

As to Bièvre, then, James Mohr was right. He may or may not have lied in the following paper, when he says that the Prince was coming over, with Lord Marischal, to the Balhaldie faction of Jacobites, who were more in touch with the French Court than his own associates. Mr. Trant, of whom James Mohr speaks, was really with the Prince, as Pickle also asserts, and as the Stuart Papers prove. Probably he was akin to Olive Trant, a pretty intriguer of 1715, mentioned by Bolingbroke in his famous letter to Wyndham. As to Ireland, James Mohr really did take it on his way to France, though his promises in the name of 'the People of Fingal' are Irish moonshine. Were arms, as James Mohr says, lodged in Clanranald's country, Moidart? Pickle refused to let them be landed in Knoydart, his own country, and thought nothing of the kind could be done without his knowledge. James Mohr may really have had news of arms landed at the House of Tough on the Forth, near Stirling, where they would be very convenient. Pickle, I conceive, was not trusted by Clanranald, and Cameron he had traduced. If James Mohr by accident speaks the truth in the following Information, more was done by Lochgarry and Cameron than Pickle wotted of during the autumn of 1752 and the spring of 1753. The arms may have been those ordered by Charles in 1750.

Here is James Mohr's Confession, made in London, November 6, 1753: {240}

'That, in June 1753, the Pretender's Son wrote to Mr. McGregor of Bolheldies, in a most sincere manner, that he wanted He should undertake His Service, as formerly: Bolheldies refused to undertake anything for him, till such time, as He was reconciled with his Father, and make acknowledgements for His Misconduct to the King of France, and then, that He was willing to enter upon His affairs only, in concert with the Earl of Mareschal, and none other, for that He could not trust any about Him: Upon which, the Pretender's Son wrote Him a second time, assuring Bolheldies, that He would be entirely advised by Him, and at the same time, that He expected no see Him soon, when things would be concerted to His Satisfaction. {241}

'About the middle of September, the Pretender's Son arrived in Paris, in company with one Mr. Trent [Trant], and Fleetwood, two English Gentlemen, who carried Him from South of Avignon [probably a lie], and when they came thro' Avignon, He was called Mr.

Trent's Cousin, and thereafter, upon all their Journey, till they landed at Paris. During his stay at Paris, He stayed at Mr. John Water's House. Immediately upon His arrival at Paris, Bolheldies was sent for, who stay'd with Him only that night: The next day, He went to Baivre [Bièvre], where He lives, Two Leagues South of Paris: How soon Bolheldies went Home, He sent Express to Mr. Butler, the King of France's Master of the Horse, and also a great Favorite: Mr. Butler came upon a Sunday Morning to Baivre, and about 3 o'clock in the Afternoon, the Earl of Marischal sent an Express to Bolheldies; and after Receipt of this Express, Mr. Butler went off to Versailles: That evening, Bolheldies told me, that now He hoped, the Prince, as He called Him, would be advised by His best friends, for that He seems to have a full view of what Folly He had committed, by being advised and misled, by a Parcel of such Fools, as has been about Him, since the year 1745. But now, providing He would stand firm to His promise, to stand by the Earl of Mareschal and His advice, that He hoped His Affairs might soon be brought on a right Footing; He added further, That he was still afraid of His breaking thro' concert; That He was so headstrong, how soon He saw the least appearance of success, That He might come to ruin His whole Affairs, as He did, when He stole away to Scotland, in the year 1745, by the advice of John Murray, Callie [Kelly], Sheridan, and such other Fools.

'I then told Bolheldies, that He had been at great pains to get the Restoration of the Family Stuart brought about, and that tho' He succeeded, he might be very ill rewarded, in the Event, and He and His Clan, probably, on the first discontent, be ruined, as that Family had done formerly, to gratify others, for that it seems, He had forgot, that very Family in King Charles's time, persecuted the whole of His Clan, in a most violent manner; {242} and I added farther, that the whole of His Clan would be much better pleased, if He did but procure Liberty from the Government to return Home, and live the remainder of His Days among His Friends. Bolheldies assured me, that He was willing to go Home, providing He had the least consent from the Government; Only, He would not chuse to be put under any Restrictions, than to live as a peaceable Subject.

'He added further, that He was so much afraid of the Pretender's Son being so ill to manage, and also that the Irish would break thro' Secret, That he could heartily wish not to be concerned, could he but fall on a Method to get clear of it; But at present, that He had engaged to enter upon some Business with the Earl of Mareschal; and especially, about those Proposals from Ireland, which He thought very probable, if Matters were carried on by people of sense, that knew how to manage, for that all this affair depended on keeping the Government ignorant of what was doing. Four days after this, there was a meeting held, Two Leagues South from Baivre, by the Pretender's Son, Earl of Mareschal, Bolheldies, Mr. Butler, Mr. Gordon, Principal of the Scots College, Mr. Trent, and Fleetwood, and some other English Gentlemen, whom Bolheldies did not inform me of.

'When Bolheldies returned Home, He told me, the Irish Proposals were accepted of, and for that purpose, that there were some Persons to be sent both to Scotland, and Ireland, and that I was appointed to be one of those for Ireland, to transact the affairs with the People of Fingal, especially as Mr. Savage had desired, that if any should be sent, that I would be the person intrusted in their affair. {243} That Col. and Capt. Browne, Capt. Bagget, were to be sent along with Mr. McDiarmid: Bolheldies also said, that He was afraid, he would be obliged to take a trip to England, some time in winter, for that some certain Great Men there would trust none other to enter on business with them, as Lord Sempil was dead, but that, if [he] could help it, He did not incline to go. That those, that were to be appointed to go to Scotland, were entirely refer'd to him, and Mr. Gordon the Principal. The management of the Scots affairs is entirely refer'd to Stirling of Kear, Mr. Murray of Abercarney, Mr. Smith, and Sr. Hugh Paterson [uncle of Miss Walkinshaw!]. That Mr. Charles has promised to manage the Duke of Hamilton, and Friends . . . Bolheldies assured me, that any, that pleased to join from France, would not be hindered: and that there was a Method fallen upon to get Two Ships of War, as also plenty of arms, and ammunition, which would be sent by the Ships, to both Ireland and Scotland. That the Irish propose to raise 14,000 Men [!], and in two days time, to have them embarked in Wherries from Dublin, Rush, Skeddish, and Drogheda, and from thence transported, in six hours, to North Wales, or, in Twenty–four hours, to Scotland, either of which as the service required; providing always, that the 2 Ships of War were sent to escort them, as also Arms and ammunition and Money. That it was proposed by both the Earl of Mareschal, and Bolheldies, that 11,000 should land in North Wales, and 3,000 in Campbelltown of Kentyre in Argyleshire; for that those in Argyleshire that were well affected to their cause, would have a good opportunity to rise, by leading 3,000 Irish. That McDonald of Largye has proposed that there will rise, from that end of Argyleshire 2,500 Men, including the Duke of Hamilton's Men from Arran; To wit, the McDonalds of Largye, the McNeils, McAlisters, Lamonds, and McLawchlans, with what Sr. James Campbell of Auchinbreck can rise; and those from Campbelltown to march to the Head of Argyleshire, and to Perthshire, where they were to be joind by the North Country Clans, which with the Irish, and those from Argyleshire, was computed to be near 14,000 Men, and to be commanded by the Earl of Mareschal, and Lord George Murray. {245}

'Bolheldies assured me . . . that the Pretender's Son made a proposal to His Father to resign the Crown in his Favor: It was refused; and it was desired of Him not to make any further Proposals of that kind. Bolheldies was desired to go to Rome, to expostulate with the Pretender, which he begged to be excused, for that it was contrary to his Opinion, and that He did not approve of the Proposal, would never desire the Old Gentleman to resign. He told me, that this Proposal proceeded from the English, as the Young Pretender had owned that He was Protestant . . .

'It consists with my knowledge, that there were lodged, in Clanronald's Country, 9,000 Stands of Arms under the care of Ronald McDonald, Brother to the late Kinloch Moydart, Mr. McDonald of Glenaladale, and the Baillie of Egg, and kept still by them, in as good order as possible. That one, John McDonald, who is my own Cousin German, and is also Cousin German to Glenaladale, met with me in the Braes of Argyleshire, in March last [James was not in Scotland at that date!]; when He told me, that if there was an Invasion that they had plenty of Arms; and told the way and manner they had then preserved: But immediately before they were lodged in their hands, that Dr. Cameron had taken away, without orders, 250 Stands. That they might be got in Order, in six days time, by very few hands; for that they had sustained very little damage. It's certain, some little pains might find them out. . . . Bolheldies assured me, that Sr. John Graham was sent by the Young Pretender's Orders, to deliver Capt. Ogelvie 8,000 Swords, which had lain at Berlin [?], since the last affair, that he was to deliver them to Capt. Ogelvie, at or near Dunkirk, concealed into wine Hogsheads; and that Capt. Ogelvie was to land them at Airth, in the Frith of Forth; and to get them conveyed to the house of Tough, where they were to remain under the charge of Mr. Charles Smith, whose Son is married to the Heiress of Tough. The House of Tough is two miles above Stirling. I also saw Mr. Binglie, Under Master of the Horse, sent by Mr. Butler, and met at Bolheldie's House, by young Sheridan, who is always with the Young Pretender. {246} . . .

'That the Irish Proposal, sent by me was thus: In way to France, I came to the Isle of Man, where I had occasion to meet one Mr. Patrick Savage, to whom I was recommended by a Friend in Scotland; This Mr. Savage is an Irishman, and was in Scotland some time before I had seen Him: He was informed by Sir Archibald Stewart of Castle–Milk near Greenock, that Sir Archibald had seen Dr. Cameron in Stirlingshire; who told Him, that He hoped the Restoration would happen soon, for that preparations were a making for it, and that He had been sent to Scotland to transact some affairs for that purpose. Mr. Savage told me, in the year 1745, if the Pretender's son had sent but the least notice to

Ireland, that He might have got 10,000 or 12,000 Men, for that they at that time had formed a scheme, for that purpose, expecting to have had a message. . . . Mr. Savage assured me, that there were two Lords concerned, who put it out of his power to let their Names be known, till I came with a commission from the Young Pretender, and then, that they would frankly see me, and take me to their Houses to make up matters . . . '

The pleased reader will observe that Mr. Macgregor's Irish myth (though here sadly curtailed) has swollen to huge proportions since he communicated his tale of long lost Macgregors to the Old Chevalier in August. Whether the Prince was really turning to Balhaldie and official Jacobitism or not, is matter of doubt. Mr. Macgregor's Information having been swallowed and digested by Lord Holdernesse, Pickle was appealed to for confirmation. We have seem his unfriendly report of Mr. Macgregor's character, as a spy mistrusted by both sides. But among other precautions an English official suggested the following:

'That, if it's thought proper, Mr. —– [Pickle clearly] should be sent to Ireland forthwith, to know the whole of those concerned in the Irish Plot of the People of Fingal, that He could have a *Trusty* in Company, sent from the Secretary, who would undergo any borrowed name, and was to be Companion in the affair to Mr. —– [Pickle]. That particularly those Lords should be known, as also such of the People of Connaght as could be discovered. That Mr. —– [Pickle] is willing to undertake whatever in his power lays, to shew the zeal, wherewith He is inclined to serve the Government, but that He will not chuse to go to Ireland, *unless a court Trusty is sent with him*, who will be eye witness to His Transactions with the Irish, as Mr. —– [Pickle] will tell that he [the English companion] is a Trusty sent by the Pretender's Son.'

I detect Pickle under 'Mr. —–,' because later he was sent in a precisely similar manner into Scotland, accompanied by a 'Court Trusty,' or secret service man, named Bruce, who, under the style of 'Cromwell,' sent in reports along with those despatched by Pickle himself. Whether Pickle really went to Ireland to verify Mr. Macgregor's legends or not,

I am unable to say. The following note of his (December 13, 1753) suggests that he went either on that or a similar errand.

Add. 32,730.

'Grandpapa,—In consequence of what past at our last meeting I have wrot to my Correspondent, fixing the time and place of meeting, and at leatest I ought seet off the 20th. pray then, when and where are we to meet? If not soon, I must undow what I have begun. Excuse my anxiety, and believe me most sincerely with great estime and affection

'Your most oblidged humble Servt.

PICKLE.
'13th December, 1753.
'To the Honble. Quin Vaughan, at his house in Golden Square.'

Here James Mohr Macgregor slips out of our narrative. He was suspected by Balhaldie of having the misfortune to be a double–dyed scoundrel. This impression Mr. Macgregor's letters to 'his dear Chief' were not quite able to destroy. The letters (Dunkirk, April 6, and May 1, 1754) are published in 'Blackwood's Magazine' for December 1817. James tells Balhaldie that he had visited England, and had endeavoured to deliver Alan Breck, 'the murderer of Glenure,' to the Government, and to make interest for his own brother, Robin Oig. But Robin was hanged for abducting the heiress of Edenbelly, and Alan Breck escaped from James Mohr with the *spolia opima*, including 'four snuff–boxes,' made, perhaps, by Balhaldie himself. In England, James Mohr informs Balhaldie, he was offered 'handsome bread in the Government service' as a spy. But he replied, 'I was born in the character of a gentleman,' and he could only serve 'as a gentleman of honour.'

James, in fact, had sold himself too cheap, and had done the Devil's work without the Devil's wages. Probably the falsehood of his Irish myth was discovered by Pickle, and he was dismissed. James's last letter to Balhaldie is of September 25, 1754 (Paris), and he prays for a loan of the pipes, that he may 'play some melancholy tunes.' And then poor James Mohr Macgregor died, a heart–broken exile. His innocent friend, in 'Blackwood's Magazine,' asks our approbation for James's noble Highland independence and sense of honour!

There was another spy, name unknown, whose information about the Prince, in 1753, was full and minute, whether accurate or not. It is written in French. {250} About the end of June 1753, Charles, according to this informer, passed three months at Lunéville; he came from Prussia, and left in September for Paris. Thence Charles went to Poland and Prussia, then to Strasbourg, back to Paris, thence to Liège, and thence to Scotland. Prussia and Denmark were next visited, and Paris again in January 1754. As a rule, Charles was in Scotland, or Liège, collecting an army of deserters. This valuable news reached the Duke of Newcastle on October 30, 1754.

As to the Irish plot reported by James Mohr, I found, among the papers of the late Comte d'Albanie, a letter from an Irish gentleman, containing record of a family tradition. Charles, it was said, had passed some time near the Giant's Causeway: the date was uncertain, the authority was vague, and there is no other confirmation of James Mohr's preposterous inventions. {251}

CHAPTER XI—'A MAN UNDONE.' 1754

Jacobite hopes—Blighted by the conduct of Charles—His seclusion— His health is affected—His fierce impatience—Miss Walkinshaw— Letter from young Edgar—The Prince easily tracked—Fears of his English correspondents—Remonstrances of Goring—The English demand Miss Walkinshaw's dismissal—Danger of discarding Dumont—Goring fears the Bastille—Cruelty of dismissing Catholic servants— Charles's lack of generosity—Has relieved no poor adherents—Will offend both Protestants and

Catholics—Opinion of a Protestant— Toleration desired—Goring asks leave to resign—Charles's answer— Goring's advice—Charles's reply—Needs money—Proceedings of Pickle —In London—Called to France—To see the Earl Marischal—Charles detected at Liège—Verbally dismisses Goring—Pickle's letter to England—'Best metal buttons'—Goring to the Prince—The Prince's reply—Last letter from Goring—His ill-treatment—His danger in Paris—His death in Prussia—The Earl Marischal abandons the Prince— His distress—'The poison.'

The year 1754 saw the practical ruin of Charles, and the destruction of the Jacobite party in England. The death of Henry Pelham, in March, the General Election which followed, the various discontents of the time, and a recrudescence of Jacobite sentiment, gave them hopes, only to be blighted. Charles no longer, as before, reports, 'My health is perfect.' The Prince's habits had become intolerable to his friends. The 'spleen,' as he calls it, had marked him for its own. His vigorous body needed air and exercise; unable to obtain these, it is probable that he sought the refuge of despair. Years earlier he had told Mademoiselle Luci that the Princesse de Talmond 'would not let him leave the house.' Now he scarcely ventured to take a walk. His mistress was obviously on ill terms with his most faithful adherents; the loyal Goring abandoned his ungrateful service; the Earl Marischal bade him farewell; his English partisans withdrew their support and their supplies. The end had come.

The following chapter is written with regret. Readers of Dickens remember the prolonged degradation of the young hero of 'Bleak house,' through hope deferred and the delays of a Chancery suit. Similar causes contributed to the final wreck of Charles. The thought of a Restoration was his Chancery suit. A letter of November 1753, written by the Prince in French, is a mere hysterical outcry of impatience. 'I suffocate!' he exclaims, as if in a fever of unrest. He had indulged in hopes from France, from Spain, from Prussia, from a Highland rising, from a London conspiracy. Every hope had deceived him, every Prince had betrayed him, and now he proved false to himself, to his original nature, and to his friends. The venerable Lord Pitsligo, writing during the Scotch campaign of 1745, said: 'I had occasion to discover the Prince's humanity, I ought to say tenderness: this is giving myself no great airs, for he shows the same disposition to everybody.' Now all is changed, and a character naturally tender and pitiful has become careless of others, and even cruel.

The connection with Miss Walkinshaw was the chief occasion of many troubles. On January 14, 1754, young Edgar wrote from Aisse to his uncle, in Rome, saying that Clementina Walkinshaw 'has got in with the Prince, borne two children to him [probably only one], and got an extreme ascendant over him. The King's friends in England are firmly persuaded of this being true, and are vastly uneasy at it, especially as his sister is about Frederick's widow (the Dowager Princess of Wales), and has but an indifferent character. This story gives me very great concern, and, if true, must be attended with bad consequences, whether she truly be honest or not.' {254}

The fact was that, being now accompanied by a mistress and a child, Charles was easily traced. His personal freedom, if not his life, was endangered, and if he were taken and his papers searched, his correspondents would be in peril. On January 4, 1754, Dormer wrote, warning the Prince that 'a young gentleman in hiding with a mistress and child' was being sought for at Liège, and expressing alarm for himself and his comrades. Dormer also reproached Charles for impatiently urging his adherents to instant action. Goring, as 'Stouf,' wrote the following explicit letter from Paris on January 13, 1754. As we shall see, he had been forbidden by the French Government to come within fifty leagues of the capital, and the Bastille gaped for him if he was discovered.

Goring, it will be remarked, warns Charles that his party are weary of his demands for money. What did he do with it? His wardrobe, as an inventory shows, was scanty; no longer was he a dandy: seventeen shirts, six collars, three suits of clothes, three pocket–handkerchiefs were the chief of his effects. He did not give much in charity to poor adherents, as Goring bitterly observes. We learn that the English insist on the dismissal of Miss Walkinshaw. To discard Dumont, as Charles proposed, was to provide England with an informer. The heads of English gentlemen would be at the mercy of the executioners of Archy Cameron. To turn adrift Charles's Catholic servants was impolitic, cruel, and deeply ungrateful. This is the burden of Goring's necessary but very uncourtly epistle, probably written from 'La Grandemain's' house:

'You say you are determined to know from your professed friends what you are to depend on. I wish it may answer your desires, you are master, Sir, to take what steps you please, I shall not take upon me to contradict you, I shall only lay before you what I hear and see, if it can be of any service to you, I shall have done my duty in letting you know your true interest, if you think it such. In the first place, I find they [the English adherents] were surprized and mortifyed to see the little man [Beson] arrive with a message from you, only to desire money, so soon after the sum you received from the gentlemen I conducted to you, and some things have been said on the head not much to the advancement of any scheme for your service. Secondly they sent me a paper by Sir James Harrington of which what follows is a copy word for word:

'"Sir, your friend's Mistress is loudly and publickly talked off and all friends look on it as a very dangerous and imprudent step, and conclude reasonably that no Corespondance is to be had in that quarter, without risk of discovery, for we have no opinion in England of female politicians, or of such women's secrecy in general. You are yourself much blamed for not informing our friends at first, that they might take the alarum, and stop any present, or future transactions, with such a person. What we now expect from you, is to let us know if our persuasion can prevail to get rid of her."

'For God's sake, Sir, what shall I say, or do, I am at my wits end, the greif I have for it augments my illness, and I can only wish a speedy end to my life. To make it still worse you discard Dumont; he is a man I have little regard for, His conduct has been bad, but he has kept your secret, now, Sir, to be discarded in such a manner he will certainly complain to Murray and others; it will come to your friends' ears, if he does not go to England and tell them himself. He knows Mac. {256} Mead and D. [Dawkins] what will our friends think of you, Sir, for taking so little care of their lives and fortunes by putting a man in dispair who has it in his power to ruin them, and who is not so ignorant as not to know the Government will well reward him. Nay, he can do more: he can find you out yourself, or put your enemies in a way to do it, which will be a very unfortunate adventure.

'As for me it is in his power to have me put into the Bastille when he pleases. Perhaps he may not do this, but sure it is too dangerous to try whether he will or no; they must be men of very tryed Virtue who will suffer poverty and misery when they have a way to prevent it, so easy too, and when they think they only revenge themselves of ingratitude; for you will always find that men generally think their services are too little rewarded, and, when discarded, as he will be if you dont recall ye sentence, what rage will make him do I shall not answer for. If, Sir, you continue in mind to have him sent off I must first advise those gentlemen [the English adherents] that they may take propper measures to put themselves in Safety by leaving the Country, or other methods as they shall like best. Now, Sir, whether such a step as this will not tend more to diminish than augment your Credit in England I leave you to determine; I only beg of you, Sir, to give me timely notice that I may get out of the way of that horrid Bastille, and put our friends on their guard, I cannot but lament my poor friend Colonel H. who must be undone by it. Ld M. [Marischal] thinks it too dangerous a tryall of that man's honour: for my part I shall not presume to give my own opinion, only beg of you once again that we may have time to shift for ourselves. I am obliged to you, Sir, for your most gracious Concern for my health; the doctors have advised me to take the air as much as my weakness will permit, are much against confinement, and would certainly advise me against the Bastille as very contrary to my distemper!

'I have one thing more to lay before you of greatest Consequence: you order all your Catholick Servants to be discarded, consider, Sir, the thing well on both sides; first the good that it will produce on the one side, and the ill it may produce on the other; it may indeed please some few biggotted protestants, for all religions have their biggots, but may it not disgust the great number of ye people, to see you discard faithfull men, for some of them went through all dangers with you in Scotland, upon account of their religion—without the least provision made for them. Your saying, Sir, that necessity obliges you to do it, will look a little strange to those people who send you money, and know how far you can do good with it. I assure you, Sir, if you did necessary acts of Generosity now and then, that people may see plainly that you have a real tenderness for those that suffer for you, you would be the richer for it, more people would send money than now do, and they that have sent would send more, when they saw so good use made of it.

'I have been hard put to it when I have been praising your good qualities to some of our friends, they have desired me to produce one single instance of any one man you have had the Compassion to relieve with the tenderness a King owes to a faithfull subject who has served him with the risk of his life and fortune. {259}

'Now Sir, another greater misfortune may happen from sending off these servants in so distinguishing a manner; you will plese to remember that in the Course of your affairs the Protestants employ the Papists; the Papists join with the Protestants in sending you money and in everything that can hasten your restoration, they are a great body of men and if they should once have reason to believe they should be harder used under your government than they are under the Usurper, self preservation would oblige them to maintain the Usurper on the throne, and be assured if they take this once in their heads, they have it in their power to undoe you.

'A man of sense and great riches as well as birth, a great friend of yours, talking with me some time past of your royal qualities (note this man is a most bigotted Protestant), was observing the happyness all ranks of men would have under your reign; he considered you, Sir, as father to the whole nation, that no one set of men would be oppressed, papists, presbyterians, quakers, anabaptists, antitrinitarians, Zwinglians, and forty more that he named, though they differ, in their Creed, under so great and good a prince as you, would all join to love and respect you; that he was sure you would make no distinction between any of them, but let your Royal bounty diffuse itself equally on all. He said further that for you to disgust any of them, as they all together compose the body, so disgusting any one set of men was as if a man in full vigour of health should cut off one of his leggs or arms. He concluded with saying he was sure you was too prudent to do anything of that kind, to summ up all, he said that he looked on you as a prince divested of passions; that the misfortunes and hardships you had undergone had undoubtedly softened your great Mind so far as to be sensible of the misfortunes of others, for which reason he would do all that lay in his power to serve you; these reflections, Sir, really are what creates you the love of your people in general, and gains you more friends than yr Royal Birth.

'Observe, Sir, what will be the event of your discarding these poor men, all of them diserving better treatment from you: they will come to Paris begging all their way, and show the whole town, English, French, and strangers, an example of your Cruelty, their Religion being all their offence; do you think, Sir, your Protestants will believe you the better protestant for it? If you do, I am affraid you will find yourself mistaken; it will be a handle for your enemies to represent you a hippocrite in your religion and Cruel in your nature, and show the world what those who serve you are to expect.

'Now, Sir, do as you think fitt, but let me beg of you to give such Comitions to somebody else; as I never could be the author of any such advice, so I am incapable of acting in an affair that will do you, Sir, infinite prejudice, and cover me with dishonour, and am, besides these Considerations, grown so infirm that I beg your R.H. will be graciously pleased to give me leave to retire. . . . I may have been mistaken in some things, which I hope you will pardon, I do not write this as my own opinion, but really to get your affairs in a true light. . . I sware to the great God that what I write is truth, for God's sake Sir have compassion on yourself . . . you say you "will take your party," alas, Sir, they will coldly let you take it, don't let your spleen get the better of your prudence and judgement . . .

'One reflection more on what you mention about ye papist servants, may not the keeping publickly in employment ye two papist gentlemen [Sheridan and Stafford] do more harm than turning away three or four papist footmen, who can, by their low situation, have no manner of influence over your affairs . . . one of the papist footmen is besides a relation {261} of the poor man who was lately hanged . . . when all this comes to be publick it will much injure your caracter. To summ up all, these commissions you give me, give me such affliction as will certainly end my life, they are surely calculated by you for that very reason. . . . I once more beg you will graciously please to permit me to retire, I will let my family know that my bad health only is the reason, and I don't doubt they will maintain me.

Charles might have been expected to answer this very frank letter in a fury of anger. He kept his temper, and replied thus:

The Prince to Stouf.

'January 18, 1754.

'Sir,—I received yours of ye 13th. Current, and am resolved not to discard any of my Cervants, that is to say, for ye present . . .

'It is necessary also you should send as soon as possible 300*l*. to be remitted to Stafford and Sheridan . . . you may give out of that sum Morison's wages for half a year . . . My compliments to Sir J. Harrington, assuring him of my friendship and when you are able remit to him fifty Louis d'ors. . . . It is true I sent to E. [England] six Months ago for Money, but it was not for ye Money alone, that served only for a pretext, however I was extremely scandalized not to have received any since I thought fit to Call for it, it is strenge such proceeding. People should, I think, well know that If it was only Money that I had at hart I would not act as I have done, and will do untill I Compass ye prosperity of My Country, which allways shall be My only Studdy: But you know that without Money one can do nothing, and in my situation the more can be had ye better. I have received nothing since ye profet [Daniel] but Mistress P.'s hundred Pounds given to Woulfe. I forgot to mention fifty pounds sterling to be given to Kely. . . . I am glad you have taken my Pelise, for nothing can do you more good than to keep yourself warm.' {263}

Goring answered on February 26. The English, he said, would not send a farthing if Charles persisted in his sentiments about their 'duty.' His repeated despatch of messengers only caused annoyance and alarm. 'They expect a Prince who will take advice, and rule according to law, and not one that thinks his will is sufficient.' Charles replied as follows:

Prince to Stouf.

'March 6, 1754.

'I received yours tother day and am sory to find by it yr Bad State of Health. You are telling me about Laws, I am shure no one is more willing to submit to ye Laws of my Country than myself, and I have ye Vanity to say I know a little of them . . . All what I want is a definitive answer, and it is much fearer [fairer] to say "yes" or "no," than to keep one in suspence, which hinders that distressed person of taking other measures, that might make him perhaps gain his Lawsute. However, I shall neither medle or make in it untill I here from you again, which I hope will be soon, for my friend has lost all patience, and so have I to see him Linger so Long.

'I wish with all my heart it may mend.'

At this time Pickle was not idle. He wrote to Gwynne Vaughan from London on February 25, 1754. He was going over to Paris, to extract information from the Earl Marischal. He signs 'Roderick Random,' and incidentally throws light on his private tastes and morals. His correspondent was, apparently, an old man, 'Worthy old Vaughan,' Pickle calls him later. He often addresses him as 'Grandpapa.' In this letter he ministers to Mr. Vaughan's senile vices.

Add. 32,734. 'Monday. London: February 25, 1754.

'Dr. Sir,—I have apointed a meeting with Mr. Alexander [Lochgarry] from whom I recevd a verbal message, by a friend now in town, that came over by Caron [Mariston] that I am desir'd by Monsr. St. Sebastian [Young Pretender] to go streight to Venice [Ld. Marshal], to settle for this summer every thing relative to his amours with Mrs. Strenge [the Highlands], and that, when we have settled that point, that he is to meet me upon my return from Venice [Ld. Marshal] in Imperial Flanders, where he is soon expected. . . . Every thing lays now upon the carpet, and if I go privately to Venice [Ld. Marshal] I will be at the bottom of the most minute transactions. Without going to Venice [Ld. Marshal] I can dow little or nothing, and *I give you my word of honour*, that I reserv'd out of the last mony not 10*l*. st., but at any rate I cross the watter to save my own credit with *our* Merchants [the Jacobites], and if I am suplayd here, without which I can dow nothing, I am certain to learn what can't be obtained through any other Chanel.

'I recev'd by old Caron [Mariston] two extraordinary patez, which surprisingly answer Pompadour's intentions. {265} I have tray'd the experiment, and as I found it so effective, I have sent one of them by a Carrier that left this Saturday last in the morning, and how [who] arrives at Bath to-morrow, Tuesday, 26th. Instant; It's simply adrest to you at Bath, It operates in the same lively manner upon the faire sex as it does on ours. (The Lord have mercy upon the Lassies at Bath!) The Patez was sent by the Wiltshire Carrier how [who] seets up at the Inn on the Market place at Bath, derected to the Honble. Quine Vaughan. I have had [several] Bucks this day dining upon the relicks of your sister pattez, which is all the apologie I make for this hurried scrawle. I wait your answer with Impatience, but allwaies believe me, with great sincerity and estime—My Dr. Sir,

'Your most affte, oblidged, humble Servt.

'RODERICK RANDOM.'

From France, when he arrived there, Pickle wrote to Gwynne Vaughan as follows:

Add. 32,735. 'Aprile: Monday 8. 1754. 4 o'clock.

'Dear Sir,—I am still in such agitation after fourteen hours passage, and sitting up with our friends *Alexr.* [Lochgarry] and *Agent* [McDonald], how [who] luckly meet me here, that I am scarse able to put pen to paper. I must here confess the difficultys I labour under since the loss of my worthy great friend [Henry Pelham, recently dead] on whose word I wholly relay'd. But now every thing comes far short of my expectations. I am now to aquent you that *Alexr.* [Lochgarry] meet me here, by order, to desire my proceeding to Venice [Ld. Marshal] as every thing without that trip will be imperfect. All I can say at this distance and in so precarious a situation is that I find they play *Mrs. Strange* [the Highlanders] hard and fast. They expect a large quantity of the very best *Brasile snuff* [the Clans] from hir, to balance which severl gross of good sparkling *Champagne* [Arms] is to be smuggled over for hir Ladyship's use. The whole accounts of our Tobacco *and wine trade* [Jacobite schemes] I am told, are to be laid before me by my friend at *Venice* [Ld. Marshal]. But this being a Chant [jaunt] I can't complay with, without a certain suplay, I must beg, if this proposal be found agreeable, that I have ane imediate pointed answer.

'But if, when I leave *Venice* [Ld. Marshal] I go to meet St. Sebastien [the Young Pretender], the remittance must be more considerable that the sume I mention'd whilest you were at Bath . . .

'Yours most affly

'ALEXR. PICKLE.

'To Mr. Tamas Jones, at Mr. Chelburn's, a Chimmist in Scherwood Street, Golden Square, London.'

Pickle wrote again from France on April 11. {267} His letter follows:

'Dr. Sir,—I hope my last to you upon landing came safe to hand. I will be very uneasy untill you accknowledge the recet of it. Tho' you can't expect an explicite or regular Corespondence from me, least our smuguling [secret correspondence] so severely punish'd in this country, should be any ways discover'd. Mr. *Davis* [Sir James Harrington] was here for a few hours last night, the particulars I reffer till meeting. Great expectations from the *Norwegian fir trade* [Sweden] which Merchants here think will turn out to good account, by offering them ane ample Charter to open a free trade; but *Davis* [Sir James Harrington] is not well vers'd in this Business, but I believe my friend at *Venice* [Ld. Marshal] is: I am certain that Mr. Oliver [King of Spain] and his principal factors would harken to any proposals of St. Sebastien's [the Young Pretender] upon this topick. Mr. *Davis* [Sir James Harrington] is of opinion that a quantity of *best mettle buttons* [Parliament men] {268} could be readly and cheaply purchas'd: *Mr. Johnson* [London] will make considerable advances, but I believe this can't arrive in time for the Market, as aplication has not yet been made to *Monsr. la force* [Paris Mont Martell]. I think I can easily divert them from this, as I can convince St. Sebastien [Young Pretender] in case I see him, that they would leave him in the lurch. This proposal comes from your side the watter. I find *Mrs. Strange* [Highlanders] will readly except of any offer from *Rosenberge* [King of Sweden] as that negotiant can easily evade paying duty for any wine he sends hir. I can answer for *Mrs. Strange's* [Highlanders] conduct, as it will wholly depend upon *me*, to promote or discourage this branch of trade. But I can't be answerable for other branches of our trade, as my knowledge in them depends upon others. I will drop this subject till meeting, and if then all my burdens are discharg'd, and done otherwise for, according to my former friend's intentions, and if satisfactory, nothing will be neglected in the power of Dr. Grand Papa

Your oblidged affte, humble Servant

'ALEXR. PICKLE.

'11 Aprile 1754.

'P.S. I can't conclude without declaring once for all that I shant walk but in the old course, that is, not to act now with any other but Mr. *Kenady* [the Duke of Newcastle] and yourself, the moment any other comes in play, I drop all business; But nothing essential can be done without going to Venice [Lord Marshal].

'To Mr. Tamas Jones, at Mr. Chelburn's a Chymist, in Scherwood Street, Golden Square, London.'

To exaggerate his own importance, Pickle gave here a glowing account of the Prince's prospects. These were really of the most gloomy character. A letter forwarded by Dormer (March 18) had proved that he was tracked down in Liège by the English Government. He tried Lorraine, but found no refuge, and was in Paris on April 14, when he wrote to the Earl Marischal. He thought of settling in Orleans, and asked for advice. But Goring now broke with him for ever, on the strength, apparently, of a verbal dismissal sent in anger by Charles, who believed, or affected to believe, that Goring was responsible for the discovery of his retreat. Goring wrote in these terms:

Stouf to Charles.

'May 5, 1754.

'It is now five years since I had ye honour of waiting on you in a particular manner, having made your interest my only study, neglecting everything that regarded myself. The people I have negotiated your business with, will do me the justice to own what you seem to deny, that I have honourably acquitted myself of my charge. I do not now or ever did desire to be a burthen on you, but I thank God I leave you in a greater affluence of money than I found you, which, though not out of my own purse, has been owing to my industry and trouble, not to mention the dangers I have run to effect it; all I desire now of you for my services is that you will be so gracious as to discharge me from your service, not being able to be of further use to you, yourself having put it out of my power; what I ernestly beg of you, since you let me know that you cannot support me further, [is] to give me at least what I think my services may justly claim, viz. a gracious demission, with which I will retire and try in some obscure corner of ye world to gain the favour of God, who will I hope be more just to me than you have been; though I despair of ever serving him so well as I have done you. My prayers and wishes shall ever attend you, and since I am able to do you no more good I will never do you any harm, but remain most faithfully yours

'STOUF.'

Charles answered angrily:

'May 10, 1754.

'Sir,—I have yrs of ye 5th. May Directed "For His Royal Highness the Prince of Wales. Signed Stouf."

'I shoud *think* since the Begining was write (id est, ye superficial superscription) the *signing might accompani it*, but *Brisons Sur Les Bagatelles*, I must speke French to you, since I am affraid you understand no other Language; for my part I am true English, and want of no Equivocations, or Mental resarvations: will you serve me or not? will you obey me? have you any other Interest? Say yes or no, I shall be yr friend iff you will serve me; Iff you have anybody preferable to me to serve, Let me alone, have you ye Interest of yr Contre at hart, or a particular one, for my part I have but one God and one Country, and Untill I compas ye prosperity of my Poor Cuntry shall never be at rest, or Let any Stone unturned to compas my Ends.'

Goring answered, and here his part of the correspondence closes.

Stouf to the Prince.

'May 16.

'I recd ye most gracious letter you honoured me with dated ye 10th. of this present, and must beg your pardon if I do not rightly understand ye Contents; first it is so different from ye Orders you were pleased to send me by Mr. Obrien who by your Command told it to Mittie, {271} who Communicated it to me, as well as I can remember in these words, or to this purpose, "that you would neither see me, or write to me neither would you send me any money to Carry me out of this Town" [Paris]. This very Town I am, as you well know, by a special order from the King of France, under severe penalties never to approach nearer than fifty leagues; for no other crime than adhering to you when Abandoned by every body; this very town that was witness to my zeal and fidelity to you at the utmost hazzard of my life, is the very place where you abandoned me to my ill fortune without one penny of money to get out of the reach of the *lettre de Cachet*, or to subsist here any longer in Case I could keep myself hid. You conceive very well, Sir, ye terrible situation I was in, had I not found a friend who, touched at my misfortunes, supplied me for my present necessities, and I know no reason for the ill usage I have now twice received from you, but that I have served you too well.

'Your friends on the other side of the water, at least those who not long since were so, can, and will when necessary, testifye with what zeal and integrity I have negotiated your affairs with them, and persons of undoubted worth on this side the water have been witness to my conduct here; and when I examine my own breast I have, I thank God, nothing to reproach myself with, nobody has been discovered by any misconduct of mine, nobody taken up, or even suspected by ye Government of having any correspondence with you, whether this has been owing to experience or chance I leave you Sir to determine. Here are Sir no Equivocations, or Mental reservations; I have, I may justly say, the reputation of a man of honour which I will carry with me to ye grave. In spite of malice and detraction, no good man ever did, nor do I believe ever will, tax me with having done an ill thing and what bad men and women say of me is quite indifferent. {273}

'You say, Sir, you will be my friend if I will serve you, and obey you. I have, Sir, served and obeyed you, in everything that was just, at the hazard very often of my life, and to the intire destruction of my health, must I then, Sir, begin again to try to gain your favour? I am affraid, Sir, what five years service has not done, five hundred years will not attain to. I have twice, Sir, been turned off like a Common footman, with most opprobrious language, without money or cloaths. As I am a bad courtier and can't help speaking truth, I am very sure it would not be long before I experienced a third time your friendship for me, if I was unadvized enough to make the tryall. No, Sir, princes are never friends, it would be too much to expect it, but I did believe till now that they had humanity enough to reward Good services, and when a man had served to the utmost of his power, not to try to cast dishonour on him to save the charges of giving him a recompense. Secure in my innocence and Content with a small fortune, having no ambition (nor indeed ever had any but of seeing my Prince great and good) I with your leave, Sir, small retire, and spend the rest of my life in serving God, and wishing you all prosperity, since I unfortuneately cannot be for the future of any use to you. 'STOUF.'

Charles now invited the Lord Marischal to communicate with him through a fresh channel, as Goring was for ever alienated. But the Earl replied in a tone of severe censure. He defended Goring: he rebuked Charles for not attending to English remonstrances about Miss Walkinshaw, and accused him of threatening to publish the names of his English adherents. Charles answered, 'Whoever told you I gave such a message to Ed. as you mention, has told you a damned lie, God forgive them. I would not do the least hurt to my greatest enemy, were he in my power, much less to any one that professes to be mine.' He had already said, 'My heart is broke enough without that you should finish it.' {274}

This was, practically, the end of the Jacobite party. Goring went to Berlin, and presently died in Prussian service. The Scottish adherents, in the following year, made a formal remonstrance in writing, but the end had come. Pickle (May 11) reported the quarrel with Lord Marischal to his employers. Lord Albemarle (May 29) mentioned his hopes of catching Charles by aid of his tailor! This failed, but Charles was so hard driven that he communicated to Walsh his intention to retreat over the Spanish frontier. After various wanderings he settled with Miss Walkinshaw in Basle, where he gave himself out for am English physician in search of health.

There are some curious notes by Charles, dated November 26, 1754. Among them is this:

'Cambel: his plot: ye poison, and my forbiding instantly by Cameron.'

Had Mr. Campbell, selected by Goring as a model of probity, proposed to *poison* 'the Elector'? Not once only, or twice, perhaps, had the Prince refused to sanction schemes of assassination. We need not forget these last traces of nobility in this 'man undone.'

CHAPTER XII—PICKLE AS A HIGHLAND CHIEF. 1755–1757

Progress of Pickle—Charles's last resource—Cluny called to Paris —The Loch Arkaig hoard—History of Cluny—Breaks his oath to King George—Jacobite theory of such oaths—Anecdote of Cluny in hiding— Charles gives Pickle a gold snuff–box—'A northern —– '—Asks for a pension—Death of Old Glengarry—Pickle becomes chief—The curse of Lochgarry—Pickle writes from Edinburgh—His report—Wants money— Letter from a 'Court Trusty'—Pickle's pride—Refused a fowling–piece —English account of Pickle—His arrogance and extortion—Charles's hopes from France—Macallester the spy—The Prince's false nose— Pickle still unpaid—His candour—Charles and the Duc de Richelieu— A Scottish deputation—James Dawkins publicly abandons the Prince— Dawkins's character—The Earl Marischal denounces Charles—He will not listen to Cluny—Dismisses his servants—Sir Horace Mann's account of them—'The boy that is lost'—English rumours—Charles declines to lead attack on Minorca—Information from Macallester— Lord Clancarty's attacks on the Prince—On Lochgarry—Macallester acts as a prison spy—Jesuit conspiracy against Charles.

As the sad star which was born on the Prince's birth–night waned and paled, the sun of Pickle's fortunes climbed the zenith, he came into his estates by Old Glengarry's death in

September 1754, while, deprived of the contributions of the Cocoa Tree Club, Charles fell back on his last resource, the poor remains of the Loch Arkaig treasure. On September 4, 1754, being 'in great straits,' he summoned Cluny to Paris, bidding him bring over 'all the effects whatsoever that I left in your hands, also whatever money you can come at.'

Cluny's history was curious. The Culloden Papers prove that, when Charles landed in Moidart, Cluny had recently taken the oaths to the Hanoverian Government. He corresponded with the Lord President, Duncan Forbes of Culloden, and was as loyal to George II. as possible. But, on August 29, 1745, Lady Cluny informed Culloden that her lord had been captured by the Prince's men. A month later, however, Cluny had not yet 'parted with his commission' in a Highland regiment. {277a} Hopes were still entertained of his deserting the Prince, 'for if Cluny could have an independent company to guard us from thieves, it's what I know he desires above all things.' {277b} Cluny, however, continued faithful to the Jacobite party. Like Lord George Murray, he was a Whig in August, a partisan of the Stuarts in September. They had, these gentlemen, a short way with oaths, thus expressed by one of their own poets:

'Let not the abjuration
Impose upon our nation,
Restrict our hands, whilst *he* commands,
Through false imagination:
For oaths which are imposed
Can never be supposed
To bind a man, say what they can
While justice is opposed.'

Acting on these principles, Cluny joined in the march to Derby, and was distinguished in the fight at Clifton. After Culloden he stayed in Scotland, by Charles's desire, dwelling in his famous Cage on Ben Alder, so well described by Mr. Stevenson in 'Kidnapped.' The loyalty of his clan was beyond praise. A gentleman of Clan Vourich, whose grandfather fought at Culloden, gives me the following anecdote.

The soldiers were, one day, hard on Cluny's tracks, and they seized a clansman, whom they compelled to act as guide. He pretended an innocence bordering on idiotcy, and affected to be specially pleased with the drum, a thing of which he could not even conceive the use. To humour him, they slung the drum over his shoulders. Presently he thumped it violently. Cluny heard the warning and escaped, while the innocence of the crafty gillie was so well feigned, that he was not even punished.

Cluny came over to France in the autumn of 1754, with what amount of treasure he could collect. In later days, a very poor exile, he gave a most eloquent tribute to Charles's merits. 'In deliberations he found him ready, and his opinions generally best; in their execution firm, and in secrecy impenetrable; his humanity and consideration show'd itself in strong light, even to his enemies . . . In application and fatigues none could exceed him.' {278}

While Charles retired in 1755 with Miss Walkinshaw to Basle, where he passed for an English physician in search of health, Pickle was not idle. He had sent in a sheet of notes in April 1754. 'Colonel Buck was lately in England, he brought Pickle a fine gold stuff–box from the Young Pretender, which Pickle showed me,' that is, to the official who received his statement. In later years, the family of Glengarry may have been innocently proud of the Prince's gift. Pickle added that 'there could be no rising in Scotland without the Macdonnells: he is sure that he shall have the first notice of anything of the kind, and he is sure that the Young Pretender would attempt nothing without him.' At the French Court Pickle only knew the financier, Paris Montmartell, and d'Argenson (not the *Bête*, but his brother), through d'Argenson's mistress, Madame de Pierrecourt. 'Pickle wishes to be admitted to an audience, and so do I,' writes an English official, 'as he grows troublesome, and I don't care to have any correspondence with him or any other northern —– !'

To this report is appended an appeal of Pickle's. He asks for a regular annuity of 500*l*., being out of pocket by his 'chants'— Highland for 'jaunts.' Pickle never got the money; so ungrateful are Governments.

On May 11, Pickle congratulated his employers on having made Charles 'remove his quarters.' He adds that Charles and Lord Marischal have quarrelled. About this time, after Henry Pelham's death in March 1754, Pickle favoured his employers with a copy of an English memorial to Charles. It was purely political; the Prince was advised to purchase seats in Parliament for his friends. But in May, Charles had neither friends nor money, and he never cared for the constitutional measures recommended.

On September 1, 1754, Old Glengarry died, and Pickle, accompanied by a 'Court Trusty,' went North to look after his private affairs, for he was now Chief of the Macdonnells. {280a} He wrote from Edinburgh on September 14. Pickle wants money, as usual, and brags as usual: he tells us that Spain had recently supplied Charles with money. The Young Lochgarry of whom he speaks is Lochgarry's son, who took service with England. The Old Lochgarry threw his dirk after the youth, adding a curse on Lochgarry House as long as it sheltered a servant of the Hanoverian usurper. Family legend avers that the house was henceforth haunted by a rapping and knocking ghost, which made the place untenable. {280b} Part of Pickle's letter follows:

Add. 32,736. 'Edinburgh: September 14, 1754.

'Dr. Sir,—I have heard fully from Lochgary, who acquaints me that the Young Pretender's affairs *take a very good turn*, and that he has lately sent two Expresses to Lochgary earnestly intreating a meeting with Pickle, and upon Lochgary's acquainting him of the great distance Pickle was off, he commanded Lochgary to a rendezvous, and he set out to meet me the 4th. Instant, and is actually now with me. I shall very soon have a particular account of the present plan of operation. I have now the ball at my foot, and may give it what tune I please, as I am to be allowed largely, if I fairly enter in Co–partnership. The French King is in a very peaceable humour, but very ready to take fire if the Jacobites renew their address, which the Young Pretender assures him of, and he will the readier bestirr himself, as the English Jacobites hourly torment him. Troops, Scotch and Irish, are daily offered to be smuggled over; but I have positively yet refused to admit any. The King of Spain has lately promised to add greatly to the Young Pretender's patrimony, and English Contributors are not wanting on their parts. {281} I suspect that my letters of late to my friends abroad are stopt, *pray enquire, for I think it very unfair dealings.*

'I am in a few weeks to go north to put some order to my affairs. I should have been put to the greatest inconveniency if “21” had not lent his friendly assistance; but as I have been greatly out of pocket by the Jants I took for Mr. Pelham, I shan't be in condition to continue trade, if I am not soon enabled to pay off the Debts then contracted. I have said on former occasions so much upon this head to no effect that I must now be more explicit, and I beg your friendly assistance in properly representing it to the Duke of Newcastle. If he thinks that my services, of which I have given convincing proofs, will answer to his advancing directly eight hundred Pounds, which is the least that can clear the Debts of my former Jants, and fix me to the certain payment yearly of Five hundred at two several terms, he may command anything in my power upon all occasions. I am sorry to be forced to this explanation, in which I always expected to be prevented. I am so far from thinking this extravagant, that I am perswaded it will save them as many thousands, by discarding that swarm of Videts, which never was in the least trusted. If the Duke of Newcastle's constituent was acquainted with this, I daresay he would esteem the demand reasonable, considering what he throws away upon others of no interest or power on either side . . .

'P.S. Pray let me not be denied the Arms I wanted, and I hope in case of accidents, you'll take care of young Lochgary.'

Now comes a letter of the 'Court Trusty' who accompanied Pickle to Scotland, a spy upon a spy. The Trusty's real name was Bruce, and, what with Pickle's pride and General Bland's distrust, he was in a very unpleasant quandary.

Add. 32,737. 'October 10, 1754.

'Dr. Sir,—I have only to acquaint you since my last, that by my keeping company with Pickle, the General has upon several occasions expressed himself very oddly of me, all which might have been prevented by a hint to him. You must perceive what a pleasant pickle I am in; It is really hard that I should suffer for doing my duty. Pickle has promised to write to you this night, if he neglects it I cannot help it. I have done what I judged right by him. I have all the reason in the world to think he will be advised by me, but he now finds his situation altered, and as such must be managed accordingly. You know him well, all therefore I shall say is, that he is naturally proud, and his Father's Death makes him no less so. I wrot you long ago for advice, whether I should go north with him, or not, to which you made me no return. This day he told me that he leaves this on Monday, and insisted for my following him. I did not positively promise, waiting to see if you write me next Post, which if you don't I will follow him, which I hope you'll approve of, as I will be the more able to judge of his affairs. I shall not remain long with him, after which you shall have a faithful Report. The General is best judge of the part he has acted, tho' I could have wished he had acted otherwise for the Interest of the common Cause, but it does not become me to prescribe Rules. I wish he had got a hint. I find the Army people here are piqu'd that I should have Pickle's ear so much, for they all push to make up to him, thinking to make something of him. I know the Governor of Fort Augustus is wrot to, to try his hand upon him, when he goes north, but he is determined to keep at a distance from them, and to keep in the hands he is now in, and I am perswaded he can, and will prove usefull, but there is a particular way of doing it, which you know is the way of the generality benorth Tay. Your Own

'CROMWELL. {284}

'Edinburgh: October 10, 1754.'

Pickle now writes again from Edinburgh, on October 10, 1754. He wants money, and, as becomes a Highland chief, takes a high tone. He has been in service as a spy for four years—that is, since autumn 1750. He asks for 500*l.* a year, and for that will do anything 'honourable.' Young Lochgarry is not well received (he wished to enter the English army), and Pickle is refused a fowling–piece to shoot his own grouse, because he has not 'qualified' or taken the oaths. This, of course, Pickle could not do, as he had, in his capacity of spy, to keep on terms with Prince Charles. Did Young Lochgarry know Pickle to be a traitor?

'When I waited,' says Pickle, 'of General Bland, he did not receve me as I expected, haughtly refusd the use of a fulsie [fusil] without I should qualifie. I smiling answer'd, if that was the case, I had then a right without his permission, but that he could not take it amiss that I debar'd all under his Comand the pleasure of hunting upon my grounds, or of any firing, which they can't have without my permission, so that I thought favours were reciprocall.'

Oddly enough, we have external testimony to the arrogance of Pickle, now a little Highland prince among his own clan.

On December 13, 1754, the Governor of Fort Augustus, Colonel Trapaud, wrote to Dundas of Arniston, the Lord Advocate:

'Glengarry has behaved, among his clan, since his father's death, with the utmost arrogance, insolence, and pride. On his first arrival to this country he went to Knoydart, and there took the advantage of his poor ignorant tenants, to oblige them to give up all their wadsetts, and accept of common interest for their money, which they all agreed to. On his return to Invergarry he called a meeting of all his friends and tennants in Glengarry, told them what the Knoydart people had done, threw them a paper and desired they might all voluntarily sign it, else he would oblige them by law, but most of the principal wadsetters [mortgage–holders] refused, on which he ordered them out of his presence. . . . He has declared that no peat out of his estate should come to this fort. . . . His whole behaviour has greatly alienated the affections of his once dearly beloved followers. I shall take all opportunities of improving this happy spirit of rebellion against so great a chieftain, which may in time be productive of some public good.' {285}

Pickle was not only a traitor, but a bully and an oppressor. Thus Pickle, in addition to his other failings, was the very worst type of bad landlord, according to the Governor of Fort Augustus.

We return to the fortunes of the Prince.

The opening of 1755 found Charles still in concealment, probably at Basle. He could only profess to James his determination 'never to go astray from honour and duty' (March 12, 1755). James pertinently replied, 'Do you rightly understand the extensive sense of honour and duty?' War clouds were gathering. France and England were at issue in America, Africa, and India. Braddock's disaster occurred; he was defeated and slain by an Indian ambush. Both nations were preparing for strife; the occasion seemed good for fishing in troubled waters. D'Argenson notes that it is a fair opportunity to make use of

Charles. Now we scrape acquaintance with a new spy, Oliver Macallester, an Irish Jacobite adventurer. {286} Macallester, after a long prelude, tells us that his 'private affairs' brought him to Dunkirk in 1755. On returning to London he was apprehended at Sheerness, an ungrateful caitiff having laid information to the effect that our injured hero 'had some connection with the Ministers of the French Court, or was upon some dangerous enterprize.' He was examined at the Secretary of State's Office (Lord Holland's), was released, and returned to Dunkirk, uncompensated for all this disturbance. Here he abode, on his private business, living much in the company of the ranting Lord Clancarty. Lord Clare (Comte de Thomond, of the House of Macnamara) was also in Dunkirk at the time, and attached himself to the engaging Macallester, whom he invited to Paris. Our fleet was then unofficially harassing that of France in America.

Meanwhile, France negotiated the secret treaty with Austria, while Frederick joined hands with England. Dunkirk began to wear a very warlike aspect, in despite of treaties which bound France to keep it dismantled. 'Je savais que nous avions triché avec les Anglais,' says d'Argenson. The fortifications were being secretly reconstructed. D'Argenson adds that now is the moment to give an asylum to the wandering Prince Charles. 'The Duchesse d'Aiguillon, a great friend of the Prince, tells me that some days ago, while she was absent from her house at Ruel, an ill–dressed stranger came, and waited for her till five in the morning. Her servants recognised the Prince.' {287}

The Duchesse d'Aiguillon, Walpole says ('Letters,' iv. 390), used to wear a miniature of Prince Charles in a bracelet. On the reverse was a head of Our Lord. People did not understand the connection, so Madame de Rochefort said, 'The same motto serves for both, *my kingdom is not of this world*.' But Charles had not been 'ill–dressed' in these old days!

As early as April 23, 1755, M. Ruvigny de Cosne, from Paris, wrote to Sir Thomas Robinson to the effect that Charles's proposals to the French Court in case of war with England had been declined. An Abbé Carraccioli was being employed as a spy on the Prince. {288} Pickle also came into play. We offer a report of his information, given in London on April 23, 1755. He knew that Charles had been at Fontainebleau since preparations for war began, and describes his false nose and other disguises. Charles was acquainted with the Maréchal de Saxe, and may have got the notion of the nose from that warrior.

Here follows Pickle, as condensed by Mr. Roberts:

Add. 32,854. 'April 24, 1755.

'Mr. Roberts had a meeting last night with the Scotch gentleman, called *Pickle.* The Young Pretender, he says, has an admirable Genius for skulking, and is provided with so many disguises, that it is not so much to be wondered at, that he has hitherto escaped unobserved, sometimes he wears a long false hose, which they call "*Nez à la Saxe*," because Marshal Saxe used to give such to his Spies, whom he employed. At other times he blackens his eye brows and beard, and wears a black wig, by which alteration his most intimate Acquaintance could scarce know him: and in these dresses he has mixed often in the companies of English Gentlemen travelling thro' Flanders, without being suspected.

'*Pickle* promises to discover whatever shall come to his knowledge, that may be worth knowing, he can be most serviceable, he says, by residing in Scotland, for no applications can be made to any of the Jacobites there, from abroad, but he must receive early notice of them, being now, by his Father's death, at the head of a great Clan of his name, but he is ready to cross the Sea, whenever it should be thought it worth the while to send him: which he himself is not otherwise desirous of doing, as he declares that those Journies have cost him hitherto double the money that he has received.

'He hopes to have something given him to make up this deficiency, and, if he could have a fixed yearly Allowance, he will do everything that lies in his power to deserve it. He insists upon an inviolable secrecy, without which his opportunities of sending useful Intelligences will be lost.'

Pickle does not come on the public scene again for a whole year, except in the following undated report, where he speaks of Glengarry (himself) in the third person. His account of an envoy sent to make proposals to Charles, like those made to the Prince of Orange in 1688, is an error. Perhaps Pickle was not trusted. The envoy from Scotland to Charles only proposed, as we shall see, that he should forswear sack, and live cleanly and like a gentleman.

Add. 32,861.

'Dear Sir,—I am hopeful you nor friends will take it ill, that I take the freedom to acquaint you, that my patience is quite worn out by hankering upon the same subject, for these years past, and still remaining in suspence without ever coming to a point.

'I beg leave to assure you, that you may do it to others—but, let my inclinations be ever so strong, my intentions ever so upright, my situation will not allow me to remain longer upon this precarious footing; and, as I never heard from you in any manner of way, I might readily take umbrage at your long silence, and from thence naturally conclude it was intended to drop me. But, as I am not of a suspicious temper, and judge of others' candour by my own, and that I always have the highest opinion of yours, and to convince you of mine, I shan't hesitate to acquaint you, that I would have wrot sooner, but that I waited the result of a Gentilman's journey, how at this present juncture has the eyes of this part of the Country fixt upon him—I mean, *Glengary*, into whose confidence I have greatly insinuated myself. This Gentilman is returnd home within these few days, from a great tour round several parts of the Highlands, and had concourse of people from several Clans to wait of him. But this you'll hear from Military channels readly before mine, and what follows, take it as I was informed in the greatest confidence by this Gentilman.

'This Country has been twice tampered with since I have been upon this utstation [Invergarry], and I find it was refer'd to *Glengary*, as the Clans thought he had a better motion of French policy, of which they seem to be greatly diffident. The offers being verbal, and the bearer being non of the greatest consequence, it was prorog'd; upon which the greatest anxiety has been since exprest to have *Glengary* t'other side, at a Conference, that he, in the name of the Clans, should demand his owne terms.

'I am for certain inform'd that a Gentilman of distinction from England went over about two months ago with signatures, Credentials, and assurances, much of the same nature as that formerly sent to the Prince of Orange, only the number mentiond by this person did not amount above sixty. I know nothing of the Person's names, but this from good authority I had for certain told me, and that they offer'd to advance a very considerable sum of mony. It was in consequence of this that proposals were made here. Prudence will not admitt of my enlarging further upon this subject, as I am at so great a distance, I must beg leave to drop it . . .'

On May 20, 1755, James wrote to the Prince. He had heard of an interview between Charles and the Duc de Richelieu, 'and that you had not been much pleased with your conversation with him.' James greatly prefers a peaceful Restoration, but, in the event of war, would not decline foreign aid. The conduct of Charles, he complains, makes it impossible for him to treat with friendly Powers. He is left in the dark, and dare not stir for fear of making a false movement. {292a} On July 10, 1755, Ruvigny de Cosne is baffled by Charles's secrecy, and is hunting for traces of Miss Walkinshaw. On July 23, 1755, Ruvigny de Cosne hears that Charles has been with Cluny in Paris. On August 16 he hears of Charles at Parma. Now Charles, on August 15, was really negotiating with his adherents, whose Memorial, written at his request, is in the Stuart Papers. {292b} They assure him that he is 'eyed' in his family. If he continues obstinate 'it would but too much confirm the impudent and villainous aspersions of Mr. D's' (James Pawkins), which, it seems, had nearly killed Sir Charles Goring, Henry Goring's brother, 'with real grief.' Dawkins had represented the Prince 'as entirely abandoned to an irregular debauched life, even to excess, which brought his health, and even his life daily in danger,' leaving him 'in some degree devoid of reason,' 'obstinate,' 'ungrateful,' 'unforgiving and revengeful for the very smallest offence.' In brief, Dawkins had described Charles as utterly impossible—'all thoughts of him must be for ever laid aside' —and Dawkins backed his opinion by citing that of Henry Goring. The memorialists therefore adjure Charles to reform. Their candid document is signed 'C.M.P.' (obviously Cluny MacPherson) and 'H.P.,' probably Sir Hugh Paterson, Clementina Walkinshaw's uncle.

Now there is no reason for disputing this evidence, none for doubting the honesty of Mr. Dawkins in his despairing account of Charles. He was young, wealthy, adventurous, a scholar. In the preface to their joint work on Palmyra, Robert Wood—the well-known archæologist, author of a book on Homer which drew Wolf on to his more famous theory —speaks of Mr. Dawkins in high terms of praise, he gets the name of 'a good fellow' in Jacobite correspondence as early as 1748. Writing from Berne on May 28, 1756, Arthur Villettes quotes the Earl Marischal (then Governor of Neufchâtel for Frederick) as making strictures like those of Dawkins on the Prince. At this time the Earl was preparing to gain his pardon from George II., and spoke of Charles 'with the utmost horror and detestation.' His life, since 1744, 'had been one continued scene of falsehood, ingratitude, and villainy, and his father's was little better.' As regards James, this is absurd; his letters are those of a heartbroken but kind and honourable parent and Prince. Villettes then cites the Earl's account of the mission from Scotland (August 1755) urging reform on Charles, through the lips of Cluny. The actual envoy from Scotland cited here is probably not Cluny, but his co–signatory 'H.P.,' and he is said to have met Charles at Basle, and to have been utterly disgusted by his reception. {293}

Now the Earl had a private pique at Charles, ever since he refused to sail to Scotland with the Prince in a herring–boat, in 1744. He had also been estranged by Charles's treatment of Goring in 1754. Moreover, he was playing for a pardon. We might conceivably discount the Lord Marischal, and Dr. King's censures in his 'Anecdotes,' for the bitterness of renegades is proverbial. But we cannot but listen to Dawkins and the loyal Henry Goring. By 1754 the Prince, it is not to be denied, was impossible.

Honourable men like the old Laird of Gask, Bishop Forbes, Lord Nairne, and Andrew Lumisden (later his secretary) were still true to a Prince no longer true to himself. Even Lumisden he was to drive from him; he could keep nobody about him but the unwearied Stuart, a servant of his own name. The play was played out; honour and all was lost. There is, unhappily, no escape from this conclusion.

Charles declined to listen to the deputation headed by Cluny in August 1755. A secretary must have penned his reply; it is well–spelled, and is grammatical. 'Some unworthy people have had the insolence to attack my character. . . . Conscious of my conduct I despise their low malice. . . . I have long desired a churchman at your hands to attend me, but my expectations have hitherto been disappointed.'

Soon he returned to the Mass, as we learn from Macallester.

He was ill and poor. {294} He finally dismissed his servants, including a companion of his Highland wanderings. He recommends Morrison, his valet, as a good man to shave and coif his father. The poor fellows wandered to Rome, and were sent back to France with money. Here is Sir Horace Mann's letter about these honest lads:

'Florence: December 20, 1755.

'. . . My correspondent at Rome, having given me previous notice of the departure from thence of some Livery Servants belonging to the Pretender's eldest Son, and that they were to pass through Tuscany, I found means to set two English men to watch for their arrival, who pretending to be their friends, insinuated themselves so well into their company, as to pass the whole evening with them. They were five in number, and all Scotch. The names of three were Stuart, Mackdonnel, and Mackenzy. They were dressed alike in the Pretender's livery, and said they had been with his Son in Scotland, upon which the people I employed asked where he was. They answered only, that they were going to Avignon, and should soon know, and in their merriment drank "the health of the Boy that is lost and cannot be found," upon which one of them answered that he would soon be found. Another reproved him, and made signs to him to hold his tongue. They seemed to be in awe of each other.'

There was not much to be got out of the Highlanders, a race of men who can drink and hold their tongues.

On January 30, 1756, Walton, from Florence, reported that Charles was to be taken up by Louis XV., to play *un rôle fort distingué*, and —to marry a daughter of France! {296a} On January 31, Mann had the latest French courier's word for it that Charles was in Paris; but Walton added that James denied this. Pickle came to London (April 2, 1756), but only to dun for money. 'Not the smallest artickle has been performed of what was expected and at first promised.' Pickle was useless now in Scotland, and remained unsalaried; so ungrateful are kings. The centre of Jacobite interest now was France. In the 'Testament Politique du Maréchal Duc de Belleisle,' (1762) it is asserted that Charles was offered the leadership of the attack on Minorca (April 1756), and that he declined, saying, 'The English will do me justice, if they think fit, but I will no longer serve as a mere scarecrow' (*épouvantail*). In January 1756, however, Knyphausen, writing to Frederick from Paris, discredited the idea that France meant to employ the Prince. {296b}

Turn we to Mr. Macallester for more minute indications.

Macallester was now acting as led captain and henchman to the one–eyed Lord Clancarty, who began to rail in good set terms against all and sundry. For his own purposes, 'for just and powerful reasons,' Macallester kept a journal of these libellous remarks, obviously for use against Clancarty. Living at that nobleman's table, Macallester played his favourite part of spy for the mere love of the profession. He writes:

'Tuesday, January 11, 1757.—When we had drunk hard after supper he broke out, saying, "By God! dear Mac, I'll tell you a secret you don't know; there is not a greater scoundrel on the face of the earth than that same Prince; he is in his heart a coward and a poltroon; would rather live in a garret with some Scotch thieves, to drink and smoak, than serve me, or any of those who have lost our estates for his family and himself. . . . He is so great a scoundrel that he will lie even when drunk: a time when all other men's hearts are most open, and will speak the truth, or what they think . . .

'He damned himself if he did not love an Irish drummer better than any of the breed. "The Prince has no more religion," said this pious enthusiast, "than one of my coach–horses." . . . He asked me if I knew Jemmy Dawkins. I said I did not. "He could give you an account of them," said he, "but Lord Marischal has given the true character of the Prince, and certified under his hand to the people of England what a scoundrel he is {297} . . . The Prince had the *canaille* of Scotland to assist him, thieves, robbers, and the like. . . "'

The Prince had confided to Clancarty the English Jacobites' desire that he would put away Miss Walkinshaw. 'The Prince, swearing, said he would not put away a cat to please such fellows;' but, as Lord Clancarty never opened his mouth without a curse, his evidence is not valuable. On March 8, hearing that Lochgarry was in the neighbourhood, Clancarty called him a 'thief and a cow–stealer,' and bade the footman lock up the plate! The brave Lochgarry, however, came to dinner, as being unaware of his Lordship's sentiments.

Enough of the elegant conversation of this one–eyed, slovenly Irish nobleman, whom we later find passing his Christmas with Prince Charles. {298} Mr. Macallester now made two new friends, the adventurous Dumont and a Mr. Lewis. In July 1757, Lewis and Macallester went to Paris, and were much with Lord Clare (de Thomond). In December, Lord Clancarty came hunting for our spy, 'raging like a madman' after Macallester, much to that hero's discomposure, for, being as silly as he was base, he had let out the secret of his 'Clancarty Elegant Extracts.' His Lordship, in fact, accused Macallester of showing all his letters to Lord Clare, whom Clancarty hated. He then gave Macallester the lie, and next apologised; in fact, he behaved like Sir Francis Clavering. Before publishing his book, Macallester tried to 'blackmail' Clancarty. 'His Lordship is now secretly and fully advertised that this matter is going to the press,' and, indeed, it was matter to make the Irish peer uncomfortable in France, where he had consistently reviled the King.

It is probable that Macallester was now engaged in the French secret police.

He admits that he acted as a *mouton*, or prison spy, and gives a dreadful account of the horrors of Galbanon, where men lay in the dark and dirt for half a lifetime. Macallester next proses endlessly on the alleged Jesuit connection with Damien's attack on Lous XV., and insists that the Jesuits, nobody knows why, meant to assassinate Prince Charles. He was in very little danger from Jesuits!

CHAPTER XIII—THE LAST HOPE. 1759

Charles asks Louis for money—Idea of employing him in 1757—Letter from Frederick—Chances in 1759—French friends—Murray and 'the Pills'—Charles at Bouillon—Madame de Pompadour—Charles on Lord George Murray—The night march to Nairn—Manifestoes—Charles will only land in England—Murray wishes to repudiate the National Debt— Choiseul's promises—Andrew Lumisden—The marshal's old boots— Clancarty—Internal feuds of Jacobites—Scotch and Irish quarrels— The five of diamonds—Lord Elibank's views—The expedition starting— Routed in Quiberon Bay—New hopes—Charles will not land in Scotland or Ireland—'False subjects'—Pickle waits on events—His last letter—His ardent patriotism—Still in touch with the Prince—Offers to sell a regiment of Macdonalds—Spy or colonel?—Signs his real name—'Alexander Macdonnell of Glengarry'—Death of Pickle—His services recognised.

After the fatal 10th of December, 1748, Charles had entertained a bitter hatred of France, though he was always careful to blame the Ministers of Louis, not the King himself. He even refused a French pension, but this was an attitude which he could not maintain. In 1756 (July 1) he actually wrote to Louis, asking for money.

'Monsieur Mon Frère et Cousin,' he said. 'With the whole of Europe I admire your virtues . . . and the benefits with which you daily load your subjects . . . Since 1744, when I left Rome, I have run many risks, encountered many perils, and endured many vicissitudes of fortune, unaided by those from whom I had the right to expect assistance, unsuccoured even by My Father. In truth such of his subjects as espoused my cause have given me many proofs of zeal, and of good will, but, since open war broke out between France and England, I have not the same support. I know not what Destiny prepares for me, but I shall put it to the touch.'

For this purpose, then, he needs money.

'If I knew a Prince more virtuous than you, to him I would appeal.'

Whether Louis was good–natured, and gave some money for Charles to O'Hagarty and Elliot, his envoys, does not appear. {301}

In these dispositions, Charles hoped much from the French project of invading England in 1759. Though he never wholly despaired, and was soliciting Louis XVI. even in the dawn of the Revolution, we may call the invasion of 1759 his last faint chance. Hints had been thrown out of employing him in 1757. Frederick then wrote from Dresden to Mitchell, the English Ambassador at Berlin:

'I want to let you know that yesterday a person of distinguished rank told me that a friend of his at Court, under promise of the utmost secrecy, told him this: The French intend to make a diversion in Ireland in spring. They will disembark at Cork and at Waterford. They are negotiating with the Young Pretender to put himself at the head of the Expedition, but he will do nothing, unless the Courts of Vienna and St. Petersburg guarantee the proposals made to him by France.' {302a}

Charles, in fact, was deeply distrustful of all French offers. As we small see, he later declined to embark with any expedition for Scotland or Ireland. He would go with troops destined for London, and with no others. The year 1759 was spent in playing the game of intrigue. The French Minister, the Duc de Choiseul, was, or affected to be, friendly; friendly, too, were the old Maréchal de Belleisle and the Princesse de Ligne. Louis sent vaguely affectionate messages. In Rome, James was reconciled, and indulged in a gleam of hope. Charles's agents were Elliot, Alexander Murray (who, I think, is usually styled 'Campbell') 'Holker,' 'Goodwin,' Clancarty, and Mackenzie Douglas. This man, whose real name was Mackenzie, had been a Jesuit, and is said to have acted as a spy in the Dutch service. He had also been, first the secret, and then the avowed, envoy of Louis XV. to St. Petersburg in 1755–1756. On his second visit he was accompanied by the notorious Chevalier d'Eon. {302b}

As early as January 2, 1759, Murray (I think; the letters are unsigned) assures Charles of the friendship of the French Court. The King ('Ellis') will lend 30,000*l.* On January 8, Murray writes, and a funnier letter of veiled meanings never was penned:

'January 8.

'I arrived on Saturday morning, I immediately call'd at Mr. Cambels, not finding him went to Mr. Mansfield and delivered in the pills you sent him . . . I met Cambel at 10 o'clock, delivered him his pills, and drank a serious bottle of Burdeaux . . . delivered a pill to Harrison who with tears of tenderness in his eyes, said from the Bottom of his heart woud do anything in his power to serve that magnanimous Bourton [the Prince], he brought me along to Mr. Budson's, who after he had swallowed the pill came and made me a Low reverence, and desired me to assure Bourton of his respect.'

What the 'pills' were we can only guess, but their effects are entertaining. Charles at this time was at Bouillon, the home of his cousin, the Duc de Bouillon, and he made the President Thibault there the guardian of his child, for Miss Walkinshaw did not carry off her daughter to Paris till July 1760. {303} Murray (or Campbell) kept besieging Choiseul, Belleisle, and the Prince de Soubise with appeals in favour of Charles. We have heard how the Prince used to treat Madame de Pompadour, burning her *billets* unanswered. Now his mood was altered. His agent writes:

'February 19.

'Campbell, I send copy of Letter to Prince de Soubise.

'I am convinced you will not delay in writting to Madame La Marquise de Pompadour and thereby show her that your politeness and gallantry are not enferiour to your other superior qualifications, notwithstanding that you have lived for these ten years past in a manner shut up from the world. It will be absolutely necessary that you inclosed it to the P. of S. [Soubise] who has given up the command of ye army in Germany in order to conduct the expedition against England.'

Charles answered in this submissive fashion:

Prince to Murray.

'February 24.

'Rien ne me flatterai plus que d'assurer de Bouche Mad. L. M. de P. de l'estime et de La Consideration La plus parfaitte. Vous scavez mes sentiments pour Elle, je Les ay aussy Expliqué a Le P. de Soubise, et je ne dessirres rien tant que trouver Les occasions de lui La prouver.'

He also tried to justify his past conduct to 'Mr. Orry' (his father), especially as regarded Lord George Murray. He declared that, in the futile attempt at a night surprise at Nairn, before Culloden, Clanranald's regiment did encounter Cumberland's sentries, and found that the attempt was feasible, had Lord George not retreated, contrary to his orders.

The obstinate self-will of Charles displayed itself in thwarting all arrangements attempted by the French for employing him in their projected invasion of England. They expected a diversion to be made in their favour by his adherents, but he persistently refused to be landed either in Scotland or Ireland. He was partly justified. The French (as d'Argenson admits) had no idea, even in 1745, of making him King of the Three Kingdoms. To establish him at Holyrood, or in Dublin, and so to create and perpetuate disunion in Great Britain, was their policy, as far as they had a policy. We may think that Charles was in no position to refuse any assistance, but his reply to Cardinal Tencin, ' *Point de partage; tout ou rien,*' was at least patriotic. The Dutch correspondent of the 'Scots Magazine,' writing on May 22, 1759, said that a French expedition for Scotland was ready, and that Charles was to sail with it, but the Prince would not lend himself to this scheme. All through the summer he had his agents, Elliot, Holker, and Clancarty, at Dunkirk, Rouen, and Boulogne. They reported on the French preparations, but, writes Charles on July 22, 'I am not in their secret.' He corresponded with the Duc de Choiseul and the Maréchal de Belleisle, but they confined themselves to general assurances of friendship. 'It is impossible for the Duc de Choiseul to tell you the King's secret, as you would not tell him yours,' wrote an anonymous correspondent, apparently Alexander Murray.

Charles prepared manifestoes for the Press, and was urged, from England, to include certain arranged words in them, to be taken as a sign that he was actually landed. These words, of course, were to be kept a dead secret. The English Jacobites had no intention of appearing in arms to aid a French invading force, if Charles was not in the midst of it. Alexander Murray wrote suggestions for Charles's Declaration. He was to be very strong on the *Habeas Corpus* Act, and Murray ruefully recalled his own long imprisonment by order of the House of Commons. He wished also to repudiate the National Debt, but Charles must not propose this. 'A free Parliament' must take the burden of the deed. 'The landed interest can't be made easy by any other method than by paying that prodigious load by a sponge.' In a Dutch caricature of 'Perkin's Triumph' (1745), Charles is represented driving in a coach over the bodies of holders of Consols. It is difficult now to believe that Repudiation was the chief aim of the honest squires who toasted 'the King over the Water.'

In August, Murray reported that Choiseul said 'nothing should be done except with and for the Prince.'

The manuscript letter–book of Andrew Lumisden, James's secretary since Edgar's death, and brother–in–law of Sir Robert Strange, the engraver, illustrates Charles's intentions. {306} On August 12, 1759, Lumisden is in correspondence with Murray. The Prince, to Lumisden's great delight, wants his company. Already, in 1759, Lumisden had been on secret expeditions to Paris, Germany, Austria, and Venice. Macallester informs us that Sullivan, who had been in Scotland with Charles in 1745, received a command in the French army mustering at Brest. He also tells a long dull story of Charles's incognito in Paris at this time: how he lived over a butcher's shop in the Rue de la Boucherie, seldom went out except at night, and was recognised at Mass by a woman who had attended Miss Walkinshaw's daughter. Finally, the Prince went to Brest in disguise, 'damning the Marshal's old boots,' the boots of the Maréchal de Belleisle, which, it seems, 'were always stuffed full of projects.' Barbier supposes, in his 'Mémoires,' that Charles was to go with Thurot, who was to attack Scotland, while Conflans invaded England. But Charles would not hear of leaving with Thurot and his tiny squadron, which committed some petty larcenies on the coast of the West Highlands.

The Prince was now warned against Clancarty of the one eye, who was bragging, and lying, and showing his letters in the taverns of Dunkirk. The old feud of Scotch and Irish Jacobites went merrily on. Macallester called Murray a card–sharper, and was himself lodged in prison on a *lettre de cachet*. Murray wrote, of the Irish, 'their bulls and stupidity one can forgive, but the villainy and falsity of their hearts is unpardonable.' Scotch and Irish bickerings, a great cause of the ruin in 1745, broke out again on the slightest gleam of hope.

Holker sent a curious account of the boats for embarking horses on the expedition. These he illustrated by a diagram on the back of the five of diamonds; a movable slip cut in the card gave an idea of the mechanism. The King of France, on August 27, sent friendly messages by Belleisle, but 'could not be explicit.' Elliot reported that Clancarty 'would stick at no lyes to bring about his schemes.' On September 5 came an anonymous warning against Murray, who 'is not trusted by the French Ministry.' On September 28, Laurence Oliphant of Gask sent verses in praise of Charles written by 'Madame de

Montagu,' the lady who lent him 1,000*l.* years before. On October 8, Murray still reports the 'attachment' of Choiseul and Belleisle. He adds that neither his brother (Lord Elibank) nor any other Scotch Jacobite will stir if an invasion of Scotland is undertaken without a landing in England. On October 21 he declares that Conflans has orders to attack the English fleet lying off Havre. The sailing of Thurot is also announced: 'I cannot comprehend the object of so small an embarkation.' As late as October 26, Charles was still left in the dark as to the intentions of France.

Then, obviously while Charles was waiting for orders, came the fatal news in a hurried note. '*Conflans beaten, his ship, the "Soleil Royal," and the "Héros" stranded at Croisic. Seven ships are come in. Ten are flying at sea.*'

Brave Admiral Hawke had routed Conflans in Quiberon Bay. *Afflavit Deus*, and scattered the fleet of France, with the last hope of Charles.

Yet hope never dies in the hearts of exiles, as is proved by the following curious letter from Murray (?). It is impossible to be certain as to the sincerity of Choiseul; the split in the Jacobite party is only too clearly indicated.

From Campbell (probably Murray).

'December 10.

'I delivered your letter this evening and had a long conference with both the Ministers: Mr. Choiseul assured me upon his word of honour that Your R.H. should be inform'd in time before the departure of Mr. de Gouillon, {309a} so that you might go with that embarquement if you thought proper, upon which I interrupted him and told him if they were destined for the Kingdom of Ireland that it would be to no manner of purpose, for I was certain you would not go, and that you had at all times expressly ordered me to tell them so; he continued his conversation and said you should be equally informed when the P. of S. {309b} embarked. I answered as to every project for England that you would not ballance one moment, but that you would not, nor could not in honour enter into any other project but that of going to London, and if once master of that city both Ireland and Scotland would fall of course, as that town was the fountain of all the riches; he then hinted that Guillion's embarkment was not for Ireland, and talked of Scotland.

'I then told him of the message you had received from my brother [Elibank] and the other leading men of the party, in that country, that not a man of consequence would stir unless the debarkment was made at the same time in England, and that every person who pretended the contrary, ought to be regarded as the enemy of your R.H. as well as of France. He then told me that in case you did not choose to go with Mr. de Guillion that it would be necessary to send one with a declaration in your name; I told him I could make no answers to that proposition, as I had never heard you talk of declarations of any sort before you was landed in England, and that you had settled all that matter, with your friends in England and Scotland. He assured me that the intentions of the King and his Ministers were unalterable as to their fixed resolution to serve you, but that they met with difficulties in regard to the transports and flat–bottomed boats which retarded the affair longer than they imagined, and that though they had already spent twenty four million every thing was not yet ready.

'This is as near as I can recollect the purport of his conversation excepting desiring to see him before my return to Your R.H. I afterwards saw your good friend the Marcel [Belleisle] who told me that every thing that depended upon his department was ready, and said pretty near what Mr. de Choiseul had told concerning the delays of the transports, seventeen of which they yet wanted. He assured me it was the thing on earth he desired the most to see you established upon the throne of your Ancestors, and that he would with plesure give you his left arm, rather than it should not succeed: I am perfectly convinced of the sincere intention of the King and Ministers, and that nothing but the interposition of heaven can prevent your success.

'I have not yet seen the P. of S. [Soubise] but shall to–morrow: your Cousin Bethune is greatly attached to you, and has done you great justice in destroying the villanous lyes, and aspersions of some of your false subjects [Clancarty], who by a pretended zeal for you got access to the ministers, and have had the impudence to present memorials as absurd and ridiculous, as their great quality, and immense fortunes they have lost by being attached to your family. I flatter myself you will very soon be convinced of all their infamous low schemes.'

Meanwhile, in all probability, Pickle was waiting to see how matters would fall out. If Conflans beat Hawke, and if Thurot landed in the Western Highlands, *then* Pickle would have rallied to the old flag, *Tandem Triumphans*, and welcomed gloriously His Royal Highness the Prince of Wales. Then the despised warrant of a peerage would have come forth, and Lord Glengarry, I conceive, would have hurried to seize the Duke of Newcastle's papers, many of which were of extreme personal interest to himself. But matters chanced otherwise, so Pickle wrote his last extant letter to the English Government

Add. 32,902.

'My Lord [the Duke of Newcastle],—As I am confident your Grace will be at a lose to find out your present Corespondent, it will, I believe, suffice to recall to mind *Pickle*, how [who] some time ago had a conference with the young Gentilman whom honest old Vaughan brought once to Clermont to waite of yr. Grace. I find he still retains the same ardent inclination to serve his King and Country, yet, at same time, he bitterly complains that he has been neglected, and nothing done for him of what was promis'd him in the strongest terms, and which he believes had been strickly perform'd, had your most worthy Brother, his great friend and Patron, surviv'd till now. He desires me aquent your Grace that upon a late criticall juncture [November 1759] he was prepairing to take post for London to lay affaires of the greatest moment before his Majesty, but the suden blow given the enemy by Admiral Hack [Hawke] keept him back for that time. But now that he finds that they are still projecting to execute their first frustrated schem, {312} there present plan of operation differing in nothing from the first, but in what regards North Britain. He has certain information of this by verbal Expresses; writting beeing absolutely dischargd for fear of discovery. He desires me aquent your Grace of this, that you may lay the whole before His Majesty.

'If His Majesty's Enemys should once more faile in their favourite scheme of Envasion, this young gentilman [Glengarry] intends to make offer of raising a Regiment of as good men as ever was levied in North Britain, if he gets the Rank of full Colonell, the nomenation of his Officers, and suitable levie Mony. He can be of infinite service in either capacity mentioned in this letter [spy or Colonel], that his Majesty is graciously pleasd to employ him. He begs that this may not be delay'd to be laid before the King, as things may soon turn out very serious. He makes a point with your Grace that this be communicated to no mortall but his Majesty, and he is willing to forfite all pretensions to the Royall favour, if his services at this criticall juncture does not meritt his Majesty's aprobation. If your Grace calls upon him at this time, as he was out of pocket upon further Chants, it will be necessary to remit him a bill payable at sight for whatever little sum is judg'd proper for the present, untill he gives proof of his attachment *to the best of Sovereigns*, and of his reale zeale for the service of his King and Country, against a most treacherous and perfidious Enemy. I have now done my duty, my Lord, reffering the whole manadgement to your Grace, and I beg youl pardon the freedom I have taken as I have the honour to remain at all times

'My Lord, your Grace's Most obedient and most oblidged humble Servt.

'PICKLE,

'February 19, 1760.

'Mack [make] mention of *Pickle*. His Majesty will remember Mr. Pelham did, upon former affairs of great consequence.

'Dirction—To *Alexander Mackdonell of Glengary* by Foraugustus [*Fort Augustus*].'

Pickle, as he remarks in one of his artless letters, 'is not of a suspicious temper, but judges of others' candour by his own.' He now carries this honourable freedom so far as to give his own noble name and address. *Habemus confitentem reum.* Persons more suspicious and less candid will believe that Pickle, in November 1759, was standing to win on both colours. His readiness to sell a regiment of Macdonnells to fight for King George is very worthy of a Highland chief of Pickle's kind.

On December 23, 1761, Alastair Macdonnell of Glengarry died, and Pickle died with him. He had practically ceased to be useful; the world was anticipating Burns's advice:

'Adore the rising sun,
And leave a man undone
  To his fate!'

We have unmasked a character of a kind never popular. Yet, in the government of the world, Pickle served England well. But for him there might have been another highland rising, and more fire and bloodshed. But for him the Royal Family might have perished in a nocturnal brawl. Only one man, Archibald Cameron, died through Pickle's treasons. The Prince with whom he drank, and whom he betrayed, had become hopeless and worthless. The world knows little of its greatest benefactors, and Pickle did good by stealth. Now his shade may or may not 'blush to find it fame,' and to be placed above Murray of Broughton, beside Menteith and Assynt, legendary Ganelons of Scotland.

CHAPTER XIV—CONCLUSION

Conclusion—Charles in 1762—Flight of Miss Walkinshaw—Charles quarrels with France—Remonstrance from Murray—Death of King James— Charles returns to Rome—His charm—His disappointments—Lochgarry enters the Portuguese service—Charles declines to recognise Miss Walkinshaw—Report of his secret marriage to Miss Walkinshaw—Denied by the lady—Charles breaks with Lumisden—Bishop Forbes—Charles's marriage—The Duchess of Albany'—'All ends in song—The Princesse de Talmond—The end.

With the death of Pickle, the shabby romance of the last Jacobite struggle finds its natural close.

Of Charles we need say little more. Macallester represents him as hanging about the coasts of England in 1761–1762, looking out for favourable landing–places, or sending his valet, Stuart, to scour Paris in search of Miss Walkinshaw. That luckless lady fled from Charles at Bouillon to Paris in July 1760, with her daughter, and found refuge in a convent. As Lord Elcho reports her conversation, Charles was wont to beat her cruelly. For general circulation she averred that she and James merely wished her daughter to be properly educated. {316}

Charles, in fact, picked a new quarrel with France on the score of his daughter. Louis refused to make Miss Walkinshaw (now styled Countess of Albertroff) resign her child to Charles's keeping. He was very fond of children, and Macallester, who hated him, declares that, when hiding in the Highlands, he would amuse himself by playing with the baby of a shepherd's wife. None the less, his habits made him no proper guardian of his own little girl. {317} In 1762, young Oliphant of Gask, who visited the Prince at Bouillon, reports that he will have nothing to do with France till his daughter is restored to him. He held moodily aloof, and then the Peace came. Lumisden complains that 'Burton' (the Prince) is 'intractable.' He sulked at Bouillon, where he hunted in the forests. Here is a sad and tender admonition from Murray, whose remonstrances were more softly conveyed than those of Goring:

'Thursday.

'When I have the honour of being with you I am miserable, upon seeing you take so little care of a health which is so precious to every honest man, but more so to me in particular, because I know you, and therefore can't help loving, honouring, and esteeming you; but alass! what service can my zeal and attachment be to my dear master, unless he lays down a plan and system, and follows it, such as his subjects and all mankind will, and must approve of.'

Young Gask repeats the same melancholy tale. Charles was hopeless. For some inscrutable reason he was true to Stafford (who had aided his secret flight from Rome in 1744) and to Sheridan, supporting them at Avignon.

'Old Mr. Misfortunate' (King James) died at Rome it 1766; he never saw his 'dearest Carluccio' after the Prince stole out of the city, full of hope, in 1744—

'A fairy Prince with happy eyes
And lighter–footed than the fox.'

James expired 'without the least convulsion or agony,' says Lumisden, 'but with his usual mild serenity in his countenance. . . . He seemed rather to be asleep than dead.' A proscribed exile from his cradle, James was true to faith and honour. What other defeated and fugitive adventurer ever sent money to the hostile general for the peasants who had suffered from the necessities of war?

On January 23, 1766, Lumisden met Charles on his way to Rome. 'His legs and feet were considerably swelled by the fatigue of the journey. In other respects he enjoys perfect health, and charms every one who approaches him.' The Prince was 'miraculously' preserved when his coach was overturned on a precipice near Bologna. Some jewels and family relics had not been returned by Cluny, and there were difficulties about sending a messenger for them: these occupy much of Lumisden's correspondence.

Charles met only with 'mortifications' at Rome. The Pope dared not treat him on a Royal footing. In April 1766, our old friend, Lochgarry, took service with Portugal. Charles sent congratulations, 'and doubts not your son will be ready to draw the sword in his just Cause.' The sword remained undrawn. Charles had now but an income of 47,000 *livres*; he amused himself as he might with shooting, and playing the French horn! He never forgave Miss Walkinshaw, whom his brother, the Cardinal, maintained, poorly enough. Lumisden writes to the lady (July 14, 1766): 'No one knows the King's temper better than you do. He has never, so far as I can discover, mentioned your name. Nor do I believe that he either knows where you are, nor how you are maintained. His passion must still greatly cool before any application can be made to him in your behalf.'

A report was circulated that Charles was secretly married to Miss Walkinshaw. On February 16, 1767, Lumisden wrote to Waters on 'the dismal consequences of such a rumour,' and, by the Duke of York's desire, bade Waters obtain a denial from the lady. On March 11 the Duke received Miss Walkinshaw's formal affidavit that no marriage existed. 'It has entirely relieved him from the uneasiness the villainous report naturally gave him.' On January 5, 1768, Lumisden had to tell Miss Walkinshaw that 'His Royal Highness insists you shall always remain in a monastery.' Lumisden was always courteous to Miss Walkinshaw. Of her daughter he writes: 'May she ever possess in the highest degree, those elegant charms of body and mind, which you so justly and assiduously cultivate. . . . Did the King know that I had wrote to you, he would never pardon me.'

On December 20, 1768, Charles had broken with Lumisden and the rest of his suite. 'Our behaviour towards him was that of faithful subjects and servants, jealous at all times to preserve his honour and reputation.' They had, in brief, declined to accompany Charles in his carriage when his condition demanded seclusion. Lumisden writes (December 8, 1767), 'His Royal Highness' (the Duke of York) 'thanked us for our behaviour in the strongest terms.'

We need follow no further the story of a consummated degradation. Charles threw off one by one, on grounds of baseless suspicion, Lord George Murray, Kelly (to please Lord Marischal), Goring, and now drove from him his most attached servants. He never suspected Glengarry. But neither time, nor despair, nor Charles's own fallen self could kill the loyalty of Scotland. Bishop Forbes, far away, heard of his crowning folly, and—blamed Lumisden and his companion, Hay of Restalrig! When Charles, on Good Friday, 1772, married Louise of Stolberg, the remnant of the faithful in Scotland drank to 'the fairest Fair,' and to an heir of the Crown.

'L'Écosse ne peut pas te juger: elle t' aime!'

Into the story of an heir, born at Sienna, and entrusted to Captain Allen, R.N., to be brought up in England, we need not enter. In Lord Braye's manuscripts (published by the Historical MSS. Commission) is Charles's solemn statement that, except Miss Walkinshaw's daughter, he had no child. The time has not come to tell the whole strange tale of 'John Stolberg Sobieski Stuart and Charles Edward Stuart,' if, indeed, that tale can ever be told. {321} Nor does space permit an investigation of Charles's married life, of his wife's elopement with Alfieri, and of the last comparatively peaceful years in the society of a daughter who soon followed him to the tomb. The stories about that daughter's marriage to a Swedish Baron Roehenstart, and about their son, merit no attention. In the French Foreign Office archives is a wild plan for marrying the lady, Charlotte Stuart, to a Stuart—any Stuart, and raising their unborn son's standard in the American colonies! That an offer was made from America to Charles himself, in 1778, was stated by Scott to Washington Irving on the authority of a document in the Stuart Papers at Windsor. That paper could not be found for Lord Stanhope, nor have I succeeded in finding it. The latest Scottish honour done to the King was Burns's 'Birthday Ode' of 1787, and his song for 'The Bonny Lass o' Albany.'

'This lovely maid's of royal blood,
  That rulèd Albion's kingdoms three,
But oh, alas for her bonnie face!
  They hae wrang'd the lass of Albanie!'

Tout finit par des chansons!

Of the Stuart cause we may say, as Callimachus says of his dead friend Heraclitus:

'Still are thy pleasant voices, thy nightingales awake,
For death takes everything away, but these he cannot take.'

A hundred musical notes keep green the memory of the last Prince of Romance, the beloved, the beautiful, the brave Prince Charlie— *everso missus succurrere saeclo*. The overturned age was not to be rescued by charms and virtues which the age itself was to ruin and destroy. Loyal memories are faithful, not to what the Prince became under stress of exile, and treachery, and hope deferred, and death in life, *de vivre et de pas vivre*—but to what he once was, *Tearlach Righ nan Gael.*

Of one character in this woful tale a word may be said. The Princesse de Talmond was visited by Horace Walpole in 1765. He found her in 'charitable apartments in the Luxembourg,' and he tripped over cats and stools (and other things) in the twilight of a bedroom hung with pictures of Saints and Sobieskis. At last, and very late, the hour of her conversion had been granted, by St. François Xavier, to the prayers of her husband. We think of the Baroness Bernstein in her latest days as we read of the end of the Princesse. She had governed Charles 'with fury and folly.' Of all the women who had served him— Flora Macdonald, Madame de Vassé, Mademoiselle Luci, Miss Walkinshaw— did he remember none when he wrote that he understood men, but despaired of understanding women, 'they being so much more wicked and impenetrable'? {323}

Footnotes:

{3} Edition of 1832, i. p. x.

{12a} *History of England from the Peace of Utrecht to the Peace of Aix–la–Chapelle.* London, 1838, iii. 279.

{12b} *An authentic account of the conduct of the Young Chevalier*, p. 7. Third edition, 1749.

{13} London, 1879.

{15a} *Letters from Italy by an Englishwoman*, ii. 198. London 1776. Cited by Lord Stanhope, iii. 556. Horace Mann to the Duke of Newcastle. State Papers. Tuscany. Jan. ½½, 174¾. In Ewald, i. 87. Both authorities speak of *blue* eyes.

{15b} A false Charles appeared in Selkirkshire in 1745. See Mr. Craig Brown's *History of Ettrick Forest.* The French, in 1759, meant to send a false Charles to Ireland with Thurot. Another appeared at Civita Vecchia about 1752. The tradition of Roderick Mackenzie, who died under English bullets, crying 'You have slain your Prince,' is familiar. We shall meet other pseudo–Charles's.

{17a} Ewald, i. 41.

{17b} *Documentos Ineditos.* Madrid. 1889. Vol. xciii. 18.

{18a} *Voyages de Montesquieu.* Bordeaux, 1894. p. 250.

{18b} *Letters of De Brosses*, as translated by Lord Stanhope, iii. 72.

{18c} See authorities in Ewald, i. 48–50.

{19a} Ewald, ii. 30. Scott's Journal, i. 114.

{19b} Dennistoun's *Life of Strange*, i. 63, and an Abbotsford manuscript.

{20a} Stuart Papers, in the Queen's Library. Also the Lockhart Papers mention the wounding of the horse.

{20b} *Life and Correspondence of David Hume.* Hill Burton, ii. 464–466.

{21a} *Jacobite Memoirs.* Lord Elcho's MS. Journal. Ewald, i. 77.

{21b} State Papers Domestic. 1745. No. 79.

{21c} *Genuine Memoirs of John Murray of Broughton. La Spedizione di Carlo Stuart.*

{23a} Treasury Papers. 1745. No. 214. First published by Mr. Ewald, i. 215.

{23b} *Jacobite Memoirs*, p. 32.

{24a} Chambers *Rebellion of* 1745, i. 71. The authority is 'Tradition.'

{24b} I have read parts of Forbes's manuscript in the Advocates' Library, but difficulties were made when I wished to study it for this book.

{25a} *D'Argenson's Mémoires.*

{25b} This gentleman died at Carlisle in 1745, according to Bishop Forbes. *Jacobite Memoirs*, p. 4.

{26a} Stuart MSS. in Windsor Castle.

{26b} Stuart Papers. Browne's *History of the Highland Clans*, iii. 481.

{27a} James to Lismore. June 23, 1749. Stuart MSS.

{28a} Stanhope. Vol. iii. Appendix, p. xl.

{28b} *Jacobite Memoirs.*

{30a} The Kelly of Atterbury's Conspiracy, long a prisoner in the Tower. It is fair to add that Bulkeley, Montesquieu's friend, defended Kelly.

{31a} Stuart Papers. Browne, iii. 433. September 13, 1745.

{32a} Macallester's book is entitled *A Series of Letters*, &c. London, 1767.

{32b} Wogan to Edgar. Stuart Papers, 1750.

{33a} D'Argenson, iv. 316–320.

{33b} Stair Papers.

{33c} Letters in the State Paper Office. S. P. Tuscany. Walton sends to England copies of the letters of James's adherents in Paris; Horace Mann sends the letters of Townley, whom James so disliked.

{35a} D'Argenson's *Mémoires*, v. 98, fol.

{35b} *Ibid.* v. 183.

{36a} Published by the Duc de Broglie, in *Revue d'Histoire Diplomatique.* No. 4. Paris, 1891.

{37a} Browne, iv. 36–38.

{38a} *Genuine Copies of Letters, &c.* London, 1748.

{38b} *An Account of the Prince's Arrival in France*, p. 66. London, 1754.

{39a} There are letters of Bulkeley's to Montesquieu as early as 1728. *Voyages de Montesquieu*, p. xx. note 3.

{40a} In his work on Madame de Pompadour (p. 109), M. Capefigue avers that he discovered, in the archives of the French Police, traces of an English plot to assassinate Prince Charles; the Jacobites believed in such attempts, not without reason, as we shall prove.

{41a} Walton. S. P. Tuscany. No. 55.

{43} *Mémoires*, iv. 322.

{46a} See *Le Secret du Roi*, by the Duc de Broglie.

{46b} *Tales of the Century*, p. 25.

{46c} *Pol. Corresp. of Frederick the Great*, v. 114. No. 2,251.

{46d} *Ibid.* vi. 125. No. 3,086.

{49a} D'Argenson, v. 417. March 19, 1749. D'Argenson knew more than the police.

{50a} Stuart Papers. Browne, iv. p. 51.

{51a} *Mémoires*, v. 417.

{51b} *Tales of the Century*, ii. 48, 'from information of Sir Ralph Hamilton.'

{51c} 'Information by Baron de Rondeau and Sir Ralph Hamilton.'

{52a} S. P. France. No. 442.

{52b} S. P. Tuscany. No. 58. Stuart Papers. Browne, iv. 52.

{52c} S. P. France. No. 442.

{52d} This may have been true.

{52e} S. P. Tuscany. No. 55.

{53a} Dr. King made a Latin speech on this occasion, rich in Jacobite innuendoes. *Redeat* was often repeated.

{53b} S. P. Poland. No. 75.

{58a} S. P. Russia. No. 59.

{61} *Pol. Corr.*, vi. 572, vii. 23.

{62a} Browne. Stuart Papers, iii. 502.

{62b} S. P. Tuscany. No. 54.

{63} Hanbury Williams. From Dresden, July 2, 1749.

{64} James had previously wished Charles to marry a Princess of Modena.

{65a} Mann, June 19, 1750.

{65b} Stuart Papers. Browne, ii. 73.

{68} *Correspondence of the Duke of Bedford*, ii. 69. Bedford to Albemarle. Also *op. cit.* ii. 15. March 13, 1749. Bedford to Colonel Yorke.

{69} Browne, iv. 57, 63.

{70a} In the Gask Papers it is said that 5,000*l*. was sent by Cluny to Major Kennedy. Kennedy himself buried the money.

{70b} All these facts are taken from the Stuart Papers, in manuscript at Windsor Castle.

{71} Le 3. A. 1749. Projet pour mon arrive a Paris, et Le Conduit de Mr. Benn. Mr. Benn doit s'en aller droit à Dijon et son Compagnion Mr. Smith a Paris; Il faudra pour Mr. Smith une Chese [chaise] qu'il acheterra a Lunéville, ensuite il prendra Le Domestique du C. P. à Ligny, mais en partent d'icy il faudra que le Sieur Smith mont a Chevall et La Chese pourra y aller come pour son Retour a Paris. La personne dedans parraitrait profiter de cette occasion. Le Sieur Bonn doit rester quelqe jours come desiran acheter une Cofre et remettra La Sienne come par amitié au Sr. Smith, tout cecy paroissant d'hazard. Ensuite Le Sr. Smith continuera au Plustot son Chemin, et son Ami ira Le Sien en attendant, un peu de jours et à son arrivé a Dij. il doit Ecrive a Personne qu'il soite excepte La Lettre au—W. Le Ch. Gre. qu'il doit voire (et a qui il peut dire davoire ete a Di—Charge par Le P., sans meme Nomer son Camerade mais come tout seule) ne sachant rien davantage, et le laissant dans l'obscuriné, comme s'il Etoit dans le meme Cas, attendant des Nouvelles Ordres, sans rien outre savoire ou pouvoire penetre Etant deja Longtems sans me voire.' Holograph of P. Charles.

{79} Under the late Empire (1863) the convent was the hotel of the Minister of War. Hither, about 1748, came Madame du Deffand, later the superannuated adorer of the hard–hearted Horace Walpole, and here was her famous *salon moire jaune, aux nœuds couleur de feu*. Here she entertained the President Hénault, Bulkeley, Montesquieu (whose own house was in the same street), Lord Bath, and all the *philosophes*, giving regular suppers on Mondays. In the same conventual chambers resided, in 1749, Madame de Talmond, Madame de Vassé, and her friend Mademoiselle Ferrand, whose address Charles wrote, as we saw, in his note–book (March 1749).

{80} Grimm, ii. p. 183.

{82} S. P. France. June 4, 1749. Ewald, ii. 200.

{83} Translated from the French original at Windsor Castle.

{86} *Histoire de Montesquieu*, par L. Vian, p. 196.

{87} *Correspondance de Madame du Deffand.* Edition of M. de Lescure, ii. 737–742.

{91} D'Argenson confirms or exaggerates this information.

{92} Browne, v. 66. Letter of Young Glengarry, January 16, 1750.

{97} Browne, iv. 68. I have not found the original in the Stuart Papers at Windsor.

{101} The Mr. Dormer who was Charles's agent is described in *Burke* as 'James, of Antwerp,' sixth son, by his second marriage, of Charles, fifth Lord Dormer.

{103} State Papers. Examination of Æneas Macdonald.

{105} July 1, 1754. Browne, iv. 122.

{106} Mr. Ewald's dates, as to the Prince's English jaunt, are wrong. He has adopted those concerning the lady's movements, ii. 201.

{107} Charles himself (S. P. Tuscany, December 16, 1783) told these facts. But Hume is responsible for the visit to Lady Primrose, dating it in 1753; wrongly, I think.

{108} Private Memorandum concerning the Pretender's eldest son. Brit. Mus. Additional MSS.

{110} A medal of 1750 bears a profile of Charles, as does one of September 1752.

{111} This may be of 1752–1753, and the 'Channoine' may be Miss Walkinshaw, who was a canoness of a noble order.

{113} Montesquieu to the Abbé de Guasco, March 7, 1749.

{118} The sequel of the chivalrous attempt to catch Keith's mistress may he found in letters of Newcastle to Colonel Guy Dickens (February 12, 1751), and of Dickens (St. Petersburg, March 27, 30, May 4, 1751) to the Duke of Newcastle. (State Papers.)

{119} *Correspondence of the Duke of Bedford*, ii. 69.

{125} *Letters*, ii. 116.

{126} Spence's *Anecdotes*, p. 168.

{127a} Browne, iv. 17.

{127b} Stuart Papers.

{127c} *Ibid.*

{128a} Potzdam, August 24, 1751. *uvres*, xxxviii. 307. Edition of 1880.

{128b} Newcastle to Lord Chancellor, September 6, 1751. *Life of Lord Hardwicke*, ii. 404.

{130a} *Anecdotes.*

{130b} Stuart Papers. Lady Montagu was Barbara, third daughter of Sir John Webbe of Hathorp, county Gloucester. In July 1720 she married Anthony Brown, sixth Viscount Montagu.

{131} Walton's *Life of Wotton.*

{132a} Browne, iv. 89–90.

{133a} S. P. France, 455.

{135} S. P. Poland, No. 79.

{137} Angleterre, 81, f. 94, 1774.

{138} Pichot, in his *Vie de Charles Edouard*, obviously cites this document, which is quoted from him by the Sobieski Stuarts in *Tales of the Century*. But Pichot does not name the source of his statements.

{139} A French agent, Beson probably, whom Charles desired to dismiss, *because* a Frenchman.

{141} Scott's *Letters*, ii. 208. June 29, 1824.

{144} For reasons already given, namely, that Madame de Vassé was the only daughter of her father by his wife, and that Mademoiselle Ferrand was her great friend, while the Prince addresses Mademoiselle Luci by a name derived from an estate of the Ferrands, I have identified Mademoiselle Ferrand with Mademoiselle Luci. This, however, is only an hypothesis.

{145} Some of Pickle's letters were published by Mr. Murray Rose in an essay called 'An Infamous Spy, James Mohr Macgregor,' in the *Scotsman*, March 15, 1895. This article was brought to my notice on June 22, 1896. As the author identifies Pickle with James Mohr Macgregor, though Pickle began to communicate with the English Government while James was a prisoner in Edinburgh Castle, and continued to do so for years after James's death, it is plain that he is in error, and that the transactions need a fresh examination. Mr. Murray Rose, in the article cited, does not indicate the *provenance* of the documents which he publishes. When used in this work they are copied from the originals in the British Museum, among the papers of the Pelham Administration. The transcripts have been for several years in my hands, but I desire to acknowledge Mr. Murray Rose's priority in printing some of the documents, which, in my opinion, he wholly misunderstood, at least on March 15, 1895. How many he printed, if any, besides those in the *Scotsman*, and in what periodicals, I am not informed.

{149a} The portrait, now at Balgownie, was long in the possession of the Threiplands of Fingask. I have only seen a photograph, in the Scottish Museum of Antiquities.

{149b} MS. in Laing Collection, Edinburgh University Library.

{150a} A note of Craigie's communicated by Mr. Omond.

{150b} Cope to Forbes of Culloden, August 24, 1745. *Culloden Papers*, p. 384.

{150c} *Culloden Papers*, p. 405.

{150d} Young Glengarry to Edgar. Rome, September 16, 1750. In the Stuart Papers.

{151a} Chambers's *The Rebellion*, v. 24. Edinburgh, 1829.

{151b} Letter of Warren to James, October 10, 1746. Browne, iii. 463.

{152a} Stuart Papers. Browne, iv. 100.

{152b} *Ibid.* iv. 22, 23.

{153a} Browne, iv. 51.

{154} Browne, iv. 61, 62.

{155a} I presume the first beautiful Mrs. Murray is in question. The second is 'another story.' See the original letter in Browne, iv. 90–101.

{155b} State Papers, Domestic, No. 87.

{156} Stuart Papers.

{157} Browne, iv. 60.

{159} Browne, iv. 117.

{160} *Correspondence of the Duke of Bedford*, ii. 39.

{161} Paris, February 14, 1752. Stuart Papers.

{162a} iv. 84.

{162b} Rome, September 4, 1750. In Browne.

{164} Browne, iv. 102.

{165} Journal, February 14, 1826.

{169} May 4, 1753. Stuart Papers. To old Edgar.

{171} His father's name was John. One of Pickle's aliases.

{172} This identifies 'Pickle' with 'Jeanson.'

{174} Cypher names.

6—Goring.
69—Sir James Harrington, perhaps.
51—King of Prussia.
80—Pretender's Son.
8—Pretender.
72—Sir John Graham.
66—Scotland.
0—French Ministry.
2—Lord Marshall.
59—Count Maillebois.
71—Sir John Graham, perhaps.

{175} That is, probably, Pickle said to Jacobite friends that his money came from Major Kennedy.

{178} Lord Elcho knew it, probably from his brother.

{180} Elcho says he was in London, at Lady Primrose's. We have seen that Charles had had a difficulty with this lady.

{181} To this illness Glengarry often refers, when writing as Pickle.

{183a} Hay to Edgar, October 1752. In Browne, iv. 106.

{183b} 'Mildmay' to 'Green,' January 24, 1753.

{184} S. P. Poland. No. 81.

{196a} Carlyle's *Frederick*, iv. 467. Compare, for the views of political circles, Horace Walpole's *Reign of* George *II.* i. 333, 353, and his Letters to Horace Mann for 1753.

{196b} *Reign of George II.* i. 290.

{197} Add MSS. British Museum, 33,847, f. 271. 'Private and most secret.'

{198a} *Politische Correspondenz Friederichs des Grossen.* Duncker. Berlin, 1879, ix. 356.

{198b} Can the Earl and the Doctor have approved of renewing the infamous Elibank plot?

{201} Many historians, such as Lord Campbell in his *Lives of the Chancellors*, condemn as cruel the execution of Cameron. But the Government was well informed.

{202} *The Active Testimony of the Presbyterians of Scotland*, 1749.

{203} xix. 742.

{208} French service. He seems to think that Archy was betrayed by French means. He perhaps suspected Dumont, who had been in the French army.

{213} Glengarry had been a captain in the French service.

{219} Brother of d'Argenson of the *Mémoires.*

{222a} *Pol. Corr.* No. 5,933.

{222b} As early as 1748 Dawkins was in Paris, drinking with Townley, who calls him *un bon garçon*. Townley's letters to a friend in Rome were regularly sent to Pelham.

{223} *Pol. Corr.* ix. 417. No. 5,923.

{224a} Droysen, iv. 357. Note 1.

{224b} S. P. France. 462.

{227} Browne, iv. p. 111.

{231a} In his article on James Mohr (*Scotsman*, March 15, 1896), Mr. Murray Rose cites some papers concerning James's early treacheries. For unfathomable reasons, Mr. Murray Rose does not mention the source of these papers. This is of the less importance, as Mr. George Omond, in *Macmillan's Magazine*, May 1890, had exposed James's early foibles, from documents in the Record Office.

{231b} *Trials of Rob Roy's Sons* (Edinburgh, 1818), p. 3.

{232a} The reader may remember that Pickle's earliest dated letter is from Boulogne, November 2, 1752. As on that day James Mohr was a prisoner in Edinburgh Castle, the absurdity of identifying Pickle with James Mohr becomes peculiarly glaring.

{232b} *Trial*, &c. p. 119.

{232c} According to Mr. Murray Rose, James Mohr applied to the King for money on May 22, 1753. This letter I have not observed among the Stuart Papers, but, from information given by Pickle to his English employers, I believe James Mohr to have been in France as early as May 1753. Pickle, being consulted as to James's value, contemns him as a spy distrusted by both sides.

{234} Add. MSS. 32,846.

{235} He *had* been, as a spy!

{236} How worthy of our friend!

{238} As James was not in France till May 1753, he cannot have written Pickle's letters from France of March in that year.

{239} Balhaldie's papers, not treasonable, belong to Sir Arthur Halkett of Pitfirrane, who also possesses a charming portrait of pretty Mrs. Macfarlane. Sir Arthur's ancestor, Sir Peter, fought on the Hanoverian side in the Forty–five, was taken prisoner, and released on *parole*, which he refused to break at the command of the Butcher Cumberland.

{240} MSS. Add. 33,050, f. 369.

{241} Nothing of all this in the Stuart Papers.

{242} Observe James's Celtic memory.

{243} Mr. Savage, according to James Mohr, was the chief of the Macgregors in Ireland.

{245} These are transparent falsehoods. The Earl Marischal, if we may believe Pickle, had no mind to resign his comfortable Embassy.

{246} He was really at Avignon.

{250} Add. MSS. 33,050, f. 409.

{251} In 'Mémoire Historique et Généalogique sur la Famille de Wogan,' par le Comte Alph. O'Kelly de Galway (Paris, 1896) we read (p. 33) that, in 1776, Charles was 'entertained at Cross Green House, in Cork.' The authority given is a vague reference to the *Hibernian Magazine.*

{254} Stuart Papers.

{256} Probably Glengarry.

{259} This too well confirms Dr. King's charges.

{261} Goring must mean a clansman—a Cameron.

{263} Goring was probably at the Convent of St. Joseph, with Madame de Vassé.

{265} See *Mémoires of Madame Hausset*, and the De Goncourts on Madame de Pompadour.

{267} These letters have been printed in full by Mr. Murray Rose (*Scotsman*, March 15, 1895). Mr. Murray Rose attributes them to James Mohr Macgregor, wrongly, of course.

{268} That is, seats for Jacobites should be purchased at the General Election.

{271} The surgeon of Lunéville, with whom Charles had resided secretly.

{273} 'Women' refers to Miss Walkinshaw. It is clear that Charles had rejected MacNamara's request for her dismissal, described by Dr. King.

{274} Browne, iv. 120, 121.

{277a} Culloden Papers, p. 412.

{277b} Robertson of Inerchraskie to Forbes of Culloden. September 23, 1745.

{278} Manuscripts in the Charter Chest at Cluny Castle. Privately printed.

{280a} Pickle was inducted into his estates, before the Bailies of Inverness and a jury, on February 2, 1758. The 'Retour' is cited in Mr. Mackenzie's *History of the Macdonalds.*

{280b} The story is in Mr. Mackenzie's *History of the Macdonalds.*

{281} All this is probably false.

{284} Mr. Bruce, October 10, 1754, to Gwynn Vaughan, Esq.

{285} *Arniston Memoirs*, edited by G. W. T. Omond, p. 153. Mr. Dundas of Arniston has kindly supplied a copy containing what is omitted in Mr. Omond's book—Pickle's dealings with his tenantry.

{286} See Macallester's huge and intolerably prolix book, *A Series of Letters* (London: 1767).

{287} D'Argenson, July 1755.

{288} S. P. France, 468.

{292a} Browne, iv. 124.

{292b} *Ibid*. iv. 125.

{293} Ewald's *Prince Charles*, ii. 223–228. From State Papers.

{294} Letter to Edgar, September 16, 1755.

{296a} Madame Adélaïde, according to gossip in the *Scots Magazine.*

{296b} *Pol. Corr.* xi. p. 37. No. 7,199, and p. 63.

{297} I have never seen this document.

{298} A full account of Macallester, from which these remarks are taken, was published by myself in the *English Illustrated Magazine.*

{301} Archives of French Foreign Office. Angleterre. 81. fol. 11.

{302a} *Pol. Corr.* xiii. 320. No. 8,660.

{302b} See *Le Secret du Roi*, by the Duc de Broglie.

{303} *Mémoire of Charlotte Stuart.* French Foreign Office. 1774.

{306} Mr. Alexander Pelham Trotter has kindly permitted me to consult this document in his possession.

{309a} D'Aiguillon.

{309b} Prince de Soubise.

{312} As is proved by Murray's letter of December 10.

{316} *Mémoire of Charlotte Stuart*. 1774.

{317} Charles, as Lumisden writes (December 3, 1760), 'positively insists on having the young filly returned to him.'

{321} The article on the *Tales of the Century* in the *Quarterly Review* (vol. lxxxi. p. 57) was not 'by Lockhart,' as Mr. Ewald says, and is not, in fact, accurate.

{323} Nothing in the Stuart Papers confirms the story that Charles was at the Coronation of George III., in 1761. In the present century Cardinal York told a member of the Stair family that the Prince visited England in 1763. It may have been then that he saw Murray of Broughton, and was seen by Murray's child, afterwards the actor known to Sir Walter Scott.

Printed in the United Kingdom
by Lightning Source UK Ltd.
111738UKS00002B/82

9 781419 141508